WITHDRAWN

HARVARD LIBRARY

WITHDRAWN

OTHER TITLES FROM RELIGION AND POLITICS

Alien Worlds: Social and Religious Dimensions of Extraterrestrial Contact
DIANA G. TUMMINIA, ed.

Contemporary Muslim Apocalyptic Literature
DAVID COOK

Learning Lessons from Waco: When Parties Bring Their Gods to the Negotiation Table
JAYNE SEMINARE DOCHERTY

Millennialism, Persecution, and Violence: Historical Cases
CATHERINE WESSINGER, ed.

Perfectionist Politics: Abolitionism and the Religious Tensions of American Democracy.
DOUGLAS M. STRONG

Priest-Indian Conflict in Upper Peru: The Generation of Rebellion, 1750–1780
NICHOLAS A. ROBINS

Religion and the Rise of Nationalism: A Profile of an East-Central European City
ROBERT E. ALVIS

William Dudley Pelley: A Life in Right-Wing Extremism and the Occult
SCOTT BEEKMAN

Missionary Politics
in Contemporary Europe

Religion and Politics
Michael Barkun, *Series Editor*

Missionary Politics in Contemporary Europe

José Pedro Zúquete

 SYRACUSE UNIVERSITY PRESS

Copyright © 2007 by Syracuse University Press
Syracuse, New York 13244-5160

All Rights Reserved

First Edition 2007

07 08 09 10 11 12   6 5 4 3 2 1

The paper used in this publication meets the minimum requirements
of American National Standard for Information Sciences—Permanence
of Paper for Printed Library Materials, ANSI Z39.48–1984.∞™

For a listing of books published and distributed by Syracuse University Press,
visit our Web site at SyracuseUniversityPress.syr.edu.

ISBN-13: 978-0-8156-3149-1
ISBN-10: 0-8156-3149-9

Library of Congress Cataloging-in-Publication Data

Zúquete, José Pedro.
  Missionary politics in contemporary Europe / José Pedro Zúquete. — 1st ed.
    p. cm. — (Religion and politics)
  Includes bibliographical references and index.
  ISBN 978-0-8156-3149-1 (hardcover : alk. paper)
  1. Religion and politics—Europe. 2. Fascism—Europe. I. Title.
BL65.P7Z87 2007
320.53'3094—dc22
                                                    2007017054

Manufactured in the United States of America

For my parents

José Pedro Zúquete is a postdoctoral fellow at the Minda de Gunzburg Center for European Studies at Harvard University. He holds a B.A. in history from the University of Coimbra (Portugal) and a Ph.D. in political science from the University of Bath (UK) and was a visiting scholar at Boston University. He has written on modernism, fascism, and contemporary populist movements in both Europe and Latin America, and, more recently, on opposition to globalization.

Contents

ILLUSTRATIONS | *ix*

PREFACE | *xi*

ACKNOWLEDGMENTS | *xv*

1 Introduction: *Missionary Politics* | *1*

2 Le Pen and the National Front | *34*

3 Umberto Bossi and the Northern League | *115*

4 The Missionary Model | *190*

5 The Future of Missionary Politics | *233*

6 Conclusion | *243*

REFERENCES | *247*

INDEX | *265*

Illustrations

1. Cover of Roger Mauge's 1988 biography of the leader of the National Front | *66*

2. Jean-Marie Le Pen at a National Front rally, May 1, 1995 | *76*

3. The acclamation of Jean-Marie Le Pen at the Nice Congress, April 21, 2003 | *92*

4. Umberto Bossi delivers a speech to militants at the annual Northern League rally in Venice, September 15, 2002 | *152*

5. Umberto Bossi giving a speech at Pontida, May 4, 2003 | *167*

6. Umberto Bossi performing the "Ceremony of the Water," Po River, September 17, 2005 | *185*

Preface

When I began my doctoral study at the University of Bath I immersed myself in the inner world of contemporary European populist parties. My aim was to analyze the rhetoric and discourse of Jean-Marie Le Pen and Umberto Bossi, two leaders who had been regularly described as "charismatic" by both pundits and academics. In pursuit of my goal, I read innumerable articles both by and about the National Front and the Northern League, and became aware of their litany of complaints against their respective national governments. Yet the more I investigated the party literature, speeches, and interviews of each, the more I was struck by the way routine political fights were viewed by followers of both movements as all-or-nothing contests, engaged in with fierce intensity and dramatic force. This passion was virtually unremarked in all of the previous scholarly literature I had read. It was as if the fervor, emotion, and missionary zeal to "save" the community in question—be it the French nation or the northern Italian homeland—that was so important within these movements did not register on the social-scientific radar (or, if it did register, it was not deemed worth recording or analyzing).

Political scientists have been conditioned by decades of methodological precedent to perceive social realities through a rationalistic and utilitarian lens. Therefore, focus has tended to be on their negative dimensions: their grievances and complaints and their racism and radicalism, so that the claims of these movements have been dismissed as not only morally objectionable but also as plain wrong and alarmist. This dismissal, however, is not a sufficient reason to ignore their positive dimensions: the totalizing worldview that gives members a sense of communal experience and a clear understanding of their principles and values in times of change and crisis. Such perceptions and beliefs, whether we agree with them or not, shape the reality of group members and motivate their actions. The history of the twentieth century has demonstrated the power of perception and faith to change the course of history and the fates of communities. We would be well advised not to ignore their reach again. Further, these movements feed off specific internal problems of contemporary liberal democracies at a time of increased globalization. For example, the growing perception that the political and civic elites are unresponsive to the "real" issues affecting the people increases the call for more authentic and involving forms of popular participation. But at a deeper level, the way these movements consolidate a politics of identity, proclaim an ethnic community's last defense, and constantly warn of the deterioration of a European civilization on the verge of plunging into an abyss is characteristic of the solutions that man seeks periodically in history when facing rapid, disruptive, changing times. In such a fertile environment, history has taught us that a worldview that seeks to integrate man through myths, symbols, and rites; to tie him to a sense of belonging and rootedness; and to promise him a way out of his alienation has the potential to increase, sometimes in extraordinary ways, its own appeal.

Therefore, in order to capture the self-understandings and motivations of members in these groups, the social scientist must necessarily both make a close scrutiny of their internal discourse and—this is a crucial step—also take their ideas and *Weltschaung* seriously rather than dismissing them as trivial, or, worse, ignoring them because they are opposed to our worldview and therefore not to be discussed for fear that they could be quietly legitimized. A defensive attitude toward what is admittedly a very delicate subject risks replacing the analysis of what these movements are with statements of what they ought to be. In his speech on "Science as Vocation," delivered in 1918 at Munich University, Max Weber asserted that in order to gain clarity in any scientific enterprise, one must necessarily separate moral judgment from analytical work. He even committed himself to "prov[ing] from the works of our historians that whenever the man of science introduces his personal value judgment, a full understanding of the facts ceases" (Weber 1958, 146). The value of studying political and social movements on their own terms is a theme of the pioneering work on historical fascism of George L. Mosse, whose own family fled Nazi Germany. "Empathy is for me still at the core of the historical enterprise," Mosse reflected in his autobiography. He then stated, "I have myself mainly dealt with people and movements whom I judged harshly, but understanding must precede an informed and effective judgment" (2000, 172). With a similar spirit, I present this book as an analysis of two populist movements in a manner that is as value-neutral as possible, without feeling the need repeatedly to reassure the readers that, as suggested by a friendly scholar, I am on "the side of the good guys." Thus, in these pages the reader will not find any moralizing, only an effort to understand and clarify what has so far been obscure.

In the following pages I develop my analysis of this form of politics that I categorize as "missionary" and that continues to exert, at least in European politics and society, a considerable impact. There is of course no unidimensional approach toward an explanation of the appeal that contemporary populism has, and my own approach of studying such movements through the lens of the "sacralization of the political" is just one among many. But within an academic environment where socioeconomic analysis of contemporary populisms reigns supreme, the cultural approach that I adopt has been neglected, and this book aims to shift the balance. If there is a message that this book purports to promote, it is this: The allure of truly secular religions led by charismatic leaders and geared toward a sacred mission of salvation and redemption has not dimmed. It persists in the twenty-first century.

Acknowledgments

The writing of this book has been a long journey, and along the path I benefited greatly from the advice, suggestions, criticisms, and support of many people. My greatest debt goes to my joint supervisors of my doctoral dissertation, from which, in a revised fashion, emerged this book on contemporary missionary politics in Europe. Roger Eatwell at the University of Bath provided pointed criticisms at different stages, helping me to refine my thinking and writing. I am grateful for his support both in academic matters and other life issues. Charles Lindholm from Boston University provided me unwavering intellectual and moral support during the writing of the manuscript, and was the main source of inspiration for the anthropological/cultural turn of my study of contemporary political movements. I owe a great debt of gratitude to his teachings, patience, and encouragement. His friendship and that of his wife, Cherry, is something I truly value.

I would like to thank my Ph.D. examiner, Anna Cento Bull, and Leonard Weinberg, whose review of my manuscript was quite constructive. I benefited much from external comments on early drafts and sections of the manuscript. I would like to thank Stanley L. Payne, Philip Smith, Brian Neve, Jean-Yves Camus, Jonathan Laurence, and Diane Lipsett. I am grateful to Roger Griffin for his criticisms, suggestions, and overall support since we started our e-mail correspondence. I would like to thank Richard Landes for commenting on the manuscript, making bibliographical suggestions, and keeping the friendship alive through the storm. David Landes's scholarly experience and insightful criticisms helped me to better frame one of the key arguments of my book.

During the preparation of the manuscript, I benefited from the use of the library at the University of Bath, and of the Mugar Memorial Library at Boston University, to whose interlibrary loan department I am especially grateful. In the final stages of revision, the incomparable resources of the Harvard libraries system, particularly Widener Library, helped me greatly. I would like to thank Daniel Ziblatt, Niall Ferguson, Arthur Goldhammer, Trisha Craig, and my Visiting Scholars colleagues at the Minda de Gunzburg Center for European Studies at Harvard University—particularly Mentor Agani, Taco Brandsen, Christine Cadot, Robert Falkner, Paul Bempechat, Francesca Leder, and Renato Camurri. I would like to thank Sandy Selesky for always being a welcoming presence at the Center, and for all the conversations on wildlife and bird-watching. I am grateful to the Portuguese Fundação para a Ciência e Tecnologia, which provided me with indispensable financial support for my research. I would like to thank António Costa Pinto and Luis Reis Torgal for their support, and Ambreen Qureshi at AP Images for her help and prompt assistance.

I would like to express my gratitude to Syracuse University Press, particularly series editor Michael Barkun for his support and constructive criticisms at different stages of the production of the manuscript, and Glenn Wright for his diligence and overall help during this project. Thanks are due to Jill Root for a very competent and meticulous copyediting. All translations from French, Italian, and Spanish are mine.

I am profoundly grateful to Matt Stefon for his edits, proofreads, and insightful observations on missionary politics. The many hours we spent talking about these issues helped in a decisive way to shape my work. I owe a great debt to him and his friendship. I am also grateful to Antonia Chayes for her hospitality and genuine interest in my work. I would like to acknowledge Richard Rice, Noam Yavor, Kurt Streed, Blaise Bettencourt, and the Elmerick and Quinn families for their friendship and constant encouragement.

Finally, my family—my parents, my grandparents, my grandmother Rafaela, my cousins, my aunt Teresa, Marta, Filipa, and Rafaela—have been always present (if not always physically) and constant sources of inspiration and strength. To my parents, and their unconditional love and support, this book is dedicated.

Missionary Politics
in Contemporary Europe

I
Introduction
Missionary Politics

> In politics we have not yet found firm and established ground. Here there seems to be no clearly established cosmic order; we are always threatened with a sudden relapse into the old chaos. We are building high and proud edifices; but we forget to make their foundations secure. The belief that man by the skillful use of magic formulae and rites can change the course of nature has prevailed for hundreds and thousands of years in human history. In spite of all the inevitable frustrations and disappointments mankind still clung stubbornly, forcibly, and desperately to this belief. It is, therefore, not to be wondered at that in our political actions and our political thoughts magic still holds its ground.
> —Ernst Cassirer, *The Myth of the State*

The occasion is important and invested with the solemnity of a Mass. In Reims, where in the sixth century Clovis I, king of the Franks, was baptized, Jean-Marie Le Pen, the historical leader of the French National Front, identifies himself as the man who picked up the French flag from the mud in which the elites left it, and calls on his followers to take an oath "to fight for France until the rebirth and recovery of our people." In Pontida, the land where the people of the north of Italy vowed to resist the troops of Emperor Barbarossa, Umberto Bossi, the leader of the Northern League, leads his followers in an "oath of loyalty to the cause of autonomy and freedom of our peoples." In Reims and in Pontida, the symbolic settings reinforce the attachment of party followers to the mission proclaimed by the leader. Their focus was not on specific policies, requests, or grievances, but rather on the holiness of the place, the cause, and the movement. Both the National Front and the Northern League, two of the most successful European examples of politics outside of the mainstream, repeat such rituals every year, heralding the leaders who will take them into the dawn of a better age. They constitute examples of messianic or missionary politics in the twenty-first century. It is both a major conviction of mine and the thesis of this book that the attachment to the holy in European politics has not subsided since the decline of the great political religions of the twentieth century. What follows is intended to provide an insight into the world of these two missionary political parties.

THE DISENCHANTMENT OF THE WORLD

Sociologists and historians have dedicated a body of literature, particularly since the 1950s and 1960s, to analyzing the decline of religion both at a societal and an individual level. Although it is not a homogeneous group of writings and explanations, this literature has been clustered into the general term of *secularization theory*. Its central argument is that, since the beginning of the Reformation in the sixteenth century through the Enlightenment, the Western world has suffered a process of multifaceted modernization that has led to the undermining of religion in the social system and in the minds and behavior of individuals.

Max Weber's philosophy of history can be considered the prime reference in all social analysis of the dynamics and effects of secularization. In a speech given in 1918, the German sociologist argued that the increased trend of rationalization and intellectualization led to a "disenchanted world." That is, "it means that principally there are no mysterious incalculable forces that come into play, but rather that one can, in principle, master all things by calculation" (Weber 1958, 139). In Weber's view, a crucial development for the construction of an increasingly disenchanted world was the Protestant Reformation, which encouraged the rise of a new work ethic that encouraged individualism and led to the emergence of modern capitalism.

In *The Protestant Ethic and the Spirit of Capitalism,* Weber distinguished between "outer-worldly asceticism," which promoted distance between the spiritual and the rest of society, and the new "inner-worldly asceticism," which saw hard work, activism, and diligence as a way of gaining God's favor (Weber 2002, 39–41). This boost to individualism would in the long term, he claimed, undermine deep-rooted ideas about hierarchy and even about the social relevance of religion for the organization and life of communities. A major feature of modernity's march toward a "rational" construction of society was the prominence of an organized group of experts, a bureaucracy in charge of human affairs. Weber described the emergence of an era in which authority would be based on rational grounds. "The bureaucratic structure," Weber wrote, "is everywhere a late product of development. The further back we trace our steps, the more typical is the absence of bureaucracy and officialdom in the structure of domination. Bureaucracy has a 'rational' character: rules, means, ends, and matter-of-factness dominate its bearing" (Weber 1978, 244).

On the whole, the theoretical spine of Weber's analysis has remained central to the current secularization paradigm. Modernization is viewed as the greatest enemy of religion. One of the main contemporary defenders of this paradigm, sociologist Steve Bruce, describes secularization as a "social condition manifest in (a) the declining importance of religion for the operation of non-religious roles and institutions such as those of the state and the economy; (b) a decline in the social standing of religious roles and institutions; and (c) a decline in the extent to which people engage in religious practices, display beliefs of a religious kind, and conduct other aspects of their lives in a manner informed by such beliefs" (Bruce 2002, 3). This is, in sum, the view of the disenchanted world described by Weber. In Bruce's words, "the clash of ideas between science and religion is less significant than the more subtle impact of naturalistic ways of thinking about the world. Science and technology have not made us atheists. Rather, the fundamental assumptions that underlie them, which we can summarily describe as 'rationality' . . . make us less likely than our forebears to entertain the notion of the divine" (Bruce 2002, 28–29). This secularizing trend, however, as generally admitted by proponents of the secularization paradigm, tends to be geographically limited to the Western world.

Sociologist Peter L. Berger, one of the fathers of the paradigm turned critic, observes the emergence of powerful movements of countersecularization in the contemporary world. He particularly emphasizes Islamism and evangelicalism as "the two most dynamic religious upsurges in the world today" (Berger 1999, 6–7). These movements are orthodox in the sense that they are characterized by an intense religious fervor and a return to traditional sources of religious authority. Similarly, Philip Jenkins argues in *The Next Christendom* (2003) that the center of gravity of the Christian world has shifted from Europe and the United States to the Southern Hemisphere. "Christians," Jenkins writes, "are facing a shrinking population in the liberal west and a growing majority of the traditional Rest. During the past half-century the critical centers of the Christian world have moved decisively to Africa, to Latin America, and to Asia. The balance will never shift back" (Jenkins 2002b).

A school of thought particularly critical of the secularization paradigm that has gained prevalence in the last decades has been the application of "rational-choice theory" to religious studies. It is essentially a supply-side theory of religion and has as a major contributor, among others, sociologist Rodney Stark. While accepting a macro-version of secularization in terms of institutional differentiation between the church and the state, the supply-side school rejects the notion that there has been a micro-version of secularization in the last centuries, that is, a general decline in religious commitment, in individual piety and belief. The demand for religion has remained constant because people always want the salvation and relief from fear that religion has to offer. Therefore the fact that the levels of subjective religiousness remain high even in the nations most often cited as examples of secularization undermines the secularization doctrine (Stark and Finke 2000, 57–79).

From this perspective, religion is seen as a product in the marketplace and, from the various options available, people choose according to their hopes, fears, and needs. The implication is that people act rationally in choosing their religion. Therefore, an environment of religious freedom (pluralism), with open competition between religions, enhances religious vitality and the level of consumption (in terms of a more active, not lazy laity). Religion is consequently subject to the laws of supply and demand. This factor explains the religious disparities within the Western world. That is why the United States is a more religious country than European countries (where religious monopoly has a stronger tradition that undermines the "religious market") (Stark and Finke 2000, 220–33).

Even if it has been challenged, the secularization theory is still a dominant one and shared by many scholars. In a recent work Ronald Inglehart and Pippa Norris have established a direct link between the process of societal modernization and the declining importance of religious values in postindustrial nations. One of their conclusions is worth quoting in its entirety:

> We conclude that due to rising levels of human security, the *publics of virtually all advanced societies have been moving towards more secular orientations*. We demonstrate that "modernization" (the process of industrialization, urbanization, and rising levels of education and wealth) greatly weakens the influence of religious institutions in affluent societies, bringing lower rates of attendance at religious services, and making religion subjectively less important in people's lives. (Inglehart and Norris 2004, 18 [emphasis mine])

"In Europe," observes sociologist of religion Philip Jenkins, "Christianity is largely a dead issue" (Jenkins 2002a). At both a popular and a scholarly level, the current assumption is that religion is on the decline in Europe, particularly Western Europe. The secularization paradigm seems to hold in European territory. In fact, if attention is paid to the religious upsurge in other parts of the world, in matters of faith Europe increasingly looks like an exceptional case.[1] This situation can be seen at two levels: at an institutional level church attendance is at an all-time low, the majority of churchgoers are overwhelmingly elderly, and the church, either Protestant or Catholic, has increasing difficulty in recruiting members for the clergy; at an individual level, very few people follow church-dictated codes of behavior and an increasing number play down the importance of religion in their personal lives (Halman 1999–2000).

In this environment it comes as no surprise that the member states of the European Union decided to exclude any reference to God in creating a European constitution (and in the Reform Treaty that replaced it). There is no mention of the Christian roots of Europe either. Instead there is a somewhat

---

1. Inglehart and Norris stress the fact that the notion of "secular exception" of Europe should be extended to all of the postindustrial societies. To them, "secularization is not taking place only in Western Europe, as some critics have claimed (though it was first observed there). It is occurring in most advanced industrial societies including Australia, New Zealand, Japan and Canada . . . But even in America there has been a lesser but perceptible trend toward secularization; the trend has been partly masked by massive immigration of people with relatively traditional worldviews" (2004, 18).

vague reference in the preamble of the document to "the cultural, religious and humanist inheritance of Europe."[2] It is a symbolic but significant episode in a continuous narrative of secularization.

THE REENCHANTING OF THE WORLD

Max Weber and Charismatic Leadership

In his analysis, Weber describes how the Western world was indeed marching toward an inexorable rationalization. However, Weber leaves open the possibility of discontinuities in this process. Weber's introduction of the concept of charisma in social science should be seen as way of counterbalancing this rationalist trend with the occasional irruption of the irrational and enchanted in the modern world. In politics, this irruption means the possibility of heroic leadership. The emphasis on heroic leadership was not new in itself; after all, thinkers such as Thomas Carlyle before him had put forward "great man" theories of leadership and historical change. "For, as I take it, Universal History, the history of what man has accomplished in this world," declared Carlyle in an 1840 public lecture, "is at bottom the History of the Great Men who have worked here" (Carlyle 1962, 239). Even in Marxist theory a Russian philosopher such as Georgi Plekhanov, though giving primacy to social conditions and needs, recognized in 1898 the role of a great man as "a beginner because he sees further than others, and desires things more strongly than others" (Plekhanov 2003 [1898], 60).

Weber's innovation is his emphasis placed both on the concept of charisma and on charismatic domination. This is a major contribution to subsequent leadership literature. Charismatic authority is the opposite of legal or bureaucratic authority. Indeed, it rests "on devotion to the exceptional sanctity, heroism or exemplary character of an individual person, and of the normative

---

2. In 2005 both France (May 29) and the Netherlands (June 1) rejected the constitution in popular referenda. For the full text of the Constitution, see <http://europa.eu/constitution/en/lstocl_en.htm>. In June 2007, the twenty-seven members of the European Union agreed on a Reform Treaty that, on the whole, preserves the substance of the rejected draft constitution. It is expected to come into force during 2009, after ratification by each member state.

patterns or order revealed or ordained by him" (Weber 1978, 215–16). *Charisma* is a religious term meaning "the gift of grace." In the New Testament the apostle Paul describes a *charism* as a divine bestowal of power incapable of being induced by human effort and manifesting itself in spiritual gifts *(charismata)* such as prophecy, healing, and glossolalia (1 Corinthians 12:27—31; see also Acts 2). Using the work of religious scholar Rudolph Sohm as a basis, Weber took the concept from its original Christian context and tried to make it operational in the historical and social domain. Therefore, there should be no surprise at the persistence of religious undertones in Weber's work on charisma. Charismatic leaders resemble the biblical prophets. "The term 'charisma,'" he wrote in his landmark study *Economy and Society,*

> will be applied to a certain quality of an individual personality by virtue of which he is considered extraordinary and treated as endowed with supernatural, superhuman, or at least specifically exceptional powers or qualities. These are such as are not accessible to the ordinary person, but are regarded as of divine origin or as exemplary, and on the basis of them the individual concerned is treated as a "leader." (Weber 1978, 241)

In the beginning, there is a revelation that proves to people that the leader should be followed. "It is recognition on the part of those subject to authority which is decisive for the validity of charisma. This recognition is freely given and guaranteed by what is held to be a proof, originally always a miracle, and consists in devotion to the corresponding revelation, hero worship, or absolute trust in the leader" (Weber 1978, 242).

A central tenet of Weber's theory of charismatic authority is the concept of mission. *Mission* is another term that Weber took from Christian vocabulary. In Trinitarian theology it means the sending into the world of the Son or Spirit by the Father, or of the Spirit by the Son, especially for the purpose of salvation. The authors of the New Testament used terminology intimately linked with a sense of mission or vocation in life (see, for instance, Matthew 28:16–20; Romans 1:1–15). "Pure charisma," Weber writes, "is specifically foreign to economic considerations. Wherever it appears, it constitutes a 'call' in the most emphatic sense of the word, a 'mission' or a 'spiritual duty'" (Weber 1978, 244). Weber makes it clear that the charismatic leader is driven by a sense of mission, of "calling" or "vocation." In "Politics as a Vocation" he declares,

> Here we are interested above all in the second of these types: domination by virtue of the devotion of those who obey the purely personal "charisma" of the "leader." For this is the root of the idea of a *calling* in its highest expression. Devotion to the charisma of the prophet, or the leader in war, or to the great demagogue in the *ecclesia* or in parliament, means that the leader is personally recognized as the innerly "called" leader of men. Men do not obey him by virtue of tradition or statute, but because they believe in him. If he is more than a narrow and vain upstart of the moment, the leader lives for his cause and strives for his work. (Weber 1958, 79)

In Weber's work, the role in history of these leaders with a sense of mission is crucial. Although he describes the coming of a world run by bureaucrats, Weber longs for a world run by true charismatic leaders driven by a cause. This charismatic leadership is particularly important for democracies, in which "there is only the choice between leadership democracy with a 'machine' and leaderless democracy, namely, the rule of professional politicians without a calling, without the inner charismatic qualities that make a leader." In a paragraph revealing of his mindset Weber observes,

> [A]ll historical experience confirms the truth—that man would not have attained the possible unless time and again he had reached out for the impossible. But to do that a man must be a leader, and not only a leader but a hero as well . . . Only he has the calling for politics who is sure that he shall not crumble when the world from his point of view is too stupid or too base for what he wants to offer. Only he who in the face of all this can say "in spite of all" has the calling for politics. (Weber 1958, 128)

Recognition of the charismatic leader and complete personal devotion to the possessor of the charismatic quality arise out of either "enthusiasm" or "despair and hope" (Weber 1978, 242). The charismatic leader's sense of mission comes into being during a period of crisis. The effect of a crisis is dual: crisis disrupts the social and psychological equilibrium and increases the need for a strong leader; crisis also leads to the development of the sense of mission by the future leader. It reinforces his inner drive to act and lead. It strengthens his own devotion and faith in his mission. In Weber's words, "The mere fact of recognizing the personal mission of a charismatic master establishes his power. Whether it is more active or passive, this recognition derives from the surrender of the faithful to the extraordinary and unheard-of, to what is alien to all regulation and tradition and therefore is viewed as divine—surrender which arises from distress or enthusiasm" (Weber 1978, 1115).

Charisma becomes the equivalent in Weber's analysis to the individual's surrender to a sacred dimension in order to escape from a threatening social and cultural "profane" reality.

Mission in Secular Religions

Though Weber attributed charismatic dimensions to modern political figures,[3] he quite understandably placed the life and mission of religious leaders at the center of his analysis of charismatic leadership. The type of devotion and inner calling described by Weber can easily be found in examples taken from the Bible or from medieval history, in times when the religious sphere was admittedly more central to the life of individuals, groups, and communities. Weber was, however, particularly pessimistic about the march of rationalization and bureaucracy, and its implications for humanity: the potential danger of a spiritual emptiness and a government of bureaucrats and technocrats removed from the people.

Thus Weber stressed the importance of the political sphere in the modern world as a last resort of freedom and creativity in history. As in the past a charismatic religious leader could affect the evolution of history, so

---

3. Of William Gladstone (1809–1898), four times Queen Victoria's prime minister, Weber wrote, "Gladstone's very personal charisma, which was irresistible to Puritan rationalism, forced the caucus bureaucracy to make an about-face and to stand with him despite the most serious objections and the prognosis of an unfavourable outcome of the elections" (Weber 1978, 1132–33). Weber's "value-free sociological analysis" also identified Kurt Eisner (1867–1919), a German and Bavarian politician, as a "type" of charismatic figure: He represented "the type of literateur, who is overwhelmed by his own demagogic success" (Weber 1978, 242).

in modernity a charismatic political leader could do the same. Charisma is in Weber's view a "specifically revolutionary force" in history. In his words, "[Charisma] may then result in a radical alteration of the central attitudes and directions of action with a completely new orientation of all attitudes toward the different problems of the 'world'" (Weber 1978, 245). It is slight wonder that Weber rejected what he saw as a "leaderless democracy," typically parliamentary democracy, and opted instead for a "plebiscitarian democracy," a case of "democracy with a leader" (Weber 1958, 113).

The sense of mission of the charismatic political leader described by Weber, unlike that of the charismatic religious leader, is not divine: It is not based on a divine revelation, and the leader does not pledge to do any of God's work, or announce any of God's words. There is, however, vagueness in Weber's description of charismatic political movements. There was no actual, detailed description of the political leader's mission. In Weber's work the religious undertones of the political charismatic leader remain powerful. The leader is somehow perceived as superhuman. There is an intense emotional attachment between the leader and the followers. The followers blindly follow their leader and his mission. The charismatic relationship has more to do with emotion than with reason. It is clear that there is a quasireligious dimension to the relationship between leader and follower, even if the final goal is not religious in the narrow sense of bringing people closer to God or to an afterlife. A movement may be religious in a broader sense, even though Weber never specifically developed his analysis of what has come to be known in the domain of social sciences as "secular religions." In a manuscript that he never finished, however, he wrote, "The earliest and most energetic manifestations of the idea [of the nation], in some form, even though it may have been veiled, have contained the legend of a providential 'mission.'" Thus, "[t]hose to whom the representatives of the idea zealously turned were expected to shoulder this mission" (Weber 1978, 925).

Such secular religions are intimately linked with the exaltation and deification of the concept of a nation typical of modernity, particularly since the American and French revolutions of the eighteenth century. The connection between the sacred and the nation can be seen in *On the Social Contract*, written in 1762 by French philosopher Jean-Jacques Rousseau. In a section titled "On Civil Religion," Rousseau defended the necessity for any new nation-state to create its own civic religion in order to strengthen the links of the citizens to the national community. The "dogmas of civil religion" were a necessary and positive thing. According to Rousseau,

> The dogmas of the civil religion ought to be simple, few in number, precisely worded, without explanations or commentaries. The existence of a powerful, intelligent, beneficent divinity that foresees and provides; the life to come; the happiness of the just; the punishment of the wicked; the sanctity of the social contract and of the laws. These are the positive dogmas. As for the negative dogmas, I limit them to just one, namely intolerance. (Rousseau 1987, 102)

French traveler and historian Alexis de Tocqueville also made some insightful observations about the links between religious faith and political action in his 1856 book *The Old Regime and the French Revolution*. Commenting on the French Revolution, he noted that it followed the lines of a religious revolution. To de Tocqueville,

> No previous political upheaval, however violent, had aroused such passionate enthusiasm, for the ideal the French Revolution set before it was not merely a change in the French social system but nothing short of a regeneration of the whole human race. It created an atmosphere of missionary fervor and, indeed, assumed all the aspects of a religious revival—much to the consternation of contemporary observers. (Tocqueville 1955, 12–13)

A contemporary of Weber's, French sociologist Émile Durkheim, would develop further a theory of the *process* of the transfer of the focus of such worship from the deity to the nation. At the very basis of Durkheim's sociology is his functional and experiential definition of religion. To him, a religion is a "unified system of beliefs and practices relative to sacred things, things set apart and surrounded by prohibitions—beliefs and practices that unite its adherents in a single moral community called a Church" (Durkheim 2001, 46). Durkheim sees all religious systems as being based on the distinction between the profane, or the ordinary world, and the sacred, the religious world. What separates these two realms is a collective system of beliefs, myths, rites, and symbols. In Durkheim's explanation, "The division of the world into two comprehensive domains, one sacred, the other profane, is the hallmark of religious thought. Beliefs, myths, gnomic spirits, and legends are either representations or systems of representations that express the nature of sacred things, the virtues and powers attributed to them, their history, their relations with each other and with profane things" (2001, 36). Although Durkheim never mentions the words *secular religion*, he does consider the nation to be the contemporary form of the religious, with its sacred objects, emblems, and rituals establishing the moral community of the sacralized state. The flag, he said, is the totem of today (2001, 165).

After the American and French revolutions, a major boost to the concept of secular religions came from the rise of ideologies such as fascism, Nazism, and communism, which had a strong component of faith, a communal dimension, and an ultimate goal of salvation not *outside* but *within* the world. Two Frenchmen, both contemporary to these political movements, were among the first to analyze the inner dynamics of these political movements through the concept of "secular religion." In a 1944 article, about the advent of secular religions relying on a fideistic rapport with the masses, Raymond Aron warned about the danger that faith could degenerate into barbarism. Aron observed that these movements gained their strength from characteristics similar to those of traditional religions: by giving their members a *global interpretation of events* and explaining the reasons behind the problems facing mankind; by providing through the *fraternal community of the party* the future image of a redeemed world; and finally by wrenching individuals from the loneliness and hopelessness of modern times, which by itself justified *sacrifices* demanded for the good and survival of the collective (Aron 1945, 289–90). A few years later Jules Monnerot, in *The Sociology of Communism*, stressed the impossibility of abolishing the "consecration of politics" in the modern world, and focused on communism's secular religious nature. Monnerot's thesis is that in modernity the sacred is never destroyed but displaced, and attaches itself to new "objects." The loosening of the grip that otherworldly religions had on Europe was followed by the emergence of such other religious phenomena as secular religions that satisfy a never-ending human hunger for the holy (Monnerot 1976, 285), that "seek the transcendent within the immanent," and, like communism, are characterized by an "active presence of a *faith*, and of *myths* and *dogmas*" (1976, 146).

After these and other initial analyses,[4] a vast literature on the politico-religious dimensions of the mass ideologies of the twentieth century was slowly but steadily built. French sociologist Jean-Pierre Sironneau studied the "undeniable" transfer of sacredness from the religious sphere to the political sphere in political ideologies and movements of the last two centuries. Both Nazism and communism share what he sees as the "four usual dimensions of religious phenomena": a mythical core, ritual, communion, and faith (Sironneau 1982, 577). But though these secular religions played the *functional* role of religion, Sironneau was careful to point out that they were not religions in the *phenomenological* sense, in terms of "essence," of a belief in superhuman beings and of solving the problem of life after death. According to Sironneau, "The transcendence aimed at by the 'political religions' is a pseudo-transcendence because the hereafter, in the future, remains prisoner of the temporality of history" (1982, 558). German historian Karl Dietrich Bracher described the "new philosophies" that took hold at the beginning of the twentieth century as "pseudo-religious ideologies with the dual claim to scientific validity and, simultaneously, to religious absoluteness."[5] A major boost to the heuristic value of the concept of political religion (and not just as a metaphor) has come more recently from historians

---

4. German philosopher Eric Voegelin was the first one to systematically study these attempts by political movements, as *political religions,* to bring about here and now a sacred kingdom. In a tract published in 1938 and confiscated by the Nazis, Voegelin denounced their anti-Christian nature, and stated that "temporal religiosity, be it mankind, the *volk*, the class, the race, or the state, which is expressed as the *Realissimum*, is a falling away from God" (1986, 79). Together with Voegelin, see, for example, the writings of another witness of the twentieth century, Waldemar Gurian, on the totalitarian and political religious nature of Bolchevism (Gurian 1952, 3–14).

5. Bracher writes that these movements "promised to reunite what modern science and secularization had divided: harmony once more between culture and technology, between politics and culture. They attempted to promise everything to everybody, to be an all-embracing movement and an all-embracing faith . . . The reverse of the medal was the emphatically one-sided militant and activist character of the totalitarian movements employing these substitute religions. Fascism and national-socialism, [as were] Leninism-Stalinism and later Maoism, were both things at the same time: promise of an eventual community—the 1000-year Reich or universal communism—but meanwhile, and above all, mobilization ideologies for battle with the total enemy" (Bracher 1984, 32–33).

who have applied it to specific case studies, and consider it a major analytical tool toward scientific understanding. In this way, Roger Griffin categorizes fascism as a political religion driven by a *"utopia* of regenerated national community saturated with *mythic* and *palingenetic thinking,* reminiscent of early modern forms of European *millenarianism,"* and aimed at "purging society of alleged sources of socio-cultural and/or racial decadence within historical time" (Griffin 2005, 46), while Michael Burleigh approaches Nazism as one of such "pseudo- or substitute religions, with eclectic liturgies, ersatz theologies, vices and virtues."[6]

A considerable improvement to a historical perspective on the theme of the "sacralization of politics" has originated in the work of Italian historian Emilio Gentile. He notes that this phenomenon emerged "after the political realm had gained its independence from traditional religion [and] acquires a sacred nature," going so far as claiming "for itself the prerogative to determine the meaning and fundamental aim of human existence for individuals and collectivity" (Gentile 2006, xiv). Gentile distinguishes between two categories. *Civil religion* relates to the sacralization of a common civic creed, and the development of a system of beliefs, symbols, and rituals aimed at celebrating the collectivity. Gentile contends that civil religions are typical of democratic regimes in order to create attachment and consensus (2006, xv).[7]

Political religion, on the other hand, is identified with the sacralization of politics by antidemocratic ideologies and regimes. Gentile writes,

---

6. "The Great War and its disturbed aftermath," notes Burleigh, "led to an intensified revival of this pseudo-religious strain in politics, which exerted its maximum appeal in times of extreme crisis, just as medieval millenarianism . . . had thrived in times of sudden change and social dislocation" (Burleigh 2000, 6–7). On a more recent discussion of the application of the concept of "political religion" to fascism, see Robert Paxton (2004, 213–15).

7. Robert Bellah, for instance, has studied the quasireligious dimension of American nationalist sentiment. In his famous essay "Civil Religion in America," Bellah has described how the American civil religion "has its own prophets and its own martyrs, its own sacred events and sacred places, its own solemn rituals and symbols" (Bellah 1967, 18). Adopting a clear Durkheimian approach, Bellah shows how this religious dimension of American democracy spawns solidarity and encourages the citizens to make sacrifices for the goals of the national community.

> Political religion is the sacralization of a political system founded on an unchallengeable monopoly of power, ideological monism, and the obligatory and unconditional subordination of the individual and the collectivity to its code of commandments. Consequently, a political religion is intolerant, invasive, and fundamentalist, and it wishes to permeate every aspect of an individual's life and of a society's collective life. (2006, xv)

This distinction also runs throughout the work of Spanish sociologist Salvador Giner, who holds a positive view of civic religion as an assembly of "myths, civic pieties and public exorcisms" that "sustain the political," and are ultimately compatible with plural democratic society and institutions (Giner 2003, 89–90). Political religions, on the other hand, are inherently totalitarian, and impose a "militant ideology hostile to any sort of ambiguity" led by elites or political parties that are "determined" to absorb civic religions and manipulate them in order to reach their ideological goals (2003, 97–100). Therefore, while civil religion is a form of sacralization of politics that serves to increase the legitimacy and allegiance to a given political system, political religion is a form of sacralized politics that is inherently "total" in the sense that it is characterized by an all-encompassing ideology and aims at a maximum consensus. Such a sacralized politics provides a worldview that gives meaning to, and shapes the perceptions of reality of, those who adhere to it. It is on this latter that my book is focused.

I find it necessary to point out that, though the concept of "political religion" has been applied mainly to the behemoth ideologies of the last century, it has also found a fertile ground in social science literature on postcolonial modernization, which emphasizes the role played by political religions—and by associated charismatic leaderships—in cementing the solidarity and collective commitment of the people to the newborn nation-states (see Rustow 1970, 18–20). Thus David E. Apter described the elevation of the "ends of the state" in the new nations to "virtually a sacred level" (1963, 66–80); Edward Shils wrote extensively about the development of sacred attachments to the new nations, and about the charismatic dimensions of the leaders who embody these attachments (see, for example, Shils 1975, 405–22); and authors such as French journalist and biographer Jean Lacouture have characterized charismatic leaders in postcolonial states as true "demigods" (1970).

My primary emphasis is of course on the modern West, and on Europe in particular, and I will now turn to the current status of the application of the concept of "political religion" to contemporary political movements.

The De-sacralization of Politics?

Notwithstanding the increase in analyses of the ways politics was sacralized by political movements and leaderships of the past century,[8] the application of the rubric "political religion" to totalitarian systems will continue to meet resistance from a considerable number of scholars who contend that the notion confuses differences between the essences of these movements and those of traditional religions. Further, these scholars note, designating such movement[s] as "religion[s]" overstates emotion to the detriment of more rationalist appeals. Historian Ian Kershaw has dismissed the political religion approach as "a currently voguish revamping of an age-old notion, though no less convincing for being repeated so persistently" (2004, 250). Richard J. Evans cautions against "pushing the religious metaphor too far" in the study of Nazism, which lacked basic features of a "genuine" religion. Nazism "had nothing to say about the hereafter or eternity or the immortal soul"; there were no equivalents in Nazism to "medieval scholastics" committed to the study of the doctrine or even a "sacred book from which people took their texts for the day"; and, lastly, Nazism lacked the universal message of salvation and a morality of "love and compassion that have always formed an important element in the beliefs of the world's great religions." Therefore Nazism's use of myths, symbols, and rituals was above all a question of style, not of substance, and the attempt to understand it through the concept of political religion is "purely descriptive" and unhelpful (Evans 2006, 257–60).

Even those who see the political religion approach in a more favorable manner seem to form a tacit consensus that political religions are, wholesale, on the wane in the contemporary world. It is as if the process of social secularization has also led progressively to a total de-sacralization of the political realm. As political scientist Juan Linz has written, "Political religions

---

8. The writings of Israeli historian Uriel Tal (2004) constitute an illuminating example. See also Koenker 1965; Maier and Bruhn 2004; and Pinto, Larsen, and Eatwell 2006.

are powerful and have shaped the life of people in the twentieth century in unique ways . . . But only because they could rely on the power resources of a totalitarian state including its coercive resources." Linz further adds that totalitarian movements "do not seem to have generated sufficient strength of belief to survive the loss of political power (2004, 109–10). Weberian sociologist Luciano Cavalli writes that while Weber's forecasts about Western rationalization and secularization have proven wrong for interwar Europe because of the advancement of secular religions, secularization has "[i]n recent years . . . attacked secular religions too. Today Weber's forecasts [about secularization] make more sense then they did for decades after his death" (1987, 324). Cavalli further notes, "Secularization considerably weakens traditional religions at first, and then the secular ones such as Marxism-Leninism" (1987, 332). Although recognizing the role of religion as a "constitutive aspect of human experience," sociologist Daniel Bell stresses in a similar manner the undermining of the sacred by rationalization. According to him, "the 'ground impulses' behind aestheticism and political religions are exhausted."[9] The same position is taken by historian Philippe Burrin. In his evaluation of the relevance of the concept of political religion, he expresses doubts about the possibility to "re-enchant a society in the clutches of modernity." Instead, political religions will likely be swept away by the march of rationalization.[10]

Scholars who excel at identifying the multivarious forms that the sacred assumes show a similar reluctance to see the permanence of political

---

9. According to Daniel Bell, "On the double level of social structure and culture, the world has been secularized and profaned." Bell states that "religion is no longer the 'collective conscience' of society . . . because society is radically disjointed, its different realms of the techno-economic sphere, with its principle of functional rationality, the polity and its surge for equality, and the culture with its demands for self-fulfillment creating increasingly intolerable strains" (1977, 439–42).

10. Discussing the inherent frailty of political religions, Burrin writes, "The type of political, moral and spiritual unity that they aim to create can only be thwarted by the massive movement toward rationalization of society, by the institutional segmentation and the technical specialization that continuously engender the splitting of social life into autonomous spheres. Even on their own privileged level of beliefs, symbols and rituals, the limits of political religions are soon evident" (1997, 342).

religions in contemporary times. Sironneau, a critic of the secularization paradigm who sees political religions as one of the resurgences of the sacred, feels compelled to note the collapse of the "modern metamorphosis of the sacred." Insofar as they are not properly "traditional religions," they tend to "de-mythicize rapidly" (Sironneau 1982, 562). The same logic is behind the work of Gentile. Although he acknowledges the fact that the sacralization of politics can eventually be "a dormant volcano," Gentile writes that

> [w]e could consider the sacralization of politics to be an imposing but extraordinary and contingent phenomenon relating to tempestuous cultural, political, economic and social changes that dominated the process of modernity through the last two hundred years. This is therefore a phenomenon that has run its course or is at least nearing the end of it, together with the epoch that created it. (2006, 136)

This line of interpretations seems to have taken hold. Giner, who has probed into the staying power of the holy in liberal democracies and the continuing sacralization of communities though the workings of civic religions—of which charisma as a manifestation of the numinous he sees as a crucial part—mainly joins political religions with bygone totalitarian movements such as Nazism, Stalinism, and Maoism (2003, 91). Somewhat analogous is Stanley G. Payne's take on the subject, which recognizes the "vitality of the sacred in ever-multiplying metamorphoses," but does not specifically identify it in any contemporary European political movement apart from a passing mention of Basque and Catalan nationalism and the ideology of "Political Correctness." As Payne notes, "[D]iverse forms [of political religion] may be found in the late twentieth and early twenty-first centuries in African and Asian countries" (2002, 125).

The concept of "political religion" has therefore been closely linked either with totalitarianism and associated with the establishment and development of specific historical political regimes—mainly fascism, Nazism, communism—or with non-Western postcolonial states. As I will show, however, the persistent scholarly focus on the totalitarian and coercive nature of these political religions has obscured less extreme manifestations of sacred politics in the contemporary context.

According to major scholars, at least regarding European liberal democracies, political religions seem to be losing ground so rapidly that they are doomed eventually to disappear altogether. It is as if movements led by a charismatic leader invested with a mission of salvation and characterized by myth, ritual, communion, and faith represent mere traces of a past doomed to be overtaken by the natural course of history. In fact, the internal dynamics of liberal democracies seem, on appearance, to be a natural corollary of a world more and more "disenchanted." They do seem to fit perfectly the secularization paradigm that opened this introduction. As argued by Steve Bruce, "What most marks the political cultures of the modern industrial societies of the West from those of other countries is that the former are largely secular." "Liberal democracies," he continues, "are distinguished by having formally secular polities, their religious institutions are largely impotent except to the extent that they accept secular rules of engagement, and the majority of the population either have no religion or adhere to religions that have mutated a long way from their orthodox bases" (Bruce 2003, 245–46). This is the taken-for-granted consensus that I intend to dispute in the following pages.

A crucial part of the decline of the sacralization of the political, at least in the Western world, is the inevitable weakening of charismatic leadership dynamics. As Ronald E. Riggio stated in an article in the *Encyclopedia of Leadership,* "currently, there is no generally accepted agreed-on definition of charisma" (2004, 158). However, if social scientists have found difficult to define charisma, major post-Weberian works on charismatic leadership have had a more defined focus on examples of charismatic leaders. The rule in choosing twentieth-century case studies has been to take them either from the more extreme examples of the interwar period or from underdeveloped societies, particularly in relation to colonial struggles or postcolonial contexts.[11] The literature of charisma studies has not paid the same attention to more stable, more modern, and, therefore, allegedly less "enchanted" environments, such as those of contemporary Western liberal democracies.

---

11. A good example of this tendency in post-Weberian charismatic leadership studies can be found in Willner (1984). On this topic, see also Cavalli (1996, 679–83).

As in the case of research on political religions, this general scenario assumes the ebb of the sacralization of the political; therefore it is not surprising that major scholars have demonstrated, for some time, uneasiness regarding the phenomenon of charismatic leadership in their analysis of contemporary Western political dynamics and situations. The following words of Jasper B. Shannon, written in 1949, testify to the mindset, not to say the hope, shared by many scholars. To him,

> Perhaps a more realistic, not to say more scientific, age will look upon our belief in leaders who can solve our social ills by political magic as absurd as we regard the divine power attributed to monarchs in the healing of bodily ills ... Confused and baffled, we follow the human practice of the ages, we make men into gods and worship or curse them as fortune, fate, or the weather make us alternately comfortable or unhappy. In any case the size and complexity of human problems have become so great that only the inordinately ambitious or the well nigh saintly unselfish will assume the task of political leadership. Institutions need to be constructed for the industrial age which will reduce mass dependence upon charismatic leadership. (Shannon 1949, 327–28)

A number of social scientists have argued that the academy should get rid of the term "charisma" in analysis of contemporary political dynamics and situations. In 1960 American historian Arthur Schlesinger, Jr., wrote, "The grounds of the democratic leader's authority rest characteristically on his capacity to gain *conditional* support from enough interests and people to put together a *temporary* majority; his method is characteristically a pragmatic balancing of forces, appeals, and policies: none of this finds room in Weber's system." Schlesinger accused Weber's analysis of having a "hypnotic effect" on leadership literature and noticed "the uselessness of charisma as a concept with which to analyze leadership in more complicated cases than those of medicine men, warrior chieftains, and religious prophets" (Schlesinger 1960, 6–7). A related skepticism regarding the use of the term "charisma" to describe modern politics can be found in the work of Weber's former student and friend Karl Loewenstein. Arguing against the validity of the category of charismatic authority in times of technological mass democracy, Loewenstein observed, "In the last analysis, as a basis of rule, it [charisma] possesses a historical reality. Or, to put it differently: charismatic authority in politics is a phenomenon of the pre-Cartesian world" (Loewenstein 1966, 86). Therefore, charisma belongs to the enchanted world that, at least in the Western setting, humanity had left behind.

Rejecting the applicability of "pure" charisma to the modern world (which is deemed too impersonal, rational, and bureaucratic), Joseph Bensman and Michael Givant posit instead the concept of pseudo-charisma—the rational manufacture of charisma through the manipulation of images and symbols by elites in order to maintain and even to achieve power—as a defining feature of an increasingly media-oriented political culture that outweighs in importance the "old" Weberian type. This strategic and calculated fabrication has therefore replaced for most part the erstwhile "extraordinary," "irrational," and "revolutionary" form of charisma (Bensman and Givant 1975, 570–614; see also Giner 2003, 172–78). But even the "manufacture" of charisma in the modern world seems to face serious obstacles, and Ronald M. Glassman has written about the consolidation of a science-driven "rational, skeptical and empirical worldview" that produces a "general rationality," whereupon the "'average' individual becomes cynical and decharismatized easily," and thus stymies the increasingly sophisticated fabrication and manipulation of charisma by the mass media (Glassman 1986, 126).

Finally, James MacGregor Burns, a major scholar of leadership studies, considers charisma to be a nuisance concept: "leaders who fill bellies," Burns writes, "can be tested on the basis of how many bellies filled." Charisma as a sociological concept addresses merely "an array of murky psychological needs," and, therefore, cannot be studied in a serious and rational manner; thus, any form of leadership that satisfies "'hungers' of the 'mind and spirit'" should be approached primarily as "an exotic or lopsided form" of Burns's own concept of "transforming leadership," that is, leadership that "accomplishes rational, planned transformational change—real, comprehensive, durable change, changes that advance the great public values" (Burns 2003, 22–27). His is a telling example of contemporary scholarly discomfort—often the mark of a dismissive attitude toward the subject—in dealing with the nonrational, charismatic dimensions of politics. .

MISSIONARY POLITICS—APPROACH AND METHODOLOGY

Anomalies to the Dominant Rationalist Paradigm

Until quite recently, like the concept of political religion, charisma had been a largely absent notion in the social scientific analysis of contemporary political life. But recent developments have challenged the dominant rationalist model in social analysis. In the last decades the world has seen the rise in liberal-democratic countries of leaders so driven by a sense of mission and so deft at creating a devoted following that they are invariably defined as charismatic. Powerful examples of these "new charismatics" come from a pool of new populist movements that are usually described as fitting into the extreme right of the political spectrum.[12] Major works have confirmed this new charismatic strain in such movements operating within liberal democracies. Herbert Kitschelt calls it the "New Radical Right" and observes that it shares in common with the fascist parties of the past "the prevalence of charismatic leadership" (1995, 32). In the same vein, Hans-Georg Betz argues that "the most successful radical right-wing populist parties are led by charismatic figures capable of setting the political and programmatic direction" (1998, 9). Yves Mény and Yves Surel observe that this increasing trend of populism "advocates the power of the people, yet relies on seduction by a charismatic leader" (2002, 17). Gianpietro Mazzoleni observes that "neo-populist movements characteristically organize themselves around charismatic and strongly personalized leaderships and are immediately and exclusively identified with highly visible and controversial leaders" (2003, 4–5). Among the characteristics displayed by the successful parties of the extreme right, notes Piero Ignazi, there is "an appealing, charismatic, and uncontested leadership which could prevent and control internal factionalism and attract the attention of the media" (2003, 203). Roger Eatwell

---

12. These movements have been categorized in many different ways, ranging from extreme, radical, or far right to populist, neopopulist, or populist radical right. On the problem of categorization, see Eatwell 2004. In my book both the National Front and the Northern League will be presented as ideal typical examples of the form of politics that I categorize as *missionary*.

brings a similar point home in writing that some voters "are strongly attracted by extreme right and populist policies on issues such as immigration and law and order, and by 'charismatic' personalities such as Le Pen" (2004, 1). Eatwell sees the personification of issues and policies in the uncontested figure of the leader as a major "rational" tool, particularly in election times. However, he does recognize the persistence of an emotional and affective relationship with the leader within these movements (2002, 17–21). Elisabeth Carter, in her study on the varying electoral fortunes of Western European extreme-right parties, concluded that the well-organized and well-led nature (by leaders described as "strong and charismatic") of some of these parties constitutes a major factor in their success (2005, especially 64–101).

Meanwhile, resurgent literature on charismatic leadership has followed Weber, and has emphasized the intimate link between the development of a sense of mission and a situation of crisis. In Weber's analysis, as mentioned above, recognition of the charismatic leader arises out of "enthusiasm, or of despair and hope" (1978, 242). Norberto Bobbio has expressed his conviction that

> [a]ny discussion of the phenomena of charismatic leadership, as in the past with [the phenomenon of] Caesarism, makes evident the fact that either one of them arise[s] in times of historical crisis, in the passage of a power system to another, in the moment in which the violent break of a system opens the road to the foundation, also violent, of a new system, [accomplished] either by a civil war or a revolution. (Bobbio 1998, 5)

Robert C. Tucker notes both that "charismatic leadership is specifically salvationist or messianic in nature" and that "the followers respond to the charismatic leader with passionate loyalty because the salvation, or promise of it, that he appears to embody represents the fulfillment of urgently felt needs" (Tucker 1970, 81). In the words of Pierre Bourdieu, "prophetic discourse is thus more likely to gain success in periods in which economic or morphological transformations determine the collapse, decline, or obsolescence of traditions or value-systems that provided the principles of a worldview and a mode of life" (Bourdieu 1987, 130). Charles Lindholm observes that a charismatic relation "is a creative and regenerating force likely to be favored particularly in times of social malaise and suffering, when fragmented social formations are especially in need of reinvigoration through charismatic participation" (Lindholm 1990, 35). Even authors such as Ann Ruth Willner, who does not see a situation of crisis as a requirement for the rise of charismatic political leadership, admit that "preconditions of exogenous social crisis and psychic distress are conducive to the emergence of charismatic political leadership" (Willner 1984, 52).

This situation points to two major problems in the social science analysis of contemporary trends in democratic societies. If the Western world, particularly Europe, is more and more secular and rational, then why does charisma, which ultimately has to do with fervor and emotion, remain an instrument in European politics? Shouldn't this "less enchanted" environment prevent the revival of charismatic leadership, as observed by several commentators? Complicating analysis is the fact that European Western democracies do not seem, on the surface, to be living through any of the dramatic crises—such as wars or disasters—that are traditionally seen as catalysts of the emergence of a discourse of charismatic mission. How then can one explain this persistence of a charismatic strain in Western European politics?

A distinction must be made from the outset. The last decades have witnessed a popularization of the term *charisma*. It has become commonplace: Everyone who is popular, appealing, or gifted in sports, arts, or politics becomes in the eyes of public opinion a charismatic figure. The consolidation of a celebrity-oriented culture—fuelled by both the media and the public's insatiable appetite for stardom—is at the very basis of the explosion of charisma in popular vocabulary.[13] Writing about the overuse of the term *fascism*, Roger Griffin notes that "in the case of words this means that they are used to embrace more and more phenomena and so progressively lose their discriminating power: the 'blanket term' or 'conceptual hold-all' is born" (Griffin 1991, 1). Indeed, the word *charisma* has been subjected to a similar process of "inflation" and, subsequently, "devaluation."

---

13. For an analysis of the nature of celebrity power in contemporary societies, see Marshall 1997, particularly 27–76. See also Marshall 2004. Neal Gabler (1998) argues that "entertainment" values—and a concomitant focus on celebrities and "human interest stories"—have been steadily shaping the reality of American society since the early nineteenth century.

In order to avoid this risk of hollowing out the descriptive power of the term, I introduce a distinction between two forms of charisma in contemporary societies. The first one I call the *popular* form of charisma. It is intimately linked with the celebrity-oriented culture and the predominance of the visual and imagery in the contemporary Western world. It is in essence superficial. (I use the word *superficial* to indicate not something trivial or insignificant but rather something that is near the surface.) It deals essentially with projection of looks and attitudes, of physical and personal qualities deemed appealing and amplified by the media, particularly the visual media. The second form of charisma, which I define as *missionary*, is the form that operates within my conceptual framework of missionary politics and on which I focus my book.

As we have seen at the beginning of this chapter, the march of rationalization has pushed to the forefront a continuous narrative of secularization that has itself ultimately led to the undermining of traditional religions and, in a later period, to the failure of political religions in Europe. In this way, according to the dominant rationalist paradigm, the sacralization of the political fell victim to a supposedly more rational, secular liberal-democratic environment. In this paradigm, the tendency has been to study the sacralization of politics either as a manifestation of the past or, primarily, as the work of exploitive and manipulative propaganda by demagogic leaders and organizations. In my work I approach the phenomenon of sacralized politics not through the lens of the conventional rationalist model but by emphasizing a different dimension of politics in the West, "missionary politics," which will guide my investigation of the reality of contemporary political movements.

An Ideal Type

My methodological approach is heuristic and follows the path of Weber's comparative-historical sociology, particularly at the level of construction of ideal types as guiding tools to understand and systematize reality. Weber's causal sociology is anchored in ideal types that provide a framework and a "mental picture" to analyze the world of experience. These heuristic devices function as yardsticks that, according to Weberian sociologist Stephen Kalberg, document "patterned action" and assist the researcher in comprehending an "amorphous and ceaselessly flowing reality" (Kalberg 1994, 93). Deeply rooted in empirical reality, these ideal types "seek to isolate, on a rigorous basis, significant causal patterns of action." Because they follow primarily systematic and internally consistent lines they constitute a "conscious exaggeration of *essential* features of the significant action-orientations for the research task at hand" (Kalberg 1994, 86). Aiming at assisting empirical inquiry, ideal types "accentuate those aspects of the empirical case of particular interest to the researcher" (1994, 85). Missionary politics should therefore be understood as a construction, an ideal type that gives a synthesis of the features of the sacralization of the political in a contemporary age.

Other scholars have attempted to capture the missionary field in contemporary liberal-democratic politics through the use of a methodology that refers back to Weber and the use of ideal-types as heuristic tools. British philosopher Michael Oakeshott put forward two ideal types that, according to him, have been predominant in the modern politics of Western Europe. These two historic styles of politics have been "the politics of skepticism" and "the politics of faith." While the politics of skepticism offers a piecemeal approach to politics, the politics of faith is geared toward a holistic vision of politics within which "the activity of governing is understood to be in the service of the perfection of mankind." Oakeshott adds, "Perfection, or salvation, is something to be achieved in this world: man is redeemable in history" (Oakeshott 1996, 23). In the politics of skepticism, "governing is understood as a specific activity, and in particular it is understood to be detached from the pursuit of human perfection" (1996, 31). For the skeptic the activity of governing is a judicial activity, "not a matter of establishing the 'truth,'" in which "discussion and 'opposition' will not be regarded as means for 'the discovery of truth,' but as a means for calling attention to something that might otherwise have been forgotten and for keeping government within its proper bounds" (1996, 37). The opposite is the case for the politics of faith, which aims at a totalizing vision that will transform the world and rid it of pollution. Oakeshott describes these two political styles as abstractions, extremes between which politics have been fluctuating since early-modern European history up to the present.

Drawing from Oakeshott's analysis, Margaret Canovan argues that there is another face of democracy that is less rational and more emotional, with a strong component of faith. It deals with redemption rather than pragmatism (Canovan 1999, 9). "Inherent in modern democracy, in tension with its pragmatic face," she writes, "is faith in secular redemption: the promise of a better world through action by the sovereign people" (1999, 11). Through the use of concepts that systematize a diffuse empirical reality, Oakeshott and Canovan have stressed that the sacred has entered into the political realm, albeit in a secularized disguise. Neither, however, has attempted to apply these ideal types systematically to specific case studies.

A Cluster Concept

Building on these contributions, I base my study of contemporary populist movements by developing an empirically derived cluster concept that I call "Missionary Politics." Historians Gentile and Griffin, among others, have blazed this methodological trail of clustering. By establishing the parameters of an ideal type, the cluster concept captures reality in a holistic or "organic" manner by emphasizing both patterns of action and dynamic, interconnected constellations of different but related phenomena. Therefore, a cluster should be understood as a central concept or "star" that lies in the middle of a constellation of adjacent and overlapping concepts and associated dimensions. According to this method, as stated by Griffin, conceptual terms "are to be approached 'synergically' as complimentary components forming an open-ended nexus of heuristic devices with which to arrive at a deeper understanding of particular aspects of reality" (Griffin 2005, 38).

Taken as a whole, my research focus on a network of interacting concepts clustering around the central concept of "missionary politics," aims at giving a multiperspective approach to a multifaceted phenomenon. Grounded in empirical reality and deduced from the material collected within the movements—not imposed from above according to a preexisting model, which precludes formulating an abstract comparative analysis—my research on missionary politics has indicated the following constellation: Missionary politics should be understood as a form of *political religion* carried out by a *chosen people* who, in a time of self-perceived deep-rooted *crisis*, sees itself as a *moral community* led by a *missionary charismatic* leader undertaking a *collective mission of salvation*. Driven by *apocalyptic* and *millenarian* dynamics, the community manifests its solidarity and belief in the mission by constant *ritualization*. In the process, the members of the community celebrate themselves as a *sacred collective*, as representatives of a *sacred nation* and heirs to a *sacred history* involved in an apocalyptic showdown with the *evil* and *conspiratorial* forces of a *new world order*.

Cultural Analysis

My adoption of clustering as a methodological procedure to investigate the dynamics of missionary politics makes my approach decidedly multidisciplinary, and I hope to give a rounded analysis of the phenomenon, open to contributions and insights drawn from an array of different disciplines such as political science, history, cultural anthropology, and sociology of religion. From the major competing theoretical schools in comparative politics—divided between rational choice theorists, structuralists, and culturalists—my approach falls within the culturalist research school in the sense that I want to give a cultural contribution to political analysis and show how the experiential, rhetorical, and ethnographic dimensions of religion shape contemporary political groups. *Culture* from this perspective, and following the path of Max Weber and anthropologist Clifford Geertz,[14] should be understood not merely as the possession of specific values or beliefs but, in the words of Marc Howard Ross, as a "worldview," a "system of meaning and identity" that "explains why and how individuals and groups behave as they do" (Ross 1997, 44–45).[15]

Owing to predominant rationalist assumptions, these populist or extreme-right groups have until now been primarily explained in terms of their relationship with issues and grievances. The implication is that these groups have been chiefly anchored in materialist frames. But in my study, I

---

14. It is useful to remember here Geertz's classical definition of culture as "an historically transmitted pattern of meaning embodied in symbols, a system of inherited conceptions expressed in symbolic forms by means of which men communicate, perpetuate, and develop their knowledge about and attitudes towards life" (1973, 89).

15. On the continuing importance of cultural frameworks and performances that provide meaning systems, see Alexander, Giesen, and Mast 2006, 1–22.

attempt to discern how such a group is sustained by nonmaterial dimensions: the cultural frames that sustain these groups, that is, the internal production of a narrative and codes that establish a symbolic world and a framework of salvation. Cultural theorist Philip Smith has argued for the need to stress cultural structures such as "binary cultural codes" that oppose good and evil, and "narratives" that mythologize reality by aligning it within a salvation framework, in order to have a broader picture of contemporary charismatic leaders (2000, 103–4). I follow Smith's line of interpretation: hence my primary focus on the discursive frames created by those who are within the movement and involved in a quest for salvation, focusing on what they *actually say and do,* and on how they experience and symbolize the collective, with a special relevance given to the status and role of the leader.

My argument that these cultural frames play a visible role in the maintenance and development of these groups does not imply a dismissal of more instrumentalist approaches. The appeal of these contemporary movements certainly is spurred by different dimensions, of which the religious is only one (albeit, in my view, a relevant and often neglected one). There are important materialist explanations for the phenomenon—economic insecurity, views on immigration, issues of crime and order, political corruption—that facilitate the identification of some sectors of the population with movements that specifically exploit those insecurities.[16] But these will not be the focus of my book. I agree with Gentile's contention that to study a political movement as a secular religion does not mean to find only in this aspect the explanation for "[the movement's] nature and historical meaning" (Gentile 2006, 145). However, instrumentalist models that emphasize primarily grievances and concepts such as "political opportunity structures" often fail to capture the positive identity and extraordinary member commitment engendered by many of these movements, the persistence of culturally specific grand narratives in them, and the role that nonmaterial forces play in the development of these movements' respective identities. At a broader theoretical level my book addresses one of the major shortcomings of political theory: what Chantal Mouffe has decried as the "incapacity to grasp the central role

---

16. For a rounded view of instrumentalist approaches to the study of these movements across Europe, see Schain, Zolberg, and Hossay 2002; Rydgren 2005; and Givens 2005.

of passions in the constitution of collective identities" (Mouffe 2005, 51; on this point see also Aminzade and McAdam 2001, 14–51).

Case Studies

As I have written above, sacralization of politics is a generally absent theme in research on major contemporary movements led by leaders who are repeatedly characterized as "charismatic" by both social commentators and scholars. It is this lack that I propose to remedy in my book. I focus here on two of the most successful of these movements: the French Front National (National Front), led by Jean-Marie Le Pen, and the Italian Lega Nord (Northern League), led by Umberto Bossi. Only a handful of studies have followed a similar approach to mine and have specifically focused on the role of religious frameworks for the implementation and sustenance of these movements—when done, it has often been in a fragmentary manner.[17]

From my research I concluded that these two cases are sufficient to suggest a pattern or cluster of attributes that can then be extended to provide the skeleton of an ideal type. Looking at both the empirical reality of these movements and the sacred dimension of their respective politics, I will document patterned actions and both integrate and systematize my findings into an ideal type of missionary politics. My hope is that I may provide a guideline against which different movements can be measured and compared. Therefore, adding new ethnographic, rhetorical, and symbolic cultural material to the empirical research of political movements commonly categorized as "populist" or "extreme-right" can shed light on dynamics that would otherwise be left unnoticed or unexplained.

---

17. Regarding populist movements in general, one would find worthwhile a look at Paul Taggart (2000, particularly chapter 9). In the case of Le Pen and his movement, a notable exception to the dominant rationalist and structuralist trends can be found in the work of Erwan Lecoeur (2003, especially chapters 9 and 10). See also Soucheter et al. 1998, especially 132–40 and 216–22; and Lafont 2001, especially 193–97. Regarding the movement of Umberto Bossi, some fragmentary references can be found in the works of Ilvo Diamanti (1996, chapters 5 and 6); Biorcio (1997, especially chapter 9); Donegà (1994); and Berzano (1994, especially chapter 9).

I need to point out that because my intention is the construction of a comparative model and mode of analysis based on the relationship between religion and politics, I deduce general principles from my case studies more than political scientists usually do. This deduction could be anathema for scholars who are reluctant to use generic concepts and wary of generalizing in academic research, particularly in social sciences and humanities, fearing abstraction, lack of discriminatory power, and the loss of "explanatory value" from a theoretical concept that could be applied "almost to anything, anywhere."[18] Yet ideal types are primarily tools of analysis, devices that serve to create "a better understanding of the 'real' thing" (Morgan 2006, 158) by discovering features that, as in the case of missionary politics, were hidden or sacrificed within standard rationalistic modes of understanding contemporary political movements. The danger of reification, or essentialism, if it exists, stems from a fundamental misunderstanding of what an ideal type is and of the purpose it serves in academic research.

I compensate for the necessary loss of the nuances and elaboration of differences between both movements under study with an exploration of the extensive ethnographic narratives employed by each, and the patterns discerned in them. There are obviously differences between both parties under study, given that each emerged in specific national contexts—the National Front as the embodiment of different sectors of the French nationalist right, and the Northern League in the regionalist and autonomist setting of northern Italy—and each has its own trajectory. Further, the missionary dimension that I identified in both movements coexists with a decidedly more bureaucratic and pragmatic one within each. In the pages that follow I argue not that the missionary style is hegemonic but that it is a crucial and often understudied dimension. I hope that my primary focus on the religious dimensions of both parties, derived from internal material, can be extrapolated in order to conceptualize patterns of thought and action that can then be applied to the study of other contemporary political movements.

My analysis focuses primarily on the immediate following of the leader, and not on the general voter or on what makes the party attractive to the

---

18. For a harshly critical view of using ideal types in social sciences and humanities, see James A. Gregor's review of Roger Griffin's work (2006, 115–22; 311–19).

broader electorate. At the end of my study I discuss global and societal dynamics that may facilitate the conversion of others to the missionary call of the group. Public opinion analysis, voting behavior patterns, and dynamics of electoral breakthrough, however, are secondary to my investigation into the missionary dynamic at work within such political groups. My focus is on those who surround the leader, from cabinet members and party officials to the militants themselves. I take a closer look at the dynamics of what Eatwell has called, in opposition to mass charisma, the "charisma of the coterie," that is, "a hardcore of supporters both in their inner courts and more locally who held that a special mission drove the leader, and who accorded this leader great loyalty and were willing to make special efforts on behalf of the cause" (Eatwell 2002, 19). In his study on Nazism, Kershaw introduced the distinction between the "charismatic community" composed of those "who formed the initial agency of transmission of the personality cult surrounding him" and "the mass of 'Hitler believers' in the population at large" (2001b, 15–17). Another study by Emrich and colleagues, drawing from the vast organizational literature on charismatic leadership, has explained this distinction in terms of "public charisma" as perceived by a broad audience of followers, and "private charisma" as perceived by a "narrower band of followers, all of whom have both direct contact and relationships with the leader" (Emrich et al. 2001, 534). It is this more personal, private, coterie form of charisma, which I call "missionary," that serves as the center of my book.

THE DATA I USE to make my argument reflect my primary concern with the self-perception of the group. My aim is to establish the phenomenological reality of the collective movement through the use of first-person accounts. Therefore speeches, party literature, election programs, party newspapers, friendly newspapers, biographies, memoirs, books by the leaders and officials, and interviews with officials and militants constitute my primary sources of evidence. In this way, my approach is similar to that of Lindholm who, in his pursuit of identifying the dynamics of charismatic movements, defended the necessity of entering the world of the participants "by listening attentively to their own accounts" and not just to the abstractions of theory (Lindholm 1990, 89). I hypothesize that these are indeed charismatic political movements whose dynamics and features are those of a political religion. If the hypothesis of the development of missionary politics is validated by the study of these case studies, then this study will help to explain the persistence of charisma in contemporary democratic politics and provide a model of the form these movements are likely to take in the future.

Plan of the Book

In the next two chapters I identify the features of the sacralization of politics in these movements, by paying attention to the actual inner workings, rhetorical tropes, ritual performances, and social organization of what I consider to be two paradigmatic examples of modern missionary political movements. In synch with my clustered approach to missionary politics, I look at how the militant group presents itself as a chosen people following its charismatic missionary leader and engaged in a battle for salvation. In the creation of this missionary narrative, the leader plays a fundamental role, and my study is thus primarily a leader-oriented approach. Because the development of a missionary discourse implies the formation of a close-knit community, however, my analysis will also inevitably focus on some of the internal dynamics of the community of followers. After exploring the religio-political dimensions of the movements led by Jean Marie Le Pen and Umberto Bossi, I follow with an analytical chapter that draws from my empirical findings and lays out the different features of the sacralization of politics within both movements, in a comparative manner that attempts to integrate all the findings in order to construct—using scholarly work from different disciplines—an ideal type of missionary politics that can serve as a baseline for further comparative research into the religious dimension of contemporary political movements. Finally, I conclude my study with a discussion of current European and global trends that, I believe, have the potential to exacerbate both the conditions and the call for a "politics of salvation" in contemporary Europe.

2
Le Pen and the National Front

In this chapter, which focuses on the political movement of Le Pen, and in the next, which is dedicated to that of Umberto Bossi, I identify the features of the sacralization of politics in each, focusing on the actual inner workings, rhetorical tropes, ritual performances, and social organization of these two modern missionary political movements.

REJECTION OF THE PRESENT—THE CRISIS

At the very basis of Le Pen's discourse is a totalistic rejection of the present. Le Pen constructs a narrative intended to imprint deeply in the public mind an image of himself as a hero ready to save a country riddled by corruption and decline, and unable to survive without help. France's "liberation" from the "crisis" of the present is a recurring theme in Le Pen's discourse. In order to understand how this concept of crisis provides the gravitational center of Le Pen's discourse, one needs a closer look at his concept of "The Nation." The party platform of the Front National (National Front) in 2001 had a section headlined "La Mémoire" (The Memory), which stated that

> [i]t is [by] respecting their founding principles that human societies can perpetuate themselves. Society is not the result of a contract but the outcome of an Order. Nothing can be done without submission to this law . . . Under abusive and intoxicating universal changes is hidden a big and profound law of immobility . . . In reality there is, in the continuity of civilizations and peoples, a pre-established harmony, reflection of the Creation, called Cosmos by the Greeks, that means Order. (National Front 2001)

According to the National Front's philosophy, the nation is not modern. Rather, the nation is primordial: It is a natural body, permanent and based on a spiritual and physical continuity between the past and the present. It is not an abstraction nor a creation of the intellect; the nation is a concrete reality. The program of the National Front uses as its main historical resource the defense of tradition and historical continuity propounded by French historians Ernest Renan and Hippolyte Taine (National Front 2001). Above all, this concept of nation represents a rejection both of the Enlightenment and of the abstraction and universalism brought by the French Revolution of 1789.

In the philosophy of the National Front, the French nation is not a group of citizens detached from their respective ethnic or religious origins and organized around a social contract or a political project. To the contrary, the nation is a community bonded by a continuity of generations, all of which share the same language and belong to the same historical France. "What we have more in common between us and with our compatriots that are abroad," said Le Pen in 1987 at a banquet with his sympathizers, "is the notion of heritage, [France's] material heritage, accumulated by centuries of work and sacrifices, by all the generations that have preceded us, [France's] immense moral and cultural heritage" (Souchard et al. 1998, 96). "It took more than a thousand years of efforts," he said in a speech in his hometown in Brittany, "to establish the French nation, in its historical homogeneity, in its culture and language" (Le Pen 1992a, 195).

Although Le Pen has always rejected the label, the National Front is commonly put on the extreme right of the political continuum. Le Pen rejects the term as being more "polemical than scientific," and has always defined his party as "a movement of the *national right,* the *national* opposition" (Le Pen 1984, 180). Thus the problems that afflict France, according to Le Pen and given center stage within his narrative—excessive immigration, lack of law and order, unemployment—are only symptoms of a deeply rooted national malaise extending back to the Enlightenment, which initiated the undermining of national identity and values, and which, inexorably, will lead to the end of the nation itself. This scenario of national crisis serves as the background in which Le Pen develops a narrative that presents the National Front, the last defenders of "The Nation," and the Front's leader,

Le Pen, the nation's savior, as united in the mission of rescuing France from the onslaught of the forces of corruption and decadence. In order to explain this narrative, I will first show how Le Pen creates and reinforces the identity of the group as the True France.

THE GROUP AS THE ELECT

Historical Continuity

In his discourse, Le Pen constantly aims to replace the dominant historical paradigm with an alternative vision of French history. The prevalent, mainstream version promotes the values of the French Revolution of 1789 through the French resistance to the Nazi occupation as the solid basis of the Republic. Le Pen sees this version of history as an artificial creation of modernity that is ultimately dismissive of the true premodern and Christian roots of the French nation. The France hailed by Le Pen is the France that is heir to the Galois, Celts, and Franks. In the words of Le Pen, "the first martyr of the national independence" (1992c) was the Gallic leader Vercingétorix, who defied the rule of the Roman emperor. A main reference in Le Pen's historical repertoire is Clovis I, the king of the Franks who, in the sixth century, unified the French territory with Paris as its capital. The National Front connects Clovis, the first French ruler to adopt Christianity, to the foundation of a unified and Christian France. "In this way [the baptism of Clovis]," declared Le Pen in a speech, "achieved the sacred union of Christianity, the Roman civilization, and the youthful vigor of the Frank people that would become, through fifteen centuries, the French people." Further, Le Pen told his faithful, "We are the heirs of this prestigious destiny" (1995). In 1996, the National Front celebrated the fifteen-hundredth anniversary of Clovis's baptism in the cathedral at Reims, with festivities and meetings all over France. In the preface of a book published by the party to celebrate this anniversary, Le Pen stressed his party's "true celebration of the foundational moments of the French Nation [that] could only come from those who have a filial relationship [with the nation]." Ceremonies derived "from the cold analysts of a disembodied history" or from "subsidized official commemorations" lacked authentic legitimacy (Le Pen 1996a, 5).

The most celebrated historical figure in the imagination of the National Front is the fifteenth-century French martyr Joan of Arc, who organized the resistance against English invaders and was tortured and burned at the stake. Le Pen's tributes to Joan are always passionate, and he constantly establishes a parallel between her fight and the National Front's battle for France. Asked in an interview which role model he would suggest to European youth, Le Pen gave the name of this "first and most complete symbol of France," for "in this national heroine, patriot saint, and champion of Christianity, we find the youth, the people, the faith and the sacrifice, all the things that compose civilization." He continued, "half a millennium ago, she was the precursor of a national France" (1989a, 154). In a speech Le Pen declared, "What was the plot 600 years ago? It was to deliver France to the king of England, with the complicity of the University of Paris, the church of France, and feudal instigators. What is the plot today? It is to put an end to the independence and inalienable sovereignty of France, and to amalgamate in a so-called European unity that knows no geographical and political limits—with the complicity of those who have the sacred mission of defending France" (1998).

The principles that inspired Joan of Arc's mission in the past are the principles that inspire Le Pen's mission in the present: "Faith in the eternal France, love for the homeland, defense of the people, authority, independence, identity, security, courage, gathering, faith, honor, and sacrifice. Those were her values. Today they are our values" (1999c).

At the same time, the French history promoted by Le Pen displays nostalgia for the old French empire. Refusing to accept what he calls the unjust official version of colonization as a shameful period, Le Pen asserts that the "advantages" of empire "were far greater than we want to admit" (1989a, 46), for "history has been unfair toward the men of the Third Republic, the founders of the second French colonial empire . . . those men who led the colonization—what today is referred to in a pejorative and unjust way as 'colonialism'—had above all the purpose of propagating European civilization to the men of the entire world" (1989a, 38).

In the eyes of Le Pen, two events symbolize, above all, the loss to France of its past imperial grandeur. The first is the military defeat at Diên-Biên-Phû (May 1954) that marked the end of the French rule in Indochina. The second is the loss of Algeria as a French colony (1962). These events above all he sees as humiliating, for they symbolize not only lack of political will but also outright treason by the French political establishment. "The defeat of Diên Biên Phû," Le Pen said to one of his biographers, "is a little like the twilight of Gods for France, a warning from history that will not be heeded" (Marcilly 1984, 109). In a phrase that reveals his mindset, Le Pen once wrote, "I was aware that the only countries that could play a role in the world would be those who had not only geopolitical but also economic and strategic space. If not, [France] would be reduced to a little hexagon in the Asiatic peninsula that is Europe" (1984, 49).

Another subject of friction between the history heralded by Le Pen and the dominant history of the French political-cultural establishment has to do with the Second World War and the role played by two major figures, General Charles de Gaulle and Marshal Pétain. Le Pen considers that the "leftist-oriented" version of the events promotes a slanderous image of the man who was the head of the collaborationist regime of Vichy between 1941 and 1944. In Le Pen's eyes, Pétain was a true patriot who thought and acted in the best interests of France. The leader of the National Front is clear about the moral equivalence he sees between those who joined the resistance and those who collaborated. "They had a common attachment to the fatherland," he noted.

> True, they worked on different sides [for the fatherland], but insofar as they were sincere and courageous they were unknowingly . . . on the same side, [the side] of the men who are capable of giving their lives and shedding their blood for a superior cause . . . Since my adolescence, I have never accepted the Manichaeism between the Resistance and the Collaboration. My life experience made me conscious of the relativity of events and engagements, and I understood perfectly well that we could want to serve our country in the resistance to the German occupation as well as in the service of the strategy of the Marshall Pétain or fighting bolshevism. (1993, xxii, xxiii)

However, Le Pen also takes issue with the official version of the resistance to the Nazis, for "it was the national right who led the combat against the occupant and the legend of a collaborationist right and a resistant left was forged by the communists after the war" (1997). In emphasizing his fight against the historical view promulgated by the "System," Le Pen said in an interview that the German occupation of France had not been "particularly inhumane," even if "there were a few excesses." To him, "It's not just from the European Union and globalization that we need to deliver our country, but also from the lies about its history" (*The Guardian*, January 13, 2005, online).[1] In this way, the leader of the National Front provides an alternative historical version of the traumatic events of World War II.

Le Pen puts much emphasis on this battle for the memory of France. To him there is a "good" memory, harkening back to Gaul and the Christian origins of France, which accentuates the natural order at the basis of the nation. There is also a "bad" memory, inaugurated by the Enlightenment, which promotes a false and artificial order. Within his discourse, Le Pen singles out philosopher Jean Jacques Rousseau as the historical figure who best epitomizes this modern subversion of "natural" order. Le Pen sees Rousseau as being guilty of creating a utopian strain in Western thought that led to attempts to create a forced uniformity of values and ways of living. To him, "The Rousseau-esque dream—which inspired socialism, communism, and liberalism—feeds off of *bluettes*, humanitarian feelings of love and utopias, but leads to civil war, anarchy, and tyranny" (1984, 118). Le Pen draws a critical example of this danger from the Reign of Terror that followed the Revolution of 1789. "You tell me," Le Pen said, "that Europe is going to celebrate the French Revolution but, unfortunately, the revolution originated the first great bloodbath of Modern Europe [for] it opened the way to mass massacres" (1989a, 152). In this light, Robespierre and Saint-Just, for example, play the role of veritable bêtes noirs in the narrative of Le Pen (see, for example, Le Pen 2001b). The Declaration of the Rights of Man that emerged during the French Revolution is merely another step in the forced shedding by distinct peoples and cultures of their specific traits, and their amalgamation into a bland, uncharacteristic, artificially "universalistic" order. In 1979, Le Pen accused then president of the Republic Giscard d'Estaing of forgetting

---

1. After the outrage that these comments provoked, Le Pen called it scandalous that "60 years later, one cannot express oneself in a coherent and calm way on these subjects and freely pass judgment on the facts of the occupation" (BBC News, January 13, 2005, online).

his right-wing credentials because of his "Rousseau-esque, humanitarian, utopian, globalist philosophy." To Le Pen, d'Estaing propounded a "philosophy of the left, not of the right" (1979, 175). One should not be surprised that in Le Pen's historical imagination the events of 1968 are "a decisive stage toward decadence" representing "the self-awareness of a country that realizes it is not a great country anymore and [thus] abandons itself . . . 1968 was nausea. It was an act of despair, of disenchantment" (1984, 54–55). Nineteen sixty-eight is a power representation, therefore, in the undermining of tradition and authority that has been corrupting the natural fabric of France since the advent of modern times.

Le Pen views the French political-cultural establishment as being guilty of dishonesty and treason by actively pursuing the redefinition of France's history. The history promoted by politicians and academics is not the true and natural history of France: "What they want, those sclerotics [political class], is to tear off, piece by piece, entire sections of our history, our collective imaginary, our memory. It is [our memory] that they want to darken, as we can see in their successful efforts, *hélas,* in our schools to sabotage the history of France" (1998).

To counterbalance this story, Le Pen and the National Front offer a truly distinct, alternative history of the nation. Around this narrative gravitate Le Pen's speeches, interviews, and symbolic gestures. His choice of historical figures reveals his intention to underscore the constant, the permanent, and the stable in the history of France. Underneath the disturbances of past and current events lies a track of continuity in which the pillars of the nation are anchored. French history is above all a spiritual heritage, as is written in the program of the National Front: "France possesses a system of values that embraces time and space" (National Front 2001).

What is most important to note is that there is an incessant effort by Le Pen to connect the National Front and its supporters to a historical continuity that harkens back to France's origin. "The National Front is the Union of the indigenous of this country" (1985, 51), wrote Le Pen. As he declared in a speech,

> Our effort [is to] rejuvenate in permanence the eternal message of which we are the guardians and bearers . . . We are the sons and daughters of the

party of the homeland. We are the sons and daughters of those who have not stopped working tirelessly, who have not spared any efforts in sacrifice in wars, in order to transmit to their children the sun, the language, the liberty, the beauty and wealth, [the] fruits of the millenarian effort of our people. We can only be proud of the mission accomplished and [have] immense gratitude regarding those who have entrusted the mission to us. (1992a, 103–7)

For the leader, not yielding to the directives of the prevalent "official" historical paradigm constitutes an essential part in the Front's combat against the putative cultural debasement of contemporary France.

The Definition of the Group

Le Pen defines the National Front, his group, his militants and supporters, as the true representatives of France. In fact, in the alternative version of history provided by Le Pen, they *are* France. Le Pen wrote,

> From Clovis to Jean de Brem . . . From Joan of Arc to Barrès, Bainville, and Maurras . . . is the same flame that has burned throughout our history. We, militants and supporters of the National Front, write a new page of our saga. We are a link in the immense chain of generations. We have no pretension of reinventing the world, but more modestly and humanely [intend] to preserve the heritage, to defend a certain idea of a strong, generous, and fraternal France. In that sense, notwithstanding it displeases our adversaries, we are literally, the last heirs of classical humanism that is an integral part of our patrimony. Our political roots are noble, good, and beautiful. To defend them is not only to defend our memory, our way of life and way of seeing the world, but also to preserve our future from the clouds of barbarism that crowd the skies of the third millennium. (1996c)[2]

---

2. In this speech Le Pen cites the name of Jean de Brem, journalist, poet, and former paratrooper, who was a member of the secret armed organization (OAS) committed to stopping—by violent means—Algeria's route to independence. This supporter of the "Algérie Française" died in 1963 at the age of twenty-seven, in a confrontation with the police, becoming a martyr in French nationalist circles.

Of particular note is Le Pen's description of those who join the National Front as a true vanguard of men and women who constitute "the best" of the French population. They are the Elect in whom is vested the sacred mission of defending France. "Our responsibility is immense," claimed Le Pen in a speech, "and let me tell you what Churchill used to say to the English pilots of June 1940: 'Never was so much owed by so many to so few.' Well, I am sure that tomorrow France will be grateful to the most courageous, the most lucid and the most devoted of her daughters and sons who have constituted the walking wing of the recovery and national renaissance" (1992a, 145).

In the discourse of Le Pen, the supporters of the National Front are indeed the remnant few, upon whose shoulders rests the responsibility of saving France. This empowerment of his followers is a chief element of Le Pen's discourse. In a speech to his militants he declared,

> Since we have engaged in political combat—you know very well, my dear comrades—we have sought power not for the sake of power, but to apply the ideas that we think are just when the France that suffers—of whom we are the voice—will call us for help. We are the watchmen, those who awaken our people, the voices in the night. It is true—we are in a hurried fight against decadence—but as long as there are men to love France and to devote themselves to her, as long there is a French people [who is] conscious of itself, there will be a serious hope of victory. (2001b)

In stark contrast to the faithful, the overall French population is guilty of allowing the evils afflicting society to take hold, thus putting the nation on the track of decline and decadence. The French themselves trusted and gave their support to the forces of corruption and, therefore, are indirectly responsible for the crisis of the nation. Within this context, the National Front sees itself as a besieged community undergoing terrible persecutions, sufferings, and sacrifices in order to keep alive the spirit of the "true France" and, in the end, to redeem the mistakes and errors of the entire community. In his discourse, Le Pen alludes to two Frances: One is passive, weak; the other is militant, strong, and spiritually pure. This "militant France" is, in the words of the leader, "a conscious France that has adhered to the analysis of the National Front, that has understood the reasons of our decadence and that fights." "This militant France," the leader adds, "is suffering also. But it is suffering with hope, because action in the good direction can pull her out from despair" (1992a, 316–17). In fact, the "other" France is composed of the part of the French population that has for a long time been brainwashed and stripped of its character, identity, and true nature. The role of the National Front is therefore literally to show the light to those who are in darkness. "A lot of our compatriots have lost sight of everything that they risk losing," declared Le Pen. "We need to enlighten and unite them" (1995). Le Pen has many times denounced the civic apathy of the population: in his diagnosis "the public spirit looks as if it is in a state of advanced coma" (1999b). On a separate occasion, Le Pen declared that "in the state of paralysis, coma-like, in which the country finds itself, it is necessary to prepare a daring and firm therapy in order to restore its strength and youth" (2004b).

This lethargy is the sole thing that keeps the rest of the French population from joining the forces of French renaissance. Although they are unaware, the French people are enslaved to corrupt forces hell-bent on cutting away their roots. "We are the true liberators of the people of France" (2002a) is a persistent mantra invoked by the leader of the National Front. In describing the Front's opposition to globalization, Le Pen sheds light on this dialectic between the passive France, seduced by the devil of globalization, and the militant France, standing for truth and goodness.

> This project [globalization], cynically conceived, is so monstrous that the majority of the people do not believe in it, do not even see that the project has already started, aggravated by the *dénatalité* [declining birthrate] of our continent and the aging of our populations. Until now, we have been the only ones to see clearly and to try to open the eyes and the ears of the future slaves. Millions have understood us and trust us but the System has created fear. That is why we are persecuted . . . [We have] an irresistible appetite for freedom and independence. That is why it would be mad and criminal to lose the hope of saving France and liberating the French. When, with our help, with the National Front, they become conscious of the danger, their cholera will be terrible. (2000)

The Group under Siege

After defining the group as the ultimate guardian of the "eternal France," Le Pen reinforces its identity by portraying the National Front as a community under siege. The discourse of Le Pen evolves around the idea of menace, of threat. It is a rhetoric of perpetual fear. The hierarchy of the enemies might change slightly over time, but the targeting of enemies is always present. Enemies loom everywhere, either internal or external to the community. Internally, close attention is paid to the political-media establishment. "You can, my dear compatriots," stated Le Pen,

> today, be proud of yourselves, proud of the National Front and of everything that it has achieved after twenty years of its foundation; like the sailor, we also have known fatigue and discouragement. Sometimes even despair. But we have surmounted it. We have been victims of lies, defamation, and persecution. And we continue to be . . . we are truly treated in our country in [the media] but also in many others, as authentic pariahs. (1992a, 299–301)

Why has the National Front been the object of persecution since its origins? Why is it that the community of True France is marginalized? Le Pen states that the reason is simple: The National Front is the only party that informs the French people of the truth about the threats imperiling the nation's survival. Such vehement denunciation of this process of marginalization by the "political-media caste" has always been a chief element in the Front's self-perception. Le Pen calls the French Republic a totalitarian democracy that aims at the destruction of the only national opposition to "the System" (see, for example, 2002d). Since the foundation of the party there has been widespread "intellectual terrorism" launched to prevent the National Front, the open-eyed "militant France," from waking up the sleepy-eyed, passive populace. The ultimate aim of this intellectual terrorism is to produce "brainless citizens":

> It serves to deny the people the knowledge of realities they should know, to reduce [the people] to a blind and deaf mass, dazed by unanimous, monolithic propaganda. It has as a goal concealing real problems like the taboo of immigration . . . Little by little, because of the criminalization of

our movement and our ideas, the French are forbidden to think, to reflect about the problems of our society . . . it is this intellectual terrorism, totally irrational, that explains why our movement is today excluded from the official political field. (2002d)

Such *internal* enemies are, therefore, all whom Le Pen sees as "foreign forces" or members of the party of "Anti-France." They include the mainstream media, the politicians of the System, and all of those considered to be servants of the powerful forces of globalization, dedicated to the destruction of France and to the creation of an artificial world order, from immigrant activists to freemasons to human rights activists. Le Pen pays crucial attention to the enemies within the group of the Elect itself—warning constantly against hidden traitors—thus keeping the group's internal mobilization and energy level high. Examples of past traitors serve as admonition about the fate of future traitors: "In this way, and men are what they are, it is convenient that no one lose sight of the fact that the risks of division that threaten all human formations cannot develop within [our group]. We have to put aside all temptation of friction, to ban all worthless oppositions and devastating defamations. Individual ambition and over-estimation of the ego have led Mégret to the criminal adventure of the split" (2002d).

External enemies are the internationalist forces that put the French nation at danger. This theme is always present in party rhetoric, though the primacy and even the face of the enemies may change over time. The National Front initially saw the greatest danger in the Soviet Empire. "If there is a threat today it is the Soviet [threat]," wrote Le Pen.

> It is a time, not of choosing between being "red or dead" or of capitulating to our anguish or fear, but, on the contrary [of opting for the road] of resistance against death [in order to] to prepare ourselves [for] a confrontation that could be military, subversive, or revolutionary [and in which] we know that there will be a winner and a loser and that our country—even Europe and the Western World—risks being lost if we do not know how to mobilize our forces to survive and win. (1984, 145)

The Soviet threat was closely linked to the other big threat: massive immigration. Le Pen has incessantly talked about the Third World hegemony that, because of "the demographic explosion in the third world, [and] particularly [within] the Arabic-Islamic World, penetrates our country and is on the verge of colonizing it" (*Le Monde,* February 15, 1984). The communists were promoting this development because immigration had the final goal of preparing the way for a communist revolution in France.

> For more than forty years, the improvement of the standard of life of the working class posed a problem to the Marxists. The members of the national proletariat, once heralded as the iron spear of the Revolution, looked thinner and thinner. How to preserve the customers? . . . The call to immigration is one of the answers to this question. In importing misery [by] welcoming a foreign proletariat, they preserve the relevance of class warfare, hoping at the same time to make those foreigners [eligible to] vote. (1985, 228)

Communism, therefore, endorsed an internationalist ideology at odds with the natural order championed by Le Pen and the National Front.

After the fall of the Soviet Empire, Le Pen immediately found as a substitute what he calls the "American empire," which itself is guilty of imposing the tyranny of globalization on the nations of the earth, with the help of cronies such as the European Union, the International Monetary Fund, the World Bank, and human rights organizations. Le Pen's indictment of the United States of America became particularly visible after the end of the cold war and the first Gulf War.[3] The United States is seen as the driving force behind the implementation of a new world order. Le Pen blasts what he calls "American universalism," which is based on the "fundamentalism of the market" (2001b) and has as its objective the creation of

---

3. It is relevant to note that, particularly in the eighties, Le Pen saw the Anglo-American liberal theory of economics favorably. The market-oriented policies of Ronald Reagan were a reference in the economic program of the party, and Le Pen was accused in some sectors of the French traditional extreme right of being an "Atlantist." Ronald Reagan was also praised because of the social conservatism of his administration. The situation changed after the end of the cold war. (On this issue see Camus 1997, 223–24; see also Bresson and Lionet 1994, 445).

a World Government that will run the world in the next century. The Europe of Brussels is, in practice, its ally. [The European Union] was created to be just another stage in the process of globalization. [We have] borders that disappear, local and cultural specificities that blur to the advantage of a universal culture, an ideology of human rights elevated to the rank of Holy Gospel, an appearance of democracy, a planetarian market economy, one currency (why not the dollar?), and the belt is buckled. The World Village is not a whim anymore. We witness, powerlessly, the edification of a true totalitarianism [that is] much more vicious than communism and much more destructive than it. It's not an outlandish scenario anymore, a scenario of science fiction, but a nightmare: a communism "light" or a totalitarianism "soft," the endgame is the same! (1999d)

The United States is charged with the crime of creating a destabilizing, worldwide "unjust Order" that has triggered a worldwide rebellion. The terrorist attacks of September 11, 2001, constitute an example (2006b). Le Pen has said that the post–cold war, American-led design of a new order characterized by the "end of history" neglected the existence of other value-systems in the world, of which "expansionist and dynamic" Islam, an all-encompassing "religious, political and societal" worldview, is one (2006b).

The European Union is implicated in this malevolent, globalizing process, determined to strangle and eventually subsume the "natural" system of the diversity of nations with an artificial, disruptive, "internationalist" system. In a revelatory statement about the project of a Europe-wide constitution, Le Pen said that

> [i]n creating a Constitution, it is therefore hoped the emergence of a [European] Nation, which means that [the goal] is to create one by force, destroying the historical nations that have shaped the essence of world history, reducing them to a range of provinces. The intention is to make a European Nation, but what will emerge is a new empire, a prison of peoples, which will meet the destiny of all multi-national, artificial constructions, that is, a quick disappearance amid probable dramatic upheavals. We are at the very heart of a new totalitarian utopia [that seeks to establish] a total break with fundamental political principles of European civilization, a civilization of free peoples, of sovereigns. (2004b)

This project of a new European constitution, then, is one decisive European step toward doomsday. Against this federal Europe, Le Pen offers the vision of a "grand Europe of Nations, from Brest to Vladivostok," that will serve as a "counterweight" to America and emerging Asian powers (2006b).[4] When the newly elected French president Nicolas Sarkozy, in a symbolic gesture, followed the example of Charles de Gaulle and delivered a speech on the need for an institutional reform of the country in the town of Epinal, the leader of the National Front reacted by noting that while de Gaulle's address was held in a free France, Sarkozy's speech was delivered in an occupied homeland controlled by European and transnational forces (2007b).

The National Front has since the late nineteen eighties intensified its opposition to the development of Islamic culture and practices in France and Europe. The party led the initial opposition to the construction of mosques in France, seen as a sure sign of the "conquering Islam" (see, for example, *National-Hebdo*, April 20–25, 1996). Le Pen has always blamed what he calls the "immigration lobbies" for this trend that threatens the survival of the "France Française." Immigrants of Muslim countries, Le Pen contends, unlike immigrants from European countries, are impossible to assimilate because they are ethnic and cultural foreigners to French identity. The immigration lobbies use Islam as a weapon "against our country," in order to "eradicate from our spiritual and intellectual universe everything that attaches us to the Western, Humanist, and Christian civilization" (Le Pen 1990; see also 1996a). In a May Day speech to his followers, Le Pen warned about the danger of "growing Muslim proselytism," particularly at a moment at which "religiosity is receding in our Christian societies" (2000). The alternative "European project" promoted by Le Pen is based on a "coherent group of peoples belonging to a Christian civilization [and] sharing a common culture" (2006e). It is hardly surprising that, as the "Islamic problem" became more salient, Le Pen began to distinguish between "Christian" (for example, immigration from Poland or Portugal) and "Muslim" immigration. Those Christian

---

4. From a narrow geopolitical perspective, the Eurasian conception in Le Pen's discourse of a Europe "from Brest to Vladivostok"—based on the refusal of European subjugation to the "imperialistic designs" of the United States—is somewhat reminiscent of the writings of Belgian author Jean Thiriart. See, for example, Thiriart 1964.

immigrants, said Le Pen to an American interviewer, "are a little like your Mexicans in the United States. They are Christians ... our immigrants are principally Muslim." Because in the suburbs these immigrants are the majority, they naturally refuse to adopt the values and principles of the broader French society. Le Pen sees an utter incompatibility between French culture and that of Muslim immigrants, "[G]uided by the precepts of Shariah, that aren't only political but religious," which makes assimilation impossible (*Wall Street Journal*, November 19, 2005, online).[5]

The French government and the politicians of the system, left and right, are nothing more than collaborators, sycophants of their masters, in this process of globalization and homogenization "launched against France" (Le Pen 1997). In this context, Le Pen sees the National Front, the group of the Elect, as absolutely essential in fighting for a France that has been attacked

---

5. In the discourse of Le Pen the issue of "Islamization" has been primarily viewed as an ominous symptom of a deeper disease: governmental policy of open borders and "massive immigration" that created unassimilated communities—living by their own customs and cultural practices—within the French territory. Thus, though an anti-Islamic strain is continually present in Le Pen's discourse, it is framed in a more general attack on immigration. This has also been the position of Le Pen's daughter, Marine Le Pen. Other voices in the party—or close to the National Front—are more strident in their denunciation of Islam. See, for example the writings of Bernard Antony and Yves Daoudal (2005). Le Pen's former lieutenant Bruno Mégret, leader of the Mouvement National Républicain (MNR), vows regularly to fight the "Islamization of Europe," and has attacked Le Pen on the basis that "he does not see a problem in the development of Islam in France as long as Muslims are given French nationality" (Mégret 2002). In a similar fashion, Philippe de Villiers, a long-time member of the mainstream French right and leader of the Mouvement pour la France (MPF), has veered his party's discourse toward a more blatantly anti-Islam direction, brands himself as "the only politician who tells the French the truth about the Islamization of France" (Reuters, April 24, 2006), and has proposed a ban on wearing veils in public places (*Le Figaro*, November 2, 2006). The leader of the National Front has spoken out against Villiers's "religious discrimination" (Le Pen 2006e). It is worthwhile to note—and this serves as a signal of the sway that Le Pen's discourse has on his supporters—that an opinion poll has revealed that the supporters of the National Front are less favorable to banning the veil in public than are supporters of the mainstream right. Again, like their leader, at least for the time being, they see immigration as the real issue, while Islamization is perceived as one dimension of a bigger problem. See "Sondage l'ifop a interrogé les Français sur la proposition de Philippe de Villiers" (*Le Monde*, November 7, 2006).

by powerful forces and abandoned by everyone *but* the National Front. Not one opportunity is missed for Le Pen to remind his followers of the crucial role they play as the remnant few, the remnant patriots, the sons and daughters of the *real* France that is struggling to maintain its integrity against overwhelming forces of evil.

> If Globalization is nothing more than a metamorphosis of History ... a consequence of the abandon of the moral and civic rules that have governed us for centuries, then we have to deal with what [globalization] is: a materialistic ideology following the example of communism, against which we have [fought] and we must fight in order to escape from it. It falls upon the most lucid, the most courageous and wise, to mobilize the peoples to assure in the world of tomorrow not only the defense of the Rights of Man, but also those of the Rights of the Soul ... [Thus] we have to take inspiration from the successes and failures of more than three millennia of civilization. (1999d)

This rhetoric of fear is intended to strengthen the perception of the group as a besieged community. It is also closely aligned with a rhetoric of conspiracy. An antinational, internationalist plan has been gaining ground since the Enlightenment. Its current face is the neoliberal and American-led globalization. By connecting the dots thus, Le Pen forms a coherent picture of a changing socio-cultural-economic reality. Everything is part of a plan that is diabolical in both scope and goal. The goal of the "Dr. Strangeloves of the twenty-first century" is to mold and shape humanity according to their own "fantasies and interests" (Le Pen 2005). The creation of a united and federal Europe, for example, is meticulously included in this powerful *mondialiste* and cosmopolitan project ruthlessly waged against the ethnic group. Le Pen talks about "a secret plan imagined by Jean Monnet," who fell under the influence of the "big international American banks" and became an apostle of a supranational United States of Europe. The implementation of this plan was made with the help of three organizations: the Council on Foreign Relations, the Bildelberg Group, and the Trilateral Commission (Le Pen 1998). This insidious plot encourages the collapse of birth rates in Europe and a policy of open borders and massive immigration, both intended to soften and ultimately destroy national identity. Le Pen explains the rationale:

> The internationalists want to organize the world according to their own utopias [which are] fundamentally anti-national, anti-religion, and inhuman. Men and women will be sacrificed to Humanity [sic], and the self-appointed experts will define and organize their happiness. This happiness will be the same on all the continents . . . We recognize [in this plan], without any doubt, the same totalitarianism responsible in the 20th century for the death and suffering of hundreds of millions of men and women. In order to accomplish this Orwellian project, it is necessary to uproot the people and to dissolve the familiar, religious, civic, social, and associational links . . . that is why the family and the Nation are their main targets: the family because it is the material link of the transmission of life and moral values; the Nation because it is a superior principle of effective solidarity, dignity, and security. (2000)

As a proof of these dark designs, Le Pen often quotes David Rockefeller as saying in a 1991 Bilderberg meeting that "[t]he supranational sovereignty of an intellectual elite and world bankers is surely preferable to the national auto-determination practiced in past centuries" (Le Pen 2005; on this issue see also Holeindre 2003, 26).

Le Pen derides all philosophy of human rights—part of the American-led, totalitarian ideology hell-bent on the implementation of a "world government by Big Brother" (1999d)—as *"Droit-de-l'hommisme."* Le Pen accuses, for example, groups such as SOS Racisme, LICRA (Ligue Internationale contre le Racisme et l'Antisémitisme) and Ligue des Droits de l'Homme of being "anti-French" (*Français d'Abord!*, February 17, 2004). Under the disguise of liberalism, these groups want to impose an abstract and rootless program of "Humanity" on the natural, rooted realities of nations. Further, Le Pen accuses them of racism against the French and of "stigmatizing patriots" by a mechanism of *reductio ad Hitlerum* that, in a totalitarian fashion, disqualifies the opponents of an "insane immigration policy" (2002a).

Behind the *complot*, the conspiracy, Le Pen sees the work of specific international organizations. He frequently mentions Freemasonry, particularly the secret Freemasonry organization Grand Orient, as wielding absolute control over a large number of French politicians. Anti-Semitic suggestions and innuendos have been a characteristic of the National Front from its inception.⁶ It is hardly surprising, therefore, that the theme of a Jewish conspiracy endures in the discourse of Le Pen. One of his favorite targets is the international organization B'nai B'rith, which Le Pen accuses

6. The young historian François Duprat played an important role in the embryonic stage of the National Front (together with Alain Robert and José Bruneau de la Salle, he asked Le Pen to lead the new party). A prominent figure of the Nationalistes Revolutionnaires (Revolutionary Nationalists), Duprat was a Holocaust-denier who contended that France was a "colonized country" exploited by "foreigner groups" that manipulated the people through the mass media. Duprat was assassinated in 1978 (see, for instance, Igounet 2000, 161–80). A more famous episode is the interview given by Le Pen on September 13, 1987, in which he called the Shoah a "detail" in the history of World War II (see, for example, Bresson and Lionet 1994, 451–52). The leader of the National Front, however, rejects any wrongdoing and denies being an anti-Semite. "I never said the Holocaust is a 'detail.' I didn't say the concentration camps are 'details.' I never said the Jews weren't massacred—I said the gas chambers were a detail of history, but not coldly. It seemed to me that one must keep the role of this criminal instrument in perspective in the history of the war. All the Jews weren't killed in the gas chambers. They were shot blindfolded, died of hunger and dehydration, of bad treatment. So that tells you that [critics] hang on to this word in a dishonest way . . . If I were an anti-Semite, I wouldn't put Jews on my electoral list" (*Wall Street Journal,* November 19, 2005, online). More recently, a highly ranked National Front official, Bruno Gollnisch, has been accused of Holocaust denial because he said in a press conference that "[t]here isn't a serious historian who totally sticks by the conclusions of the Nuremberg trials . . . I'm not questioning the existence of concentration camps, but on the number of deaths, historians can discuss it. As to whether gas chambers existed, that's up to the historians to determine" (*JTA—Jewish Telegraphic Agency,* October 15, 2004). For these words Gollnisch was given a three-month suspended prison sentence and fined (EJP—*European Jewish Press,* January 18, 2007, online). He denied being a "racist or a [Holocaust] denier." In his defense he mentioned a document named "Liberté pour l'histoire," a 2005 public call by French historians to repeal laws that criminalize "revisionist" writing because, in their view, "History is not a juridical object. In a free country, it is the job neither of Parliament nor of the judicial authorities to define the historical truth." For Gollnisch the existence of such laws only reinforces the National Front's perception of the totalitarian nature of the "System" (*FDA,* December 2006; *Le Figaro,* December 22, 2005). Anti-Semitism, however, has been absent in the discourse of Marine Le Pen. She immediately condemned Gollnisch "without ambiguity" and added that such statements nurture the "suspicion of anti-Semitism" that weighed on the National Front (*Le Monde,* October 19, 2004). In her autobiography Marine Le Pen decried the fact that the teaching of the Holocaust, among other subjects, has been made more difficult in French public schools because of pressures from religious groups, in this case Muslims (M. Le Pen 2006, 316).

of having a powerful grip on the French political system and of being a driving force toward world government. The leader of the National Front accused Jacques Chirac of being beholden to "Jewish organizations, especially the famous *B'nai B'rith*" (*Le Monde,* March 3, 1997).

Le Pen says repeatedly that the National Front is free of the influence of such obscure forces. "It is true," he declared, "that we do not obey the talking points of any organization, whether foreign like the *B'nai B'rith,* or internal as the *Grand Orient* . . . [as do] so many of the elected officials of the so-called Republic" (1997; on this issue see also Camus 1997, 269–72). The neoliberal Trilateral Commission formed by David Rockefeller in 1973 is accused of putting minions in important political positions and controlling them behind the scenes, thus playing an important role in the army of "Big Brother." All of these groups are depicted as "forces that aspire to establish a reductive, global and equalizing ideology [by] playing a non-negligible role in the creation of an anti-national spirit" (*Le Monde,* September 9, 1989).

In sum, by claiming a worldwide conspiracy against his small group, Le Pen manages to give his followers an idea of their crucial role as defenders of France and French values in a period of rapid change. His claim provides his people a model with which they may understand the world, one that makes both a complex and seemingly chaotic situation more rational and the role of the National Front more morally compelling. This "hidden-hand" mentality depicts the enemies of the group as power-grabbing, mischievous, and diabolical, which removes any sort of ambiguity in the combat against evil.

The rhetoric of Le Pen is also catastrophic. To emphasize the deep crisis imperiling the nation and the dangers that lie ahead for the remnant patriots, Le Pen uses a catastrophic vocabulary. Below are some typical examples of Le Pen's litany of catastrophic threats to France (and to the world).

Communism

> It is necessary to remind the French that their existence, their freedoms, their prosperity are linked to the survival of the homeland, to the survival of a free Europe—and she is objectively threatened. And if this threat is not fought off, we will be in the gulag before the end of the century. (1984, 165)

I tell the young men and women of my country: What is being prepared under your eyes is the establishment of the Marxist revolution that leads to the gulag, slavery, and death. (1985, 166)

There is no national defense, no matter the material means employed, without a "spirit of defense," that is without an awareness of the danger, of its nature, its amplitude, its imminence, and without the will to preserve ourselves. The choice to be made is between life and death, between self-chosen sacrifice and slavery. (1989a, 63)

Immigration

The disastrous policy of our government has had catastrophic consequences because it opened the door, in an uncontrollable manner, to a migratory flux that we don't even know the reality or the statistics . . . it is truly a tidal wave. (1984, 100–101)

We are going to witness a real invasion, of which we have only seen the beginning, that will literally submerge our indigenous populations. (1985, 288)

We are the victims of a worldwide mutation, of an invasion apparently peaceful but that, evidently, is a deadly threat to our identity, our security, our culture. (1992a, 213–14)

Immigration . . . the opening and suppression of our borders . . . and the attribution of social benefits have given it a torrential character [that will be] cataclysmic in the future. It threatens us with engulfment and, soon, submission, which means extinction. (2002a)

Declining Birthrate

In effect, the gravest danger that threatens the earth is the collapse of birthrates in the Western World confronted with the birthrate explosion in the Third World. That is why I estimate that homosexuality, if it keeps growing, will drive us to the end of the world. (*Le Monde*, June 13, 1984)

Declining birthrate is a mortal phenomenon. If continued, by the decline in vitality coupled with the demographic pressure from the Third World, we will be, before the arrival of the year 2000, submerged. (1985, 167)

While the lack of newborn makes us decadent, the rest of the world explodes, literally . . . the conditions for a world cataclysm are assembled, and this cataclysm will happen. We have to make sure that this cataclysm does not happen among us. (1992a, 110–11)

Even more [we should remember], the famous phrase of [Algerian president] Houari Boumedienne [in a 1974 speech at the United Nations] that resonates daily like an oracle, "The time is coming when the starving masses of the South are going to mount an attack on the North. And this immigration will be neither peaceful, nor fraternal" . . . At the doors of Europe, [we are faced with] the pressing reservoirs of populations of the very young who will overtake us in twenty years, 100 million Turks, 100 million in the Maghreb (Tunisia, Morocco, Algeria), 100 million in Egypt, without talking about Eastern Europe and the Asian continent with inexhaustible reserves." (2002a)

Globalization

We are in the presence of a patient [France] who suffers from cancer and whose pain has been attenuated with palliatives, but where everyone is resigned to its imminent death. Our governments have abdicated! They don't believe in France anymore, or in Europe. They serve Globalization. (1999d)

Let's remember the newest apocalyptical threats that weigh on our country: the frantic dictatorship of King-money, the complete miscegenation imposed on our people by a massive immigration, and an anti-birthrate policy monstrously organized, the disappearance of our civilization, our culture. (2000)

[The world faces] a geology of dangers. On the surface we witnessed the tsunami. But at a profound level, from the depths of the West and the world, huge tectonic changes are occurring and are setting off demographic, pandemic, religious, philosophical, and political earthquakes of such a big scale that even humanity might be itself at risk. (2005)

Le Pen's rhetoric is elaborated to create shock. It deliberately accentuates the seriousness of the times, of an ever-deepening crisis in which the survival of France is at stake. Le Pen constantly uses biological images and metaphors to express his idea of the nation as an organic living entity. "We know," wrote Le Pen, "that like all the terrestrial homelands [France] is mortal, notwithstanding the appearance of its exceptional longevity, and because we know that we are even more attached to her" (1984, 74). The issues are always literally about life and death. There is no middle ground. "The National Front," he said on another occasion, "is a bio-political movement, a reaction of health against the threat of death contained in the decadence, subversion and foreigner invasion" (1989a, 108). Le Pen has described himself as a "doctor in times of an epidemic outbreak . . . when the doctor arrives the people are happy" (*AFP* 2003).

In the discourse of Le Pen, France is depicted as a body in decomposition, decaying, putrefying, attacked by all sort of problems that are indeed described as diseases. "The crimes against the nation are all of those which attack its physical, moral and spiritual substance," said Le Pen, "all of those who explicitly or not want the violent destruction or the rotting of this great organic entity that constitutes the nation" (1997). He has mentioned that "foreigner invasion" creates "gangrene" within France (1985, 32). Unemployment is also described as a "social cancer" (1985, 51). Regarding the proliferation of immigrants and security concerns, Le Pen noted that "this proliferation resembles cancer cells—I'm not referring to the immigrants, but the [immigration] process in itself: If it's not stopped immediately, we will soon face forms of civil war or foreign subversive war in our territory" (1996b). He denounced the "mental AIDS" that afflicts society and called his followers to "reconstruct the natural immunities" (*Le Monde*, October 3, 1989). A campaign of the National Front in the nineties consisted in establishing a parallel between AIDS and socialism: "In politics, in economy, in morality Socialism is AIDS!" (Bariller and Timmermans 1994, 130).

Intimately linked with the life-death rhetoric and the conflation of his enemies with disease is the constant use of a Social Darwinist philosophy in describing the threats and dangers to the French nation. In a typical manner Le Pen said, "Generally, any weak country is potential prey to another who is stronger. Since the beginning of time, the surface of the earth has been agitated by conflicts for influence between conquering countries and submissive countries. Entire nations and civilizations have disappeared because they could not fill the necessary conditions for their own survival" (1989a, 12).

In this world where only the strongest will survive and the feeble are doomed to demise, France is in real danger. "The weak countries are the targets of all the predators of the world," declared Le Pen in a speech. "When we are not capable of defending our identity, territory and culture, there will be others who will come to impose [their culture] by force, sometimes with fusils, sometimes with *babouches* [elegant Moroccan slippers]" (*Le Monde*, April 19, 1988). On a similar note he pointed out in a speech that

> [c]ivilizations are, alas, mortal and in different dimensions obey the rhythms of the universe and, it seems, with stupefying parallelism . . . the evolution [of civilizations], their birth, growth, life and death have a common trait noted by Toynbee and Oswald Spengler, Bruyas and [Jacques] Dupâquier, they come to an end due to foreign demographic submersion, when allogenic elements become too great in number to be assimilated, and when [civilizations] let their own vital dynamism weaken. What is known in History as the "great invasions", which led to the death of a civilization, is what we are on the verge of living in our times, *hic et nunc*. (2002a)

This focus on fear, enemies, threats, and danger is a powerful mechanism aimed at inducing a sense of dire threat among the besieged community. This sense of impending tragedy pervades the rhetoric of Le Pen. He repeatedly calls immigration a "demographic bomb," "immigration-invasion" that is out of control, and he warns against its "cataclysmic" consequences. Intimately connected is the urgency to act. "The danger that threatens our country is a specific danger in the short term," he wrote. "Our fate will be sealed before the end of the century [twentieth century]" (1985, 85). He said on another occasion, "Before the end of the century we will have reached a point of no return. Then, decadence will be irreversible and irreparable. We have only a couple of years of respite left, very short, to inverse the course of the political choices that could create a fundamental change" (1992a, 127). "What they hide from you," Le Pen warned his supporters, "is that France is threatened with disappearance . . . before the end of the century, before four years. What Chirac asks from us is to be accomplices of this national suicide" (*Le Monde*, May 3, 1997).

For Le Pen the issue of mass immigration needs to be confronted urgently because it is "five minutes to midnight" for France and Europe (2006d).

Symptomatic of this sense of impending cataclysm is the way Le Pen describes France's position in regard to globalization and the European Union:

> We must break off from this politics of Death [leading toward a Federated Europe] and announce that cooperation with the peoples of Europe must be organized around nations. . . . We must combat boldly the Europe of Brussels and break France away from it, with the growing help of all its victims. Europe is working to kill [both] France and all the historical nations of the continent. At the end of this road there is nothing but servitude and war (1999d).

> It is clear that the project, better to say the global conspiracy of which the European Union of Brussels is a Trojan horse, is committed to the goal of destroying the nations for exactly the opposite reasons we want to defend and save them . . . it is clear that the Europe of Brussels prepares the death of France. (2000)

The "true patriots" of the National Front are the only force that will allow France to hold its ground against the innate evil of this global conspiracy.

The National Front's Exceptionality

In its depiction of this national tragedy, Le Pen's discourse obeys a permanent logic of polarization. The National Front is portrayed as a community of the Elect, the true patriots, the representatives of millenarian France. They are unremittingly described as sane, healthy, and pure. Opposed to them are the "mighty," the false patriots, those powerful evil forces who want to subvert the structures and history of millenarian France. They are repeatedly described as corrupt traitors beholden to secret forces.

Le Pen's vocabulary is belligerent: He talks about "battalions" (the militants) and says that the National Front is waging the "battle for France" (see for example, 2002d). The National Front, the defender of True France, is engaged in a mortal fight against the "Anti-France." As Le Pen said in a speech, "Only the Front incarnates and carries the national idea in the French political landscape" (2002d). "If the National Front has acquired today the political importance that [it] has, it is also because France has returned," Le Pen wrote in his book *La France est de retour* (France Is Back) (1985, 14). Included on the side of "Anti-France," the "France of the foreigners," are all the mainstream political parties that Le Pen derides as "Gang" or "Band of Four," and the entire media establishment. They too know that there is a mortal war developing between them and the National Front, the "national opposition," the only obstacle to the implementation of their "monstrous" project of ending millenarian France. As stated by Le Pen,

> The National Front, which honors itself as being the Party of the French, suffers, like her [France], in its combat for the liberation of our people, from a systematic persecution from those who hold the power . . . This persecution is visible in all domains [yet] it needs to end, together with the decadence of the State and the Republic, the persecution of the patriots, and the servitude of France and the French . . . Enough of failure, corruption, putting the homeland in danger—enough. The time has come to chase away from power the liars, the corrupt, and the thieves. The time has come for the people to make its voice heard and its will expressed. (1992a, 65–93)

Because of its exceptionality as the last and only defender of the nation, the National Front has been the victim of a "nefarious" and "relentless" campaign orchestrated by the establishment. In the narrative of the party, several episodes epitomize this persecution: the 1990 profanation of the Jewish cemetery in the southern town of Carpentras that was wrongly attributed to the National Front,[7] for example, or the accusations by the

---

7. In 1997, four neo-Nazis were sentenced to jail for the desecration of the cemetery (*Le Figaro*, April 25, 1997). Le Pen successfully sued for defamation the then president of SOS-Racisme, Fodé Sylla, who had accused Le Pen of "having blood on his hands" for the profanation of Carpentras (*Le Monde*, April 28, 1997). Marine Le Pen associates Carpentras with a persistent attempt by "a certain number of groups and politicians" to stigmatize Le Pen as the "new Hitler" and, thus, to divert the public's attention from the economic and social realities of France (M. Le Pen 2006, 139–40). In the discourse of the party, this episode serves as firsthand evidence of the malicious persecution of the National Front by the political and

mainstream media of Le Pen's engaging in practices of torture during the Algerian war, which led the leader of the National Front to file lawsuits— some successful, others not (see, for example, *The Daily Telegraph,* June 4, 2002, online). The establishment of an electoral majority system that has hurt smaller parties is also viewed as part of this campaign against the National Front, and has led to denunciations that the French Republic is a "false democracy." "In my view, is not normal that democracy should eliminate the non-conformist political families, such as ours," noted Le Pen in an interview (*Paris Match,* May 6, 1995). The leader of the National Front posited that the "crisis of democracy" could only be answered by letting all currents of opinion be represented through the adoption of an electoral system of proportional representation (*Les Français d'Abord!,* October 27, 2006). Le Pen has championed referenda as a way of giving a true voice to the people and creating a true democracy (see for example, Le Pen 2001a). In view of the self-perpetuation of the System, Le Pen declared, "I, and only I, incarnate democracy" in France (2006a). After all, "The popular sovereignty has been seized by an illegitimate French and European oligarchy" (*FDA,* January 2007).

In his discourse, Le Pen puts forth a framework in which the opposites are clearly defined and the options are unambiguous. To highlight differences between the two camps, Le Pen demonizes opponents, occasionally physically, but especially in terms of moral features. Writing about what distinguishes "France" from the "Anti-France," Le Pen asserted, "the gap is widening between the ruling intelligentsia, amoral and indulgent to all disorders, and the people [who are] fundamentally sane and who are the victims of those disorders" (*Le Monde,* June 16, 1983). "Authority is mostly

---

media establishment. Carpentras became a symbol of all the "injustices" and "wrongs" heaped on the National Front by the "System." A prime example of this can be seen in the reaction of the party to the episode in November 2006 in which a Paris Saint Germain (soccer team from Paris) supporter was killed by a police officer protecting a Jewish fan of an Israeli team. Prosecutor Jean-Claude Marin declared that the Paris Saint Germain supporters had made Nazi salutes and shouted, "Le Pen, [for] president." Le Pen immediately sued for defamation, and the *National-Hebdo* asked if this episode would turn out to be a "new Carpentras," a "Carpentras *Bis*" (*National-Hebdo,* November 30–December 6, 2006).

moral," noted Le Pen about his opponent in the presidential elections, "but Chirac is a man with no reputation, a[n] *immodèle,* an anti-example" (2002b). Attacks on the morality of his opponents are intended to increase repulsion toward those who serve the interests of a "foreigner France" against those of the community of patriots. In this polarized manner, the National Front becomes the only possible solution to deal with the dangers faced by the nation.

To counterbalance the forecast of France's imminent demise, Le Pen offers hope. The National Front is the only path toward salvation. As written by Le Pen, "there is still time, there is always time to refuse annihilation and slavery" (1984, 152). "Before the end of the century," stated Le Pen to supporters, "either we [in France] have carried out the Salvationist burst or we will be taken away by a cataclysm whose guidelines are already in place" (*Le Monde,* March 19, 1993). Only the embattled moral community of the Elect has in itself the power to turn around the decline of France and propel the grandiose project of recovery, renaissance, and salvation. In the discourse of Le Pen, the Elect are constantly characterized as the last hope of the nation, as is evidenced by the following quotes:

> The National Front, whatever the case, persists in its will of creating, soon, at national level, a pivotal center of resistance to the decline and decadence . . . (*Le Monde,* June 20, 1989)

> [The National Front is] the shield of France against which crash all of the projectiles emanating from people who are in rivalry with France or who wish to destroy her, to dissolve her, to demean her, or to reduce her to slavery . . . (*Le Monde,* October 3, 1989)

> That explains undoubtedly, ladies and gentleman, the hatred that follows the National Front, its militants and officials, because they constitute, truth be told, the only bolt that allows the nation to remain [held together] and, tomorrow, to prosper to the detriment of the cosmopolitan interests. (Le Pen 1992b)

Le Pen's discourse of fear is intimately paired with a discourse of hope and change. The National Front embodies hope. In fact, Le Pen has often concluded his speeches by stressing that the National Front has "a rendezvous with Destiny" (2002d). As asserted by the leader in a speech to his followers, "in the face of the decadent political System there is only one opposition that can put forward a national politics, the only one capable of assuring the future of France and the French" (2002d). The burden of saving France is, consequently, on the shoulders of the Elect—the members of the community under siege, the National Front.

So far I have illuminated how, through his discourse, Le Pen solidifies the identity of the group as the representatives of France who are engaged in a mortal fight with the obscure but omnipresent forces of "Anti-France." Le Pen empowers his followers by repeatedly emphasizing their nature as the remnant few patriots who have the aggrandizing mission of the salvation of France. In the next section I will show how Le Pen manages to portray himself as the guide and savior of the Elect along their missionary road toward national salvation. Such a savior is necessary because the danger is so great and the forces of evil are so many and powerful. There has to be a great leader to lead the minority in heroic combat. The way to victory is through moral rectitude against the cowardice of the enemy, who will collapse when confronted resolutely.

LE PEN THE SAVIOR

The Le Pen Industry

Since the foundation of the National Front in 1972 there has been a persistent trend by the movement to shift Le Pen's position in the collective consciousness from the level of history to the level of myth. There has been a consistent effort to mythologize his achievements and life stories in order to imprint deeply upon the minds of his followers an image of Le Pen as the avatar of millenarian France. The work of Le Pen's closest collaborators, the central role of the leader in the party machine, and the discourse of Le Pen himself have fueled this process of mythologization of the leader of the National Front—what could be called the "Le Pen industry."

The Inner Circle. At the very basis of this Le Pen industry is the incessant work of Le Pen's inner circle. They are not merely collaborators: Their work could be more logically described as the work of disciples, and even apostles, who sanctify the image of their leader.

In writings and speeches they proclaim a sense of destiny about Le Pen. François Brigneau has written that the fact that Le Pen was born on June 20, 1928, at the "perfect" midpoint between the end of World War I and the beginning of World War II, "proves" that Le Pen's birth was no mere coincidence but that of a man marked by destiny to play a crucial role of combatant in history (*Le Monde,* September 21, 1991).[8] Other sympathetic biographers have made a similar point (for example, Marcilly 1984, 97). These biographers have also highlighted Le Pen's Celtic roots, which seem only to add to the perception of Le Pen as a man of destiny. François Brigneau notes that "there were two fairies around the cradle of Jean-Marie. Two Celtic fairies. . . . The first one was the fairy of Eloquence, the second one the fairy of Imagination. It was them who gave the child his most precious gifts, also the most typically Briton" (Brigneau 1984, 8). "Le Pen is a Celt, a man [with the gift of] verbal enchantment," writes another commentator. "His hands, his face, his pose become, due to their expressiveness, the mirror of his thoughts" (*National-Hebdo,* May 30–June 5, 1996). According to Jean Marcilly, "[Le Pen was born] on June 20, that is, the day of the summer solstice, the most important celebration of the Celts, his ancestors, of whom we know more and more that they were a people carrying a profound religious sentiment. Bearers of a unique civilization for the time, turbulent, belligerent, conquerors—we can say that the leader of the 'National Front' resembles them" (Marcilly 1984, 97).

Such an image of the leader of the National Front as a man of destiny pervades the accounts of those close to him. Bruno Mégret, the one-time general delegate of the party, describes his first encounter with Le Pen as a life-changing moment: "I felt springing up inside of me something indefinable, called trust. Was it set off by [Le Pen's] talent of persuasion, by the shrewdness of his analysis, or the strength of his convictions? I still don't know. In any case, a simple certitude had invaded me: This man is one of those who force destiny!" (Mégret 1990, 9–10).

8. Le Pen has many times made reference to the fact that he was born midway between the two world wars (See Le Pen 1992a, 340; France 5, November 26, 2006).

Yvan Blot, a former party member of the European Parliament, argued that the trajectory of Le Pen's career fulfilled a heroic "historical destiny" of rectifying the excesses of the Enlightenment. To Blot, Le Pen "is the man who incarnates the return of the baroque in the French political life. His combat against the cosmopolitans, his [combat] for the French soul against the idolaters of the mind . . . " (Blot 1992, 251). Pierre Monnier makes a similar point: "*Voilà!* . . . Jean-Marie Le Pen, is the irruption of the baroque in an anemic, politically paralyzed, neo-classic, narrow, Marxist, and decadent world . . . [he] is the emerging of creative pleasure and freedom . . . [Such] innovators of the baroque, at once wise and restless defy the paralysis of the establishment. The breath of life blows off ideology" (Monnier 1994, 130). Le Pen's life and achievements are therefore integrated in a grandiose and mythical historical framework.

Another topic regularly stressed by the National Front's inner circle is the image of Le Pen as a natural leader. The literature of the National Front makes a point of emphasizing that in the French-Celtic dictionary the French word *chef* (leader) translates as "Pen." "For those who believe in destiny," one of the photo books in honor of Le Pen proclaims, "Le Pen's destiny was already planned" (Maréchal and Gauthier 2001, 8). One of his childhood friends wrote, "Le Pen in Breton means head [and], therefore, the leader. Jean-Marie saw himself [as being] naturally at the head of all the expeditions organized by us" (Buisson and Renault, 1984, 15). Biographer Roger Mauge notes how, even early in life and in school, Le Pen "was the head of the game, the one who took the lead, who spoke louder, the one whom we were driven to admire and follow" (Mauge 1988, 41). One of his fellow soldiers in Indochina remembered that "like everyone I had my confrontations with him and I've suffered from rejection after the confrontation: he had become the uncontested leader and inspired strong attachments, with his natural authority of a good leader" (Buisson and Renault 1984, 26–27). His biographer Marcilly wrote that Le Pen has a "permanent behavior of leadership" (1984, 21). As written by Martin Peltier,

> Listen to [Le Pen] talk about Rwanda, about the Carlos affair, all kind of affairs—he has a clear and coherent language that slices through the silence of some or the weak and embarrassed explanations of others . . . Briefly,

Le Pen has the language of a leader. As indicated by his name: Le Pen, the leader. The French people . . . need a leader. A real one. A look that discerns, a voice that speaks, a hand that holds . . . Our Republic today is a woman without a head. That is why the French suffer, that is why they desert the traditional parties, that is why they need Le Pen. (*National-Hebdo*, August 25–31, 1994)

Such emphasis on Le Pen's natural leadership qualities is coupled with an intense portrayal of Le Pen as a unique man. In the preface to a photo book dedicated to Le Pen, long-time loyalist Roger Holeindre writes that "this album is a symbol, a homage to an exceptional man, a herald of the homeland: Jean-Marie Le Pen" (Holeindre 2001, 5). In fact, in the eyes of his closest collaborators Le Pen is a man of rare qualities. His eloquence is praised. In the words of François Brigneau,

Brother of the great Irish orators, of whom he has the power of evocation, the inspiration, the generosity, the gift of the images and magical rhythms, [Le Pen] does not speak only to please. He speaks to achieve, to teach, to learn, to bring a little of his knowledge, as well as his intuitions and convictions that follow . . . [T]hat is why he entered politics . . . To transmit verbally the secrets of tradition, without which the genius of a community is swept away by the wind of history . . . [Le Pen] excels himself and reveals himself as one of the last natural orators of the epoch. (Brigneau 1984, 10)

A history of the National Front praises Le Pen's performances on the tribune as being "of a rare charisma" (Bariller and Timmermans 1994, 20). One of Le Pen's biographers states that he is "probably the last French *tribun*. He is an accomplished orator, speaking as much as with the heart as with the head, due to the fact that he has something to say and something in his guts that help in the delivery" (Marcilly 1984, 147). "We know that of all [French] politicians," writes Pierre Monnier, "he is the one who handles the French language the best, the one who expresses himself with the most ease and who is never short of words even if he has embarked in one of his meanderings à la Proust." His ability to deliver unscripted, off-the-cuff speeches is also praised by Monnier, who notes that "we also know that he can occupy

1. Cover of *La Vérité sur Jean-Marie Le Pen* (The Truth about Jean-Marie Le Pen), Roger Mauge's 1988 biography of the leader of the National Front. The sea, the boat, and Le Pen as the captain are all recurrent images in the party's narrative. Courtesy of Éditions France-Empire.

the stage for two hours without the help of notes" (1994, 65). This last of the great orators is, therefore, at the service of France.

Le Pen's perseverance occupies a central place in this exaltation of his rare qualities. The fact that his father's boat was named *Persévérance* is noted in all of the biographies or books honoring Le Pen (for example, Mauge 1988, 19). He is without fail described as a man who is persistent in adhering to a course of action and to his ideals, and he is noted for showing an uncommon steadfastness in the face of so many obstacles. As stated by Mégret, in Le Pen "you have a man who has remained faithful to his ideas all of his life. He could have had a more peaceful and interesting life outside politics. Nevertheless he has pursued, against winds and tides, a combat that for the moment has only brought him insults and slander. Isn't this a sign that he is driven by an ideal and that he possesses those two qualities, so rare today, [those qualities of] conviction and courage?" (Mégret 1990, 151)

Pierre Monnier makes a similar point: "In a world where everyone looks over his shoulder, [and] is afraid of taking a step without guarantees . . . *He advances, he fights, sturdy and indifferent to all hostility around him* . . . Ten years have passed during which he has fought without success yet confident of achieving what others have always thought impossible" (1994, 165, emphasis mine).

"We cannot deny," writes François Brigneau, "[Le Pen's] courage, his political straightness, his perseverance, his refusal of all politicking compromises" (1992, 37). In one of the photo books dedicated to Le Pen, in the chapter significantly headlined "Tenacity," it is written that "obstinate, Jean-Marie Le Pen holds the bar firmly and, despite the difficulties, he remains faithful to his ideas" (Buisson and Renault, 1984, 84–85). Blot writes that Le Pen's perseverance is closely linked with his sense of mission. As he notes in an article,

> Jean-Marie Le Pen has the conviction that he has a message to deliver to the French so that France can remain France. Twenty years ago he knew that his message would not have had hardly any echo, but still he continued to act because he felt that was his duty, his mission in this land. "Do what you have to, no matter what happens!" It is the motto of an ethic that is as

old as the *Iliad* of Homer which has [been around for] 2,800 years. It is the ethic of honor, based more on the sentiment of duty than the avidity of power. (*National-Hebdo,* March 8–14, 1999)

Le Pen is many times described as a "Menhir," which not only connects him to France's prehistoric Celtic origins but also coveys a perception of someone who does not give way to pressure or persuasion. In the work of those close to him, Le Pen is a man of unyielding character. Pierre Monnier says that his character is of "a granitic nature" (1994, 95). In anticipation of the presidential elections of 2002, the National Front published a book in praise of Le Pen that stated, "For the fourth time, Jean-Marie Le Pen aims at reaching the supreme magistrature. His political career is outside the norms. Never before has a public man been as slandered as he has. Nevertheless he kept firm, against winds and storms, with his convictions and ideals fixed in his heart. The menhirs cannot be knocked down. *Rendez-vous* in 2002" (Maréchal and Gauthier 2001, 168).

In order to highlight further the distinction between Le Pen and all of his opponents, Le Pen is constantly portrayed as an honest man. As stated by Marcilly, "The morality of the political action of Jean-Marie Le Pen is the reason why he prefers taking the risk of being unpopular in order to defend what he sees as the truth, informing his fellow citizens in spite of everything. It is his honor" (1984, 169). Eric Domard, a journalist with *Les Français d'Abord!,* takes the point further in saying that, in Le Pen, one finds "the constant refusal of the *langue de bois* [officialese], the search to speak the truth, denounced by his adversaries as politically incorrect, which has the merit of saying out loud what the militants and the voters think." He adds, "It is this anti-conformism, this temerity of language that cements the strong relationship between the president of the National Front and the militants" (Domard 2004, e-mail interview, May 25). Yvan Blot draws a stark contrast between the archetype of the "honest man" personified by Le Pen and the archetype of the *énarque,* the mainstream politician groomed at an elite school such as the École Nationale d'Administration. The *énarques* are denounced as an "inbred" political caste, connected by privilege. They are characterized by laicization, technocracy, aloofness, and the doctrine of politically correctness, bent on imposing their vision of society on the rest of the population. Le Pen is different. In the words of Yvan Blot,

> In face of the sclerosis of the dominant neo-classicism that transforms the thought and the action of our political class into a technocratic attitude to the detriment of the aspirations of the French people, Le Pen reintroduces the baroque in French political life. He incarnates its cultural type, that of the "honest man." Everyone who knows Jean-Marie Le Pen knows of his love for the truth. That love for the truth characterized also the baroque century . . . the *énarque* prefers Descartes to Pascal. He prefers certitude to the truth. He is much more at ease dealing with clear and distinct ideas than in facing the unstable and contradictory reality. (1992, 248)

Along with Le Pen's honesty, his loyalty in all realms of life, from politics to his personal life, is emphasized. The depiction of Le Pen's loyal side pervades not only his biographies but also the entire literature of the National Front. "Every time Le Pen talks about France," writes *National-Hebdo* director Yves Daoudal, "About the past of France, [about] the future of France, he emerges as the one who passes the baton of the French civilization, as the holder of the flame, that French flame that comes from faraway [and] which we do not have the right to let fade. His first ambition, regardless of his own personal destiny, is to remain faithful to this duty" (Daoudal 2002a, 21).

Le Pen is depicted as someone who has remained loyal to all of those who lived in overseas territories, such as in Algeria or New Caledonia, and who wanted to remain part of France (Maréchal and Gauthier 2001, 44–53; 86–89). Le Pen's loyalists stress his unwavering loyalty and recognition to all of his friends and National Front members who either died or were the target of persecutions and aggression. The photo books of the party show Le Pen in the company of and giving comfort to those who were persecuted (Buisson and Renault 1984, 62). A widespread image shows Le Pen with a patch on his eye after campaigning for a friend. Although it is a controversial episode (on this point see Bresson and Lionet 1994, 179–82), the literature of the National Front notes that "in campaigning for his [Algerian] friend Ahmed Djebbour, Le Pen lost an eye" (Buisson and Renault 1984, 68–69).

Along with the depiction of someone committed to ideas and friends, Le Pen is also described as a family man. Photos abound of Le Pen with his wives (first Pierrette, then Yann), three daughters, and grandchildren. However, his devotion to his cause disrupted his private life—thus the fact that his wife left him for another man (and former biographer) is viewed as a consequence of the all-embracing mission of someone who "didn't have a minute for himself to organize his personal life" (Mauge 1988, 236). Le Pen remarried and continued to be portrayed as someone who, despite all, is committed to what the literature of the National Front calls his "clan" (Buisson and Renault 1984, 139). As told by Yann Le Pen to one of her father's biographers, "My dad, because of politics, has lost a lot of money, an eye, his health, his family life, and now his wife" (Mauge 1988, 227). His younger daughter, Marine, wrote that the family life was a "collateral victim" of Le Pen's political combat. When her father says that, for him, France is above everything, "it's not a simple slogan, or a joke . . . it is his deep reality" (M. Le Pen 2006, 38–39).

Clairvoyance is another of the rare qualities possessed by Le Pen. His collaborators and friends emphasize the fact that Le Pen has the gift of prediction. According to François Brigneau, Le Pen "[s]aw correctly, before everyone else, the essential problems of immigration, education, birthrate, families, security, national security, relationship with the Muslim world etc. He saw correctly due to his lucidity but also due to the guiding principle of his action: France and the French in the first place" (*National-Hebdo*, September 15–21, 1994).

A volume dedicated to celebrating the twentieth anniversary of the National Front underlined how Le Pen was correct in predicting a variety of themes from immigration to the propagation of AIDS (Bariller and Timmermans 1994, 15, 150). Pierre Monnier praised Le Pen's "anticipating clairvoyance" (1994, 114). Roger Holeindre calls Le Pen a "visionary," because "in the name of the people he tells the truths [that] are sometimes misunderstood, but without which every hope is vain" (2001, 5). Dominique Martin expresses a similar opinion: "[Le Pen] has been in politics for more than fifty years and has demonstrated that he is a visionary. Everything he has announced has materialized and, many times, his solutions are taken by his political adversaries, although in a different fashion" (Martin 2004, e-mail interview, July 20). Marine Le Pen noted that her father "has been the only one who has predicted the problems that we face today. To govern is to predict [and] he has predicted: the time has come for him to govern" (*Les Français d'Abord!*, March 4, 2004). Following the suburban riots in heavily immigrant communities in the fall of 2005, where thousands of cars were torched and property was destroyed, the National Front released a poster stating "Immigration, explosion of the suburbs, Le Pen said so!"[9] The image of Le Pen as a leader who is always right ahead of time is present throughout the discourse of his inner circle.

Above all, the imagery incessantly promoted by the National Front portrays Le Pen as a true patriot. This literature translates Le Pen's life experience, from the military to political action, into the image of Le Pen as the embodiment and incarnation of millenarian France. Le Pen's life has lent itself to this process of mythologization: He is, in the words of Pierre Duran, "a show of examples, a gathering of French virtues" (Buisson and Renault 1984, 1). Le Pen encompasses in himself and in his life "the best" that France's history, culture, and character has to offer: "[He is] a Frenchman that comes from far away in time, nurtured by Greco-Roman and human wisdom," asserts Monnier. "This Breton carries with him everything that is specific to our people [in] ethics and culture" (Monnier 1994, 184). The following words of Yves Daoudal shed a light on this mythically patriotic image of Le Pen.

> Jean-Marie Le Pen is not a Party man, and that is undoubtedly why career politicians reject him. He is the spokesman for [a] France gathered in all its history, in all its components, in all its generations. He assumes all the heritage [of France], [that] of the saints and scientists, peasants and workers, heroes and soldiers, that of the monarchy and of the republic, the victories and defeats, the shadows and the lights, in one big movement that carries the pearls and the scoria of history . . . No other politician [so] underscores that our role is to collect respectfully what was given to us, to transmit what we have received, and to make our heritage bear fruit . . . that is the true

---

9. This and other posters can be seen on the National Front's website, <http://www.frontnational.com/militantisme_tracts.php>.

"national" dimension of Jean-Marie Le Pen. [That is] his historical dimension. (Maréchal and Gauthier 2001, 60)

Le Pen is the quintessential Frenchman. He is the *rassembleur*, the man who combines in himself the spirit and history of the Eternal France. Because of his patriotic credentials, he is the only one who can lead the remnant patriots of France to achieve their grand mission of recovery and renaissance. It is not surprising that the former general secretary of the National Front, Carl Lang, sees Le Pen as "the only man who incarnates the hope of renaissance" (*Le Monde*, April 3, 1990). The literature of the National Front, particularly by releasing photo books in which Le Pen is the main character, casts the image of a man who, from the very beginning, has made great sacrifices in order to serve his nation, first in the army and then in politics. The attempts on his life and the overall hostility he faced (see for example Buisson and Renault 1984, 92–99; *National-Hebdo*, November 2–8, 2006) have only added to the picture of a man who remained faithful to his principles and committed to serving the nation. The way Le Pen overcame adversity, many times "alone against everybody" (Buisson and Renault 1984, 100), and was able to stay the course and develop a national movement, has enhanced his status as a hero in the eyes of his followers. In the collective consciousness of the National Front, the life of Le Pen symbolizes the triumph of commitment and vision over inhospitable conditions. Le Pen has become a myth, a living symbol of potency and hope in the renaissance of France.

In this context it is slight wonder that, in the minds of those who at some point or another were his closest disciples or collaborators, Le Pen has acquired a quasi-supernatural dimension. Louis Aliot has stated that the continuing strength of the National Front comes from "the providential-like meeting between a man who speaks clearly and knows how to point the way for the patriot electorate seeking justice and truth" (*National-Hebdo*, August 26–September 1, 2004). The National Front published a book called *Passionately French: The Life of Jean-Marie Le Pen in Cartoon Strips* that describes the rise of Le Pen from his humble origins to messianic leader. Its authors noted that, like a superhero, "his life has the taste of the essential, the flavor of the emotion, the force of the ideal" (Bariller et al. 1995, 3).

The headline of one of the issues of *National-Hebdo* was "Clovis—Jeanne d'Arc—Le Pen, the same combat!" (April 18–24, 1996). François Brigneau described Le Pen as an "inspired prophet" comparable to the heroes of the Flemish poet Verhaeren (Brigneau 1984, 10). Bruno Mégret put Le Pen in the category of the "great men" of history who "position themselves always outside the norm because, as history teaches us, nothing great can come from a respect of conformity. Is our society so low in its decline that it is not capable of admitting [that Le Pen is a great man]?" (Mégret 1990, 151). Patrick Binder sees at the core of the "very strong" relationship between Le Pen and the militants "the exceptional charisma of the President of the National Front, seen by everybody, justly, as one of the greatest French politicians of the century" (Binder 2004, e-mail interview, July 2). Yvan Blot wrote about Le Pen's "refusal of resignation, of a heroical type" (1992, 225). Roger Holeindre, reminiscing about Le Pen's life episodes, declares that "I believe . . . that it was necessary for this man [to have] a supernatural, almost divine, strength of character, for him not to abandon his combat" (Holeindre 2001, 5). In the literature of the National Front Le Pen emerges as an anointed man who, in a time of crisis, has taken up the mission of rescuing France from decadence. The following description of the context in which the leader of the National Front emerged, found in a book addressing the militancy of the party, testifies to this deep-rooted belief.

> Never has the world been more dangerous. Never has the future been more unpredictable. And, yet, never have the men who have the honor of being at the head of our country appeared less confident in themselves. It is as if, in the face of the enormous [and] scary challenges of this end of the 20th century, their only answers are uncertainties. The reason for this arises from the fact that they don't know anymore whom they govern for. And, when they know it, they don't dare say it anymore. In the face of adversity, the only recourse is the will to fight. But this historical will must be rooted in faith. In these times of feeble values and tottered convictions Jean-Marie LE PEN *[sic]* is a man of faith. For him, decline is not ineluctable. (National Front 1991, 21)

Le Pen is, therefore, the charismatic missionizing hero with all of the rare qualities necessary to save France.

The Leader's Discourse. Le Pen himself plays a prominent role in the development of the "Le Pen industry." In his discourse Le Pen accentuates on one hand the urgent need for a true leader who can fight decadence and lead a national renaissance and, on the other hand, his own role and attributes as the right man for the mission.

Le Pen is outspoken about the need for strong leadership. "The French, when they are helped by great ideas and true leaders," he writes, "either in the domain of enterprise or the army, go further than the entire world" (1984, 25). He warned in an interview about a widespread decadence that cried out for leadership, "[a] crisis both moral and spiritual that our country knows," that demanded a strong resolve from the nation, "[w]ithout which there will be no recovery and renaissance." He continued by affirming that "I deeply believe that many French have hope in new formations and hope in new men" (1984, 211). In fact, Le Pen repeatedly promotes a "Great Man" interpretation of history. In his words, "All peoples who have let themselves slide and became soft, either because of materialism or the abandon of the great principles of collective and individual virtues, have been swept away by the barbarians. We believe that what lifts the peoples, what allows them to live, are the saints, the heroes, the martyrs. We do not say that we are saints, or heroes, or martyrs, but we say that the peoples need them as they need poets and artists" (1979, 180).

The fact is that in his discourse Le Pen sometimes implicitly and yet other times openly includes himself as a member of the "Great Man" club of history. He is able to insert himself into a long tradition of historical heroes. At a time of internal dissent led by Bruno Mégret, Le Pen made the following analogy: "I was told: Is there any possibility of reaching an agreement? Any chance of putting water on the fire, or that Caesar issues a pardon? . . . The difference between Caesar and me is that when Brutus approaches Caesar holding the knife in his hand, it is I who pulls the sword and kills Brutus before he kills me!" (*Le Monde,* December 14–15, 1998).

Le Pen makes an effort to infuse a mythic character into his public persona. Explaining the charismatic nature of his persona, Le Pen mentions a magical dimension:

> We only transmit what [charisma] we have. Thus, to spread one's faith or ideal, it is necessary [to have] a strong belief and its vigorous defense. It is

this faith in action that attracts and creates what we called the phenomenon of charisma. [This charisma] may be heightened by qualities of expression, however a good orator is not necessarily charismatic . . . I think there is something magic in the will of persuasion of a man. There are people who have a magnetic radiance and [there are] also publics of strong conductibility. When there is a match between the message transmitted and the aspirations of the masses, there is abruptly synergy. Yet [as] nothing can be transmitted without emotion, this synergy resembles love. (Bariller et al. 1995, 6)

He has repeatedly defined himself as the "Robin Hood who takes from the rich," and as the "Zorro of the poor and of the French" (*Le Monde,* June 9, 1984), the "avenger that no one sees" (*Le Figaro,* April 26, 2006). Asked about what the National Front would be without him, Le Pen answered, "What would have been *gaullisme* without De Gaulle, the empire without Bonaparte, Communism without Lenin? Probably very little. At the beginning of all great human enterprises there is always a man and an idea that unite and give impetus" (*Le Figaro-Magazine,* February 17, 1990). He concluded his 1990 speech to the National Front congress in Nice with the legendary words of General La Rochejaquelein during the revolutionary period in France: "If I advance, follow me; if I die, avenge me; If I retreat, kill me!" (*Le Monde,* April 3, 1990). The prospect of losing elections does not bother Le Pen. As noted by him, "before becoming the president of the United States, Lincoln was defeated forty times" (*Le Monde,* September 20, 2003). Even the fact that Le Pen has named his private boat *General Cambronne,* a detail pointed out many times in the literature of the National Front (see, for example, Maréchal and Gauthier 2001, 132–38), adds to the perception of Le Pen as a legendary figure. After all, General Cambronne led the Old Guard in the battle of Waterloo and, when asked to surrender, his last words became etched forever in the popular imagination: "The Guard dies, it does not surrender!" Le Pen hardly misses an opportunity to tell the faithful that "in our march we have the company, invisible but present, of the Saints, the Martyrs, the Heroes of our long History" (2002b).

Le Pen's emphasis on such heroes of the past as Joan of Arc, and on the similarities between her time and the present, only helps the listener to reach the natural conclusion of what is being implied: In the same way that Joan

2. During the National Front's traditional May Day rally in Paris, Jean-Marie Le Pen gestures to his supporters as he stands before a giant banner of Joan of Arc, the fifteenth-century nationalist burned at the stake, who has become a party icon; May 1, 1995. Photograph by François Mori, courtesy of AP Images.

led France in fighting off the decadence of the past, Le Pen will lead France in fighting off the decadence of the present. In the words of Le Pen, "She shows us the road of courage and faith. She teaches us that nothing is lost when we have courage, a pure heart, and tenacity" (1996c). This comparison between himself and Joan of Arc is always present in the discourse of Le Pen.

Le Pen promotes a biographical account in which he, like the heroes of the past, personifies all of the necessary qualities of the leader that France dramatically needs. The leader of the National Front not only charges himself with the task of being the spokesperson for the people but also identifies himself as someone who comes from the people. As he noted in an interview, "I think that [France] trusts men like me, who do not have to bend in order to reach the people, but who come from the people to express its aspirations and hopes, and maybe to build with her [France] a future of freedom and hope" (1984, 246). In the preface to one of the photo books dedicated to his life story, Le Pen emphasizes his common touch:

> The images gathered here, could have been those of your personal album . . . They are those of a Frenchman like you, proud of his homeland, of his people, his kith and kin . . . anyone can find here a reflection of things of his or her life, of life: the family, the childhood, the mothers, the women and girls, friends, school, army, work and the face of those who do not live anymore but in our hearts. A simple story, in short. (Buisson and Renault 1984, 4)

He repeats the same point in the preface to another book. Writing about his life story, he states, "This story is a simple story, in short. [It is] a French story that, although it is mine, could have been perfectly well yours also" (Maréchal and Gauthier 2001, 7). In his discourse Le Pen frequently mentions his family lineage of peasants and fishermen. He repeatedly states that he comes from an unprivileged upbringing. Reminiscing about his childhood, he wrote, "We were poor, but happy. Love of family was the surrogate for comfort" (1984, 32). As he said in a speech to the militants in the northeastern city of Metz, "I am a man of the people . . . born in a two-room apartment with no running water, my grand-parents didn't know how to read or write" (*Le Monde,* December 14–15, 1998). By stressing his unprivileged background, Le Pen not only underscores his similarity with the people but also sends a message that he, unlike the privileged elitist mainstream politicians, can relate to the hardships of the people. This is a common line of Le Pen's attack. He assails the technocrats for being out of touch with the people: "They cannot imagine what happens to one who is unemployed, they have never imagined and they never will . . . they believe that the fishing industry and agriculture do not deserve to exist because they despise hard jobs." Further, "they are afraid of making their hands dirty but it's not the land that is dirty, it is corruption" (*Le Monde,* March 14, 1995). At the speech that launched his presidential campaign for the 1995 elections, Le Pen declared, "I was poor, I suffered from cold and hunger. And the poor, those who have known cold and hunger . . . the lonely, the desperate, will always have a privileged place in my heart" (*National-Hebdo*, September 22–28, 1994). In an interview from the 1980s, he declared, "I am one of the rare political men who earn their lives in an ordinary way, that is, to earn my living I founded a record label" (1984, 217). Accused of being a populist, Le Pen replied, "It's not an insult, to be the people's candidate, it's valuable" (*Les Français d'Abord!*, October 27, 2006). What, above all, gives status and dimension to a political man, declared Le Pen, at a speech in Le Bourget (a suburb of Paris) that formally launched his 2007 presidential campaign, is the "connection of spirit, heart, and soul with the people, and not [the signing of] contracts with polling and marketing agencies that sell [politicians] like yogurts" (2006e). In order to distinguish himself from an opponent, Le Pen said, "There are many voters on the left who, between Sarkozy and Le Pen, will vote Le Pen, because I am a true man of the people" (*Les Français d'Abord!*, October 24, 2006).

To legitimize himself even further with the people, Le Pen underscores his selfless attitude toward politics. This unselfishness is particularly important in an era in which the mainstream political class has been hit hard by corruption, one of the "two taboos of the French political life, together with immigration," according to Le Pen (*Les Français d'Abord!*, February 7, 2004). "I'm not like one of those who want power for the sake of power," he once said (*Paris Match*, May 6, 1995), and he observed that "I'm in politics not to 'make money' but to defend and advance my ideas. That's what I ask from life—and that's what life has given me—to live honorably and to give good conditions to my kith and kin" (Marcilly 1984, 30). "I have a tendency," he maintained, "to imagine the people as I am: that is, straight, loyal, honest, and genuine" (Habbad 1998, 126).

In fact Le Pen constantly evokes a homespun persona and carefully conveys an image of frugality although, since inheriting the fortune of a personal friend, he lives very comfortably in the rich Paris suburb of Saint Cloud. However, he said in an interview to TV channel TF1, "I don't have any [expensive] passions, I don't have a yacht or a sports car . . . I live my life in simplicity, as often as possible with my family . . . but I would be happy as well as long as I was surrounded by books, in a small room. . . . I don't have a lot of needs" (Habbad 1998, 131). To further his identification with the people, Le Pen promotes in his speeches a self-image of being a traditional family man. Photos capture him in the midst of everyday life with his wife, daughters, and grandchildren. Such imagery helps people to identify with Le Pen, who enjoys the same pleasures as any ordinary man, and to contrast his lifestyle with the more reserved approach regarding family matters of typical French politicians.

This ordinariness plays a pivotal part in Le Pen's strategy of saying what seems self-evident. He presents a reputation of being someone "who tells it like it is," and his arguments are usually presented as obvious facts. He writes, "I express, I think, ideas of common sense" (1984, 173). He frames historically the "woeful plight" of the National Front as the journey of a group of men and women who, for more than thirty years, fought back "with [only] our common sense and the sound intuition that our view was the right one" (2006e).[10] A typical example of what Le Pen calls "hierarchical affinities and attachments" (1989a, 102) comes from the way he chooses to justify his policy of national preference. He repeats the following excerpt over and over again:

> The beautiful spirits and souls of Paris [political class] refer to the politics that we defend as selfish, xenophobic, and racist. It is nothing like that. In fact, what we do is to apply in politics what is the most elementary rule of good sense, that is, to apply our duties first to oneself and then to those close to us. I've said this many times: I love my daughters more than my nieces, my nieces more than my cousins, my cousins more than my neighbors. It's the same in politics; I love the French the most. And no one will make me say something different. (1985, 170)

"However," said Le Pen in an interview, "that doesn't mean that we detest our neighbors. Being a Francophile doesn't require being a xenophobe. The fact that I prefer the French does not mean that I detest the English. I like them less than the French—overall" (*New Yorker*, April 28, 1997). Le Pen prides himself on speaking a language that is at odds with

---

10. The authors of *Le Pen Les Mots* see Le Pen's discourse as a deliberate strategy that "links the speech to an absolute knowledge, accepted by everyone, always true, that cannot be contradicted without challenging the most elementary good sense, the common sense, the knowledge ordinarily shared." In Souchard et al. 1998, 22.

the perceived politically correct and "sensitive" language of mainstream politicians and media. According to him this pervasive political correctness is a way of avoiding the real issues and problems faced by France: immigration, lack of law and order, loss of national independence, and erosion of values. Le Pen sees himself as a "free man." According to him, "politicians speak a stereotyped language—not me!—because they fear the censorship of the media . . . they are afraid 'to slip' [to say something offensive], to say something outside of the normative system defined by the media" (*Le Figaro–Magazine*, February 17, 1990).

The choice of words at the beginning of his statements is intended to advance an image of Le Pen as someone who is in touch with the most elementary common sense: "It's clear that," "We all know that," "As you have already figured out," "We know very well," "The truth is," "The people know very well," and so forth. To bolster his credibility as a common man, Le Pen sometimes uses a very crude and vivid language. "France," he said on one occasion, "has been sold to the left by conservatives who are [acting like] an old lady who, on the verge of being raped, folds up her skirt and blouse, to see if at least she can save her own clothes." He concluded by saying, "France is not a brothel to six million immigrants" (Plenel and Rollat 1984, 29). At a debate Le Pen asserted, "the day we have in France not five but twenty-five million Muslims, they will be the ones in command . . . and the French will have to keep their eyes down. If they don't do it they will be told, 'Are you looking at me? Are you looking for a fight?' And you will have to behave, or you will be beaten up. That is why the National Front finds a lot of support in the popular neighborhoods" (*Les Français d'Abord!*, April 30, 2003).[11] Le Pen is also known for telling jokes to his audience, reciting poems from such authors as Verhaeren, Péguy, or Brasillach, and regularly singing local, regional, or popular songs from such performers as Yves Montand and Edith Piaf (see Maréchal and Gauthier 2001, 100). This creates intimacy and further accentuates his image as a popular man.

Le Pen claims he has the credentials to be a true leader for France because he comes from the people and he is, above everyone else, a true patriot.

---

11. For these comments Le Pen was convicted by France's highest court of inciting racial hatred against Muslims (*Le Figaro*, May 11, 2006; *The Scotsman*, May 12, 2006, online).

In fact, Le Pen repeatedly highlights his unwavering commitment and loyalty to France since the early days of his childhood. "I was lucky," remembered Le Pen in a speech, "because my natural instinct of attachment to my land and my region was nurtured from the beginning of my life. Because I belonged to those generations who learned to love the homeland and to pray to God in the lap of our mothers" (1992a, 340). The fact that, after the death of his father, he was adopted by the State as a "pupil of the nation" is a pivotal reference in the patriotic pedigree Le Pen exalts for himself:

> I felt, as a child, a particular emotion in regard to that administrative formula that was issued by the civil courts when your father had died for France: "The nation adopts the minor Jean-Marie Le Pen." All my life I felt that I had, because of this formula, not two times the rights as the others, but two times the duties. And if I accepted responsibilities in the student world and, later, in politics, if I decided to volunteer for the army, to go to Indochina . . . it is because I had the feeling not only that at stake was the battle against communism . . . but also because if France did not receive the support of the youth she would die of sadness and despair, because in order to fight it is at least necessary that those whom we fight for are conscious [that we fight for them]. (1992a, 342)

Le Pen describes this "adoption by France" as the driving force of his mission: "I felt that I had a particular role [in life], of being more French than the others" (France 5, November 26, 2006). He never misses an opportunity to instruct his audience that his life experiences testify to his patriotism and entitle him to the leadership of the nation. In announcing his candidacy to the 1988 presidential elections, Le Pen returned to La Trinité-sur-Mér, the town where he was born on Brittany's south coast, to reaffirm his patriotism.

> [C]hild of the people, pupil of the nation, I was raised by my mother in the love of God and country. I myself have devoted my life to my family and homeland, to which I gave my best to serve for more than forty years, under the flag, in my military and political life. It is because I have the profound conviction that the homeland is in grave danger and that the French are threatened with being ruined, submerged, and enslaved that I

have decided to engage in this decisive battle for the future of France. (*Le Monde,* April 27, 1987).

In the run-up for the presidential campaign of 2002, Le Pen wrote about the role of the public man in the contemporary world. This writing provides a particularly relevant testimony to Le Pen's use of his biography to bolster his sense of entitlement, as a true patriot, to become the head of the nation.

> Only child, alas! Pupil of the nation when I was fourteen years old, I've always been in search of that brotherhood that I have lacked, and maybe that is the principal source of my vocation as a public man . . . [The public man] makes an effort to act in the general interest of his people and of his nation. [The public man] is a patriot. In any case, it was in this spirit that I have dedicated myself to politics: the most difficult art and the noblest service together with the army . . . Adopted by the nation after my father was "killed for France," I have always felt more responsible [to the nation], more in debt to her than my fellow citizens. When I was a child we did not doubt God, because we were Christians, or the homeland, because we were French. (Maréchal and Gauthier 2001, 175–76)

Le Pen, therefore, plays a substantial part in the "Le Pen industry" that consolidates his image as the leader who is necessary, in his words, to "guide [France's] surge and its renaissance" (*Le Monde,* April 27, 1987).

The Personalized Party. The overall structure and dynamics of the National Front as a political party also play an important function in the strengthening of the process of mythologization of the leader. Since Le Pen accepted the leadership of the National Front he has maintained a powerful grip over the party. The party has a centralized power structure based around its president. Every three or four years the National Front holds a congress. A pool of delegates chosen from regional mini-congresses constitutes the participants. The party congress elects the members for the central committee of the National Front. From these members Le Pen chooses those whom he wants for the party's political committee, the *bureau politique* (composed of thirty to fifty members). Finally, from these members Le Pen personally chooses those who will be part of the executive committee, the *bureau exécutif.* The party has a defined hierarchical structure that has the president of the party at the top. Le Pen has always justified it as a necessity: "[T]he National Front has always been hierarchical and disciplined because that is a fundamental necessity for its unity, a guarantee of its survival and its progress in a milieu that it is very hostile" (2004b). The party's political committee has a strong hold on the party's regional expansion, and there have been cases of local and regional leaders being replaced by Le Pen for displaying too much autonomy (see, for example, Pedahzur and Brichta 2002).

Le Pen's discretionary power was evident in the April 2003 congress of Nice. Even though his daughter, Marine Le Pen, came in only 34th out of 137 candidates voted by the delegates in the election for the central committee, Le Pen appointed her as vice president, thereby giving her an automatic seat on the party's executive committee. He dismissed all accusations of nepotism as "some small pitiful upheavals, and some small sourness," and wrote off all criticisms of Marine's capacity because "[t]alent always creates some irritations" (*Le Monde,* April 21, 2003). Le Pen later accused the critics of "confusing their personal interests with the interests of the cause, which is essential" (*Le Monde,* May 22, 2004). Le Pen made sure to let everyone know that he, as always, was in command. He addressed reporters by saying that "the mission of the president of the National Front is to maintain both the unity and dynamism of the movement" (*Le Monde,* April 21, 2003). The executive committee (composed of eight to ten members) is composed of advisors who discuss the general policies of the movement, but Le Pen is always the one who has the final say. Yann Piat, a former member of the political committee in the eighties, described the meetings in the following terms: "Around the table there was supposed to be an exchange of ideas. In reality, apart from the very technical and straightforward reports of Stirbois [former general secretary] no one dared to discuss, much less criticize . . . when Le Pen speaks everyone is silent; when Le Pen decides no one risks murmuring the smallest contradiction. At that time, the Front, the executive committee, was the court of King Jean I" (Piat 1991, 129).

The decision process for choosing the president of the National Front parliamentary group is elucidative. Le Pen declared, "'I will be a candidate for the presidency. Anyone running against me?' Half of the members laughed. The other half looked down. 'Very well, if no one is a candidate against me, I am therefore elected president unanimously'" (Bresson and Lionet 1994, 436). In every congress, Le Pen is reelected president of the National Front by acclamation from the delegates (see for example, *Le Monde*, April 3, 1990). Another relevant example of Le Pen's hands-on leadership in the party was his "executive decision" in October 2005 to replace Carl Lang as secretary general of the party with the younger Louis Aliot. "I submitted my resignation immediately and in the most loyal manner," declared the deposed Lang, because "the President must have total freedom of choice and action in light of the upcoming [2007] Presidential election" (*Les Français d'Abord!*, October 13, 2005).

Under Le Pen's leadership the National Front has had a high level of cohesion. Le Pen does not tolerate any sort of opposition. For Le Pen, dissent is potential insurrection or rebellion against his rule. Over the years Le Pen has regularly reminded his troops that he is the leader. As he said in a speech,

> We have to remain vigilant [and thus] it is necessary to clearly dissipate all ambiguities. [As] founder and twenty-five-year president of the National Front . . . I will continue to assume the plenitude of my functions that your trust has not ceased to confirm. There is none but, and I say that in friendship and affection, only one number, the Number One, elected unanimously by the congress. Then, I announce that I will be the head of the list for the [1999] European Elections." (*Le Monde*, December 12, 1998)

A similar warning was issued at the end of the 2003 Congress of Nice. Le Pen made clear that any talk of a successor would be a waste of time since, in perfect health, he was "the only master on board" (*Le Monde*, April 22, 2003), and "would remain at the head of the party until I'm 95" (*New York Times*, April 27, 2003). He has jokingly asked his audiences to start calling him "Jean-Marie Methuselah," an allusion to the bible patriarch said to have lived 969 years (*Le Monde*, September 20, 2003). At the start of his campaign for the 2007 presidential election—his fifth presidential campaign since 1974—Le Pen paid tribute to French statesman George Clemenceau, toured his hometown (*Libération*, October 23, 2006), and noted in an interview that he had the exact same age as "The Tiger" when he guided France to victory in World War I (France 3, October 29, 2006).

In the spring of 2004, during a period when some party officials criticized the lack of debate inside the party and Le Pen's choices of candidates for the European Parliament elections, Le Pen again reminded everyone of his supreme authority. He reiterated that "it is up to the president to decide according to the superior interests of the movement, as understood by him" (*Les Français d'Abord!*, May 29, 2004). Le Pen's way of dealing with this internal tension followed a familiar pattern that he had been using since the early moments of the National Front and continues to use.

In any case, if there is a perception that a National Front official has a growing influence within the party, Le Pen relegates him or her to the sidelines. The process can be slow or fast, but it inevitably ends with a purge from the party. The most famous case is the purge of Mégret at the end of the nineties; however, there have been various expulsions in the history of the party. In the mid-eighties Le Pen saw one of his deputies, Jean-Pierre Stirbois, as a potential threat to his rule, and a process of marginalization was under way when the forty-three-year-old Stirbois died in an automobile accident in 1988.[12] In order to solidify his primacy in the party, Le Pen has opted for a "divide and rule" philosophy. The political apparatus of the National Front is made up of two rival structures: the general Delegation that supervises the ideological orientation of the party, and the general Secretariat that supervises the local implementation of the party. Many times their tasks collide, and there is not a distinct separation of roles. In this context, Le Pen becomes the arbiter and the one to whom everyone looks to resolve the rivalries. This situation only adds to Le Pen's control over different factions of the National Front.

There is a powerful identification between the National Front and Le Pen. Party literature is oriented toward the promotion of the leader. For

---

12. Le Pen's appointing of Bruno Mégret in 1988 to the post of general delegate of the party is interpreted, partially, as an example of his "split and rule" leadership and as a way of counteracting Jean-Pierre Stirbois's growing influence. Bruno Mégret, on the other hand, was expelled from the party ten years later, in 1998, as the leader of a rebel faction opposed to Le Pen's leadership; he founded his own (rather unsuccessful) party. In December 2006, however, Mégret withdrew his own candidacy for the presidential elections and backed Le Pen's, in the name of a "Union of the patriots" seen as "the great alternative force that France needs" (Mégret 2007).

some time the newspaper of the movement was called *La Lettre de Jean-Marie Le Pen* (The Letter of Jean-Marie Le Pen). The official party periodical, *Les Français d'Abord!*, is promoted as "the magazine of Jean-Marie Le Pen." The party has launched video games within which Le Pen fights his political opponents (*National-Hebdo,* February 15–21, 1996). Visitors to the party's website may access Le Pen's video-blog, in which he discusses different political, social, and cultural events and gives details of his personal life, such as vacations, trips, and so forth. In the marketing department militants can buy badges, key rings, and even champagne with photos of Le Pen. On the official website of the National Front, cybernauts can listen to "Radio Le Pen" audio files that contain excerpts of his speeches. On the website there is also evidently a strong emphasis on the patriotic biography of Le Pen. Under the headline "A Fervent Patriot" is asserted that "Jean-Marie Le Pen is one of those rare contemporary political men who put his life at risk for his homeland and ideas."[13] The mythologization of Le Pen is only a click away on the Internet.

The "industry Le Pen" is arguably a collective work that involves the discourse of Le Pen, the work of his inner circle, and the solid identification of the political party with the leader. The end result is the sacralization of Le Pen, which creates an image of himself as the embodiment of millenarian France and as the sole guide to salvation.

Political-Religious Symbolism

Rhetoric. Le Pen has always denied any supernatural dimension to his persona or to the National Front. Asked about the total devotion that his inner circle expressed for him, sometimes comparing him to a prophet, Le Pen replied, "We live in a State-spectacle . . . I have never encouraged that kind of vision, but it is true however that I believe that if people knew me better, they would like me better" (*Le Monde,* June 8, 1984). He always rejected any comparison between his role as the leader of the National Front and that of the prophet leading his people to the Promised Land. In fact he puts his disbelief

---

13. The National Front's website can be viewed at <http://www.frontnational.com/accueil.php>.

in terrestrial paradises at the very center of the core difference between a right-wing and a left-wing ideology. "The Right is modest, the Right says: Regarding men, almost everything is known, almost everything has been thought out and written, and men will remain as they are. The big difference is that the man of the Right, when he believes in paradise, he knows that it is not on the earth; the man of the Left, I don't know if he believes it, but he claims that it [the paradise] is on the earth" (1979, 177).

In fact, one of Le Pen's favorite mottos in his assailing of the left was for a long time, "No to paradise! Neither red nor rose" (1992a, 315). In an interview he noted, "The golden age is a notion of the Left. It's a constructivist, Rousseau-esque notion. It's the Enlightenment . . . I don't believe in earthly paradise. My paradise is in another world. [Happiness] is a personal conception. [T]here are conditions of unhappiness . . . Without having the pretension of creating a happy world, we try to create the conditions of a less unhappy world" (*New Yorker*, April 28, 1997).

However, as I have mentioned, the dominant story line set forth by the leader of the National Front is centered around an apocalyptical face-off between the forces of True France and the army of Anti-France. This battle is regularly described by Le Pen as a final confrontation between purity and corruption, light and darkness, good and evil. In his discourse, which is both oral and symbolic, Le Pen casts himself as a man who has embarked on a mission to lead the remnant few patriots, the community of the Elect, into combat against evil in order to redeem and save France. Many times he depicts this confrontation in specific religious terms. According to Le Pen the values that drive the National Front are "simple values," "those [values] that have governed the development of our civilization. They are the basis [of civilization], through the respect of God, the respect of man, the respect of fraternity, they are the rules of the Decalogue [as] imposed on our civilization" (1991, 155). In his book *Les Français d'Abord*, Le Pen, writing about the communist threat, prophesizes that "the first rider of the apocalypse, the one who all the world slowly knows by its name, without daring to affront it with clarity and firmness, is international communism" (1984, 144). "A surge of Frenchmen," he added, "can still stop the apocalypse" (1984, 152). "International communism," he said on another occasion, "has given examples of the variety of methods that it is capable of employing in order to reach its supreme and, we can say, satanic, goal: the domination of the world by one religion, by a monstrously inhuman dogma" (Marcilly 1984, 186).

In one revealing statement to his militants, Le Pen declared his "confidence in the instinct of our people, following the example of Saint *Michel*, [Archangel Michael] to combat the demons of renunciation, decline, decadence and servitude" (*National-Hebdo,* November 12–18, 1987). In a speech given at the annual National Front tribute to Joan of Arc, Le Pen stated emphatically that

> [t]oday we live in an identical crisis of civilization [to that facing Joan of Arc's time], with extremely comparable social and sociological consequences regarding the corruption of power, the dissolution of customs, and the preference given to the material over the spiritual. Today the riders of the Apocalypse are called immigration-invasion, murder of nature and life, economic and social ruin, loss of security, and death of public freedoms. (1991, 25)

As he noted in another meeting with his militants,

> The fact that we have faith in her [France], in her destiny, not comparable to any other, is at the basis of our renaissance. Our crusade will not be realized, in fact, without fighting hostile powers that came out apparently from hell, what we justly call the "anti-France." Those who hesitate should remember the flamboyant expression of Joan [of Arc]: "Warriors will fight and God will give the victory." As stated in the holy gospel: 'Unless the Lord watches over the city, the watchmen stand guard in vain.' (2000)

To convey an idea of how grave the crisis of France is, Le Pen said in a speech to his militants that "[t]he country is, evidently, ladies and gentleman, engaged in a downward spiral that will throw it into the eternal fire" (1992a, 307). The use of the metaphor of a descent into hell is regularly used by Le Pen as a way of describing the deep-rooted crisis of France (see, for example, 2003c). Le Pen constantly uses biblical metaphors. The ideologues of internationalism, he tirelessly repeats, are worshippers of the Golden Calf (the image adored by Israel when they wandered in the desert) and devotes of Moloch (the Philistine deity worshipped by idolatrous Israelites) (see, for example, Le Pen 2003a). In both cases the implication is of a Jewish plot to dominate world affairs in anticipation of the apocalypse. The European Union, in Le Pen's mindset a crucial component of internationalism, is many times regarded as a "Tower of Babel" that, sooner or later, will collapse (*FDA*, January 2004).

Le Pen renders a portrait of an ongoing apocalyptic battle between the forces of good and the forces of evil. The natural order of the world is being maliciously destroyed and, "between good and evil, the state cannot remain neutral" (1984, 78). In a meeting with his followers, the leader declared that time had come "to put order in the house—let [those who are] evil tremble and [those who are] good be reassured" (*Le Monde*, April 22, 1995). The final stages of the confrontation having been reached, the National Front's leader prophesied the signs announcing the radicalization of the battle: "We are going to enter an agitated period; without being millenarian, we can perceive the first signs of multiple clashes. I may be wrong, but I think that at that moment it is better to have holding the helm a Captain who still has strong arms than people with less experience" (*Le Monde*, April 11, 1995). Le Pen often employs maritime metaphors to describe the dangers ahead and his providential role: "We are experiencing for the moment a calm sea, but when the winds become severe, Force Eight, it will not be [socialist politician] Royal that will be called 'Captain'" (2006d). Throughout the discourse of Le Pen are references to upcoming dramatic events—characterized by widespread disorder, violence, and destruction—that will push France either to annihilation or to salvation. The following excerpt from a speech that Le Pen delivered to his militants during one of the traditional meetings in honor of Joan of Arc testifies to his apocalypticism:

> The time has not yet brought generalized disorders, although they are getting close, [I hope] at least that the youth start to open their eyes and look beyond the present times to the events that will force their destiny . . . Even if they don't know it [the youth] is in the frontline . . . only the French people, awakened by the proximity, the imminence of the mortal danger, can, with the best, the most lucid and courageous of their sons engage in the Battle till victory. (2004a)

On another occasion Le Pen warned about "a torrent of social, political, and moral decadence that seems to drive the world toward unknown yet suggested by the political and social climate, apocalypse" (1999d). Former general delegate Bruno Mégret sees in what he calls the "catastrophism" of Le Pen an "excessive behavior." As stated by Mégret, "[Le Pen has the] idea that we can only change the situation after the arrival of chaos . . . [E]vidently, it is necessary to radically change politics, but within the legal system at our disposal, without calling for the destruction of everything that exists" (2004, e-mail interview, September 30). In the discourse of Le Pen, God is not neutral. Sometimes ambiguously, other times openly, Le Pen stresses his belief that a supernatural agency will help him in his quest for the salvation of France. As noted by Le Pen, "History, in its intimacy, is not a simple succession of causes and effects but an abrupt apparition of founding events," of what he calls "hours of destiny . . . one of those manifestations of Providence" (1996a, 7). In a meeting with his supporters in Marseille the leader of the National Front invited the French people, using an expression made famous by John Paul II, to "cross the threshold of hope," adding, "we are not alone. The people of France have begun their liberation and Providence supports us in its invincible arm" (2002c). At another meeting Le Pen said, "In truth I tell you, I need you, [I need] your forces, your spirits, your will, your hearts, your souls, for the service of only one cause: the sacred cause of France. But the worse is not always certain, men and Providence can by their will and their efforts change the direction of destiny" (2001b).

But "having God on their side" is not an invitation to passivity. Though the history of France has "always included a providential dimension," the leader warns his devotees that "we can only count on the help [of Providence] if we ourselves act, as we [at the National Front] do, with our own means, our honesty, our good will"—the only way to trigger the "salvationist spark" (2006c). As asserted by Le Pen to his followers, "Providence may act no matter how weak is the spirit of resistance. But [Providence], as we know it, only helps those who help themselves" (1999d). In the "Battle for France" Le Pen has challenged the militants of his movements to "listen [to Joan of Arc], to battle, and God will give us the victory" (2000). Such use of religious rhetoric by Le Pen has been opposed by some sectors of the Catholic Church. During the presidential electoral campaign of 2002, Paris Archbishop Cardinal Jean-Marie Lustiger asserted in a press release that "[t]he Church and the Christians cannot accept that the meaning of religious symbols and convictions be changed to serve the political debate" (*Le Monde,* April 25, 2002).

The deeply embedded apocalyptic scenario in Le Pen's discourse has made members within his party uncomfortable. For instance, during the defection of Mégret and his supporters, Le Pen's apocalyptic mindset was invoked as a reason to leave the party. The National Front's College Student's Association announced that a major cause of their separation from Le Pen was because they could not recognize themselves in a man who "declares that he will come to power—which testifies to a national surge in his eyes—in the aftermath of exceptional, even apocalyptic events in our country . . . We want to come to power not in chaos but after convincing a majority of our compatriots" (*Le Monde,* January 24–25, 1999). The fact of the matter is that such a vision of the apocalypse has always fueled the discourse of Le Pen.

Rituals. The National Front has regularly promoted rituals that continually reinforce the identity of the group as the last of the patriots and saviors of the country and the role of Le Pen as their guide toward salvation. These organized mass events occur several times every year. Among them are the celebration since 1981 of the Fête des Bleu-Blanc-Rouge (BBR) (Party of the Blue-White-Red, the colors of the French national flag); the tribute to Joan of Arc, held since 1979 on May first of every year to celebrate the fifteenth-century French heroine; the *Université d'été* (summer school), where the ideology of the party is debated and discussed; the *rentrée politique,* the start of the political season, held many times in Le Pen's hometown in Brittany, La Trinité-sur-Mér. The focal point of all these celebrations is a *grand discours,* a solemn speech by the leader of the National Front. Alongside these events, the National Front organizes several street protests and parades, many times headed by the leader himself, to denounce either the wrong policies of the establishment or the persecution of the National Front by the "political-media caste." All of these rites help to foster a sense of collectivity and play a crucial role in legitimizing the soteriological function of Le Pen. In these events there is often an interchange between the political and the religious realms, and Le Pen deliberately positions himself not as a mere political person but as a preacher with a message of salvation. This ambiguity is dominant in the rites of the National Front.

3. April 21, 2003. Jean-Marie Le Pen is acclaimed by party faithful during the twelfth National Congress of the National Front Party, in Nice, southeastern France. The banner on the left of the French National flags reads "With Le Pen, even higher." Photograph by Lionel Cironneau, courtesy of AP Images.

For example, in his campaign against the treaty of Maastricht, Le Pen decided to give a speech to his militants in the historical city of Reims, where Clovis converted to Christianity, a pivotal moment in the consolidation of "eternal France." This speech became known in the literature of the National Front, appropriately, as "the Sermon of Reims" (see, for example, Maréchal and Gauthier 2001, 91). Originally Le Pen's plan was to give a "solemn declaration" inside the square of the cathedral of Reims. To his outrage the authorities barred the environs of the cathedral to Le Pen by invoking the 1905 law that codified the separation of church and state. At the occasion the spokesman of the bishops of France noted, "It seems that the National Front likes to keep alive some sort of ambiguity" (*Le Monde*, September 2, 1992). Le Pen went ahead with the meeting, his militants positioning themselves slightly outside the cathedral grounds. In his "sermon,"

Le Pen abundantly stressed his mission of saving France. In a typical manner he emphasized that "many times [in history] the idea of homeland was kept alive by a few men," and noted that "the peoples do not forge their destiny alone. To guide them, heroes, wise men, saints, and martyrs are needed" (1992c). These words served as the background for a prime example of Le Pen's missionizing messianic rhetoric. He declared,

> My dear Frenchmen and Frenchwomen, my dear compatriots, people ask you, what is the authority that Jean-Marie Le Pen has to talk as an equal to the authorities of the Republic? To pose as an expert on diplomacy? And who has given me the power to make myself heard, through you, to millions of our compatriots? . . . History teaches us that in a battle when the general is injured, or dies, or betrays, the most senior office replaces him. And on and on until, if necessary, the simple soldier, the most courageous, raises the flag. Well, that's what we do. True, the leaders of France have not died, but they have deserted combat [and] betrayed the interests of the nation . . . I accuse therefore the authorities of France of having sullied the flag of France by the incessant display of their corruption and their renunciation . . . I accuse the French government and their accomplices of wanting to deliver our flag to an anonymous synarchy . . . [I]n this context of dereliction, suffered from the people of France, I, myself, in your name, picked up the flag from the mud where they have left her. And I hold her tight to my heart. (1992c)

After identifying himself as a hero who guides the army of true France in the battle for its salvation, Le Pen read a solemn declaration with all the attributes of a prayer, an act of communion between the leader and his followers.

> [The Maastricht treaty] initiates a process [that will] ultimately lead to the loss of our freedoms, the dissolution of the state, the erasure of our language and, finally, to the death of France. Assembled in Reims, this sacred altar of the homeland, symbol of its foundation, rootedness, and perpetuity, we solemnly declare that we refuse the treaty of Maastricht, whose signature and ratifying are sullied of nullification . . . we swear to demand justice for the heinous crime and betrayal that would result from abandoning any small fragment of our national sovereignty; we swear to defend the freedoms, the independence, the identity of the French people, its culture, language, and

humanist and Christian civilization against the political genocide that constitutes the infamous Maastricht treaty; we swear to fight until the renaissance of our homeland and the recovery of our people. (1992c)

In order to stress the "suicidal" path that is leading France to enslavement and "death," Le Pen holds rallies at sites that evoke the sacred nature of the French nation. At these events and in these sacred places, Le Pen delivers his most passionate missionizing sermons, enjoining the community to persist in its mission of saving the nation. In January 1999, just before the approval by the French parliament of the treaty of Amsterdam that furthered European integration, Le Pen rallied his militants in the city of Versailles. After leading a cortege Le Pen delivered an appeal to the French people. In it the history of France is elevated to the condition of myth.

In the difficult moments of women and men, and it is the same for the life of nations, destiny sends us signs. It speaks, it manifests itself, it adverts, and it shows the way. It is maybe because France, our country, lives today [through] very difficult moments that destiny has decided to multiply those signs. Look firstly around you. Something mysterious is talking to us . . . We are on a Sunday, January 17, 1999. 206 years ago, in the same day, Louis XVI was sentenced to death and, with him, the monarchy's sovereignty was sentenced. Today it is the sovereignty of the Nation that the men of the Europe of Maastricht and Amsterdam, the men of a federal order, are getting ready to sentence to death. (1999a)

In Versailles, living symbol of France, Le Pen, in an emotional manner, reminded his militants of the majesty of the nation, a living and holy communion of people, history, territory, and destiny, threatened with debasement and extinction:

France, mother of Saints, Heroes, Martyrs, mother of the French people born from the Celts, the Greeks, the Galois, Romans, Visigoths, Franks, Britons, Normans, and others, that commune in one of the most beautiful languages of the world, the clearest one, the classiest. France of the menhirs and dolmens, of chapels and cathedrals, caves and palaces. France that doesn't stop its downhill trend, that doesn't cease to give itself away to the point of forgetting its own children. France—are you at the end of your path of suffering and glory? A few hundred felon parliamentarians are going to sell you to the Europe of merchants and financers, under the indifferent eye of the dumbfounded people? (1999a)

Le Pen concluded by identifying the struggle of the National Front as "the combat of good and [of] life."

Le Pen, surrounded by close advisers and militants, regularly visits sites that for him represent the sacredness of the nation, the land of "Saints and Martyrs." For example, in August 2001, on the day he delivered in his birthplace the speech that inaugurated the political season, Le Pen toured different sites. He started with a prayer in the Basilica of Saint Anne, followed by an homage at the memorial of the Bretons who died for the homeland in World War I, and finally a visit to the mausoleum of General George Cadoudal, French Royalist who remained true to his cause after the revolution and was sentenced to death after a failed attempt to kill Napoleon. When asked in a press conference about why he committed so much time to visiting these sites, Le Pen replied,

I choose the symbolic places of the history of our country. Since many people accept, without knowing what is going to happen to them, that France will cease to exist tomorrow, I remind them of what this people has been, what was demanded not too long ago of the French: the possibility of sacrifice of one's life for *the defense of sacred notions*, those of territory, of the Republic, of the nation and its people, with its freedoms and independence. (2001a, emphasis mine)

Intimately tied to Le Pen's self-promotion of his messianic role is his relentless promulgation of the sacred nature of his message. His words gain the stature and symbolism of prophecy. Le Pen elevates himself to the status of the bearer of a sacred truth that the forces of Anti-France are constantly conspiring to hide from the French population. The rituals of the National Front foster an alternative symbolic system to the one encouraged by the establishment. The construction of this alternative world of symbols and rites is essential in the solidification of the identity of the group.

The alter world of the National Front has at its base an alternative history, a interpretation of the present and a different concept of truth competing with that of the status quo. In this narrative, only a minority shares and valiantly defends the truth announced by Le Pen. But slowly the truth will be delivered to the rest of the French population, and they will be set free from the false truth that has brainwashed them over the years. As noted by Le Pen, "to survive is not only a right but a duty for everyone . . . but in order to survive it is necessary to know. That is why nothing is more worthwhile than creating the truth. [When the truth] starts its march, nothing will stop her" (1984, 152). In a solemn speech to his militants assembled at one of the Blue-White-Red celebrations, Le Pen declared,

> That is why our political combat is firstly and above all a combat for the first of the values, the truth. Because, as stated by John the Evangelist, "It is the truth that will set us free" . . . It is normal that our courage and lucidity be recognized. [Our] perspicacity to discern the truth and the courage to tell it at any cost . . . be it about immigration, unemployment, insecurity, finance, demography, national defense, moral laxity, drugs, AIDS, we were proved right. And I could legitimately display all over France: "Le Pen was right." He was right and he continues to be right! Together with you! (1995)

As observed by Le Pen, "I think that one of the fundamental missions of the public man, in a democratic world, is to reveal the truth" (1989a, 148). In fact a typical way that Le Pen describes any surge of support for the National Front is by declaring that "the French are finding the truth" (1992a, 237). "We want to tell our compatriots the truth that will set us free" is a regular motto in Le Pen's meetings with the militants (*Le Monde,* April 22, 1995). "Our country is not ready for the truth," lamented Le Pen failing to become president in the 2007 elections (*Français d'Abord!,* July 2007). The identification of Le Pen with the truth is a constant in the imagery of the National Front.

At the same time Le Pen is heralded as a liberator because, when people come to know the sacred truth revealed by Le Pen, they become liberated and join the community of the Elect. His arrival at one of the party congresses was accompanied by the sound of "The Choir of Slaves" from Verdi's opera *Nabucco* (Schonhuber 1998, 91). This not mere folklore but rather a powerful symbolism revealing the mission of Le Pen "The Liberator." A series of posters promoted unfailingly by the National Front showed Le Pen gagged under the headline "Le Pen tells the truth, they gag him!" or "They want to gag France!" (Bariller and Timmermans 1994, 62). Throughout his political career, Le Pen has never failed to describe himself as a common-sense politician, and has said many times that he "says out loud what most French people think" (1984, 12). At the same time he indicts the French population for being bystanders, for not coming forward, for not having the courage to join the community of the patriots, and for letting themselves be methodically brainwashed by the forces of Anti-France. They are letting their natural defenses, their instinctual common sense, be destroyed by unnatural ideologies. As written by Le Pen,

> France is in a bad state, much worse than it seems. She is on the verge of a decline that can rapidly lead to her disappearance and the people, drugged socially and by the media, does not know it, though many have a presentiment about it. In order to avoid her terrible tests she must react as soon as possible. The truth must help her to find herself and to resume in the twenty-first century the glorious road that she has drawn during the centuries. (Maréchal and Gauthier 2001, 177)

A poster distributed all over France promoted a personal message from Le Pen to the French people: "I ask Providence to inspire within all the French the lucidity, the courage, the pride that is too often lacking in them today" (Bariller and Timmermans 1994, 86).

To further his dimension as a truth-bearer, Le Pen hardly misses an occasion to stress his clairvoyance. Le Pen has repeatedly stated that the ability to predict should be characteristic of politicians. "We are," he said, "those who light up the politics [of France], that is why our logo is a flame" (1989a, 111–12). Regarding communism, Le Pen asserted that it was the National Front "who saw clearly, who saw far," and that "this prescience, this prediction of [the evils of] communism was imprinted in our permanent action and in the denunciation of communism we were the first" (1992a, 280–81). The same can be said about the phenomenon of AIDS, "A few years ago I was the first one to cry out public alarm for the danger" (1989a, 147). Regarding excessive immigration Le Pen observed, "It was the National Front, I claim, that put this affair at the center of public discussion. Historically it will be our honor . . . I had a presentiment about it and I said it at a time when it was not easy to be heard" (1985, 84–85). To him the controversies surrounding the French state's ban on headscarves in public schools are just an offshoot of the real issue, "anarchic and uncontrolled immigration" (*FDA*, January 2004). The headscarf ban, the street protests by Muslims that followed, and bomb attacks and vandalism acts on Jewish and Muslim sites are prima facie evidence that the National Front was right in alerting the public to the disruptive and dangerous phenomenon of immigration (France 2, January 29, 2004). The Islamic terrorist attacks in Spain constituted a "solemn warning" because France was "the most vulnerable European country due to a mad immigration policy for more than thirty years" (*Les Français d'Abord!*, March 18, 2004). As Le Pen said in a speech, "Who has had up until now the courage to tell the truth about the unemployment, immigration, insecurity, AIDS, infected blood, Chernobyl, mad cow disease? The National Front! . . . Therefore it was our analyses that for thirty years have been proven right, our criticisms have been proven just, and our solutions constructive" (2003b).

In the aftermath of the suburban riots in predominately North African communities in the fall of 2005, Le Pen, speaking in the third person, declared to a journalist,

> People say you can love him or hate him but you must admit that Le Pen was right. Le Pen was clear. He said, "*voilà*, this will happen if we continue down this political path." And we do continue on, listening to Jacques Chirac's pretty words and not stopping immigration, not cutting the supply pipelines, not reclaiming sovereignty over our frontiers. It can only get worse. The next explosion will be even more violent. (*Wall Street Journal*, November 19, 2005, online)

In another interview he sounded an alert: "[The riots] could constitute the premise of a civil war . . . I predicted the consequences of massive immigration . . . [The riots] do not surprise me, actually I think things may get worse" (*Le Figaro*, November 8, 2005). "The politically correct," says Le Pen, "forbids any link be established between immigration and the riots. Everybody knows it, but you can't say it" (*Jewish World Review*, January 10, 2006, online). Because, in his own eyes, Le Pen is always right, sooner or later his ideas and policies become more acceptable and copied by mainstream politicians. He applied the same logic after the 2005 fall riots: "Politicians now copy entire sections of our discourse, which they still ranted against a few months ago," he said. "Countless personalities reacted to the crisis last November by shamelessly copying the analysis and the proposals of the National Front" (*International Herald Tribune*, January 13, 2006, online). When during the 2007 presidential election campaign the conservative candidate Nicolas Sarkozy unveiled his plan to create a "ministry for immigration and national identity," Le Pen sarcastically commented in a press release that his rival was "soliciting on National Front territory" (National Front 2007a). The degree to which mainstream political parties and politicians adopt the vocabulary and the proposals of the National Front regarding immigration policies and increased criticism of current models of immigrant integration is directly related to the party's internal perception that, after decades of "preaching in the desert," Le Pen's worldview is finally starting to be vindicated. Therefore—and this is an argument put forward over and over again by Le Pen and his acolytes—why should France choose the "copyists" when the "original," who had been proven "right," is available?[14] Though Le Pen deplored the electoral loss in the 2007 presidential elections, he took comfort in the fact that the top issues of the campaign were "nation and patriotism, immigration and insecurity," which meant that the National Front had *de facto* "won the battle of ideas" (2007a). The "Lepenization" of minds and souls authenticates Le Pen's role as the *only* French politician who foretells the future.

This image of Le Pen as a truth-teller is linked to an image of Le Pen as a victim. Because Le Pen "tells the truth," the powerful forces of Anti-France persecute him. In one speech to the party faithful, the leader of the National Front compared himself to the Greek mythological figure Cassandra (2006e). Owing to his thirty-plus years of "true predictions," Le Pen remains

---

14. Le Pen has jokingly said that, to some voters, Nicolas Sarkozy appears as a sort of "Le Pen Lite" or "Le Pen wearing a tie"; yet he has warned sternly that Sarkozy "is the opposite of me" (2006a). The party frequently accuses the Mouvement Pour La France, (Movement for France) led by right-wing politician Phillipe de Villiers of "plagiarizing" the National's Front proposals.

the continuing target of the establishment's wrath. He becomes in this way the martyr, the one who makes great sacrifices and endures suffering for his beliefs and his unconditional defense of the French people. The "campaign of demonization" launched by the politico-media establishment against Le Pen during the runoff for the 2002 presidential elections became, in the narrative of the party, the epitome of Le Pen's martyrdom. To the militants of the National Front, the defenses of the elitist "System" that rules France had been breached by the "popular surge" personified in Le Pen; in order to survive, it thus unleashed all its might against the "candidate of the people," and in "totalitarian fashion" stigmatized him in the public eye as a mortal threat—while masking it in slogans such as the need to "defend democracy and the republic."[15] Yves Daoudal wrote that, to the establishment, "Le Pen is not the candidate defending French independence and putting France on the right track: He is Fascism, Hitler, he is the absolute Evil: He is the devil" (Daoudal 2002b, 11). Daoudal called it a "media lynching" (2002b, 41). "The men of the System," declared Louis Masson, fearing the end of their regime, orchestrated the "execution of Le Pen" (Masson 2003, 59).

Many times, when Le Pen perceives bias either from the political establishment or from the print and broadcast mainstream media against himself or the National Front, he promotes a campaign with solemn declarations, street protests, and parades denouncing the "persecution." After being barred as a candidate in the regional elections of 2004, for example, because he failed to prove that he lives in the Provence-Alps-Riviera region, Le Pen lambasted what he saw as a "mini-conspiracy" against him and cast himself as a victim: "As in Iran with the guards of the revolution, in France the guards of the corruption eliminate their opponents in advance" (*Les Français d'abord!*,

---

15. Roger Holeindre described the anti–Le Pen campaign as "an immense farse" that would "remain in the political and electoral history of the peoples as a model of disinformation and brainwashing—with no parallel in any other country." For Holeindre, the propagandists of Nazi Germany and the Soviet Union "pale in comparison to our great democrats" (see Holeindre 2003, 33). Le Pen, on the other hand, explained that a "member of the French masonry" told him that the campaign against him in the second round of the presidential election was motivated by the "fear that a populist surge" would destroy the system of compromises that "took decades to build." (See *National Hebdo*, November 2–8, 2006.)

February 25, 2004). A demonstration of support was organized, and Le Pen gave a speech to his militants in which he declared himself the victim of a bureaucratic-administrative persecution. The weekly newspaper of the National Front, *National-Hebdo*, put Le Pen on its front page under the headline "The guards of corruption persist in their fight against their only opponent" (February 26–March 5, 2004). This is a typical manner in which Le Pen props himself up in times of adversity and at the same time deeply imprints his status as a martyr and hero upon the collective imagination of the community of loyal party members. This rite of martyrdom is repeated with regularity.

These party rituals correspond both to a worshipping of Le Pen, as the interpreter through whom the will of the nation is expressed, and to the sacredness of the collective mission of the community of patriots. As written by a militant, "in his meetings Le Pen becomes the prophet and he infuses in his public the great poetry that is born from the nationalist sentiment, that meeting of conviction, courage and faith" (*National-Hebdo*, January 28–February 3, 1999). François Brigneau called the party's Blue-White-Red celebration a liturgy, a "Mass," because "[French] that come from all the regions of France, from all sorts of creeds and social status, and who in the past have had disagreements, *commune* together, and fervently demonstrate the love that they feel for the homeland, the land of the fathers." At the same time the Blue-White Red celebration is "above all a tribute to Jean-Marie Le Pen." In Brigneau's words,

> A whole little people, swarming with life and hope, express to him their gratitude for having managed to create, progress, and defend (sometimes against his own self-interest) this unprecedented national gathering. For the simple people, whom bourgeois conformism has not ruined, the man they call Jean-Marie possesses a number of rare qualities in today's [world]. He has physical and intellectual courage . . . that is why the BBR are a day of celebration for Jean-Marie Le Pen. It rewards him for so many hardships, disappointments, blows. (*National-Hebdo*, September 15–21, 1994)

Pierre Monnier expressed similar sentiment writing about the National Front's annual tribute to Joan of Arc. Monnier wrote that the mainstream technocratic political establishment could never understand the attachment between Le Pen and his people. According to him,

They don't understand, those beautiful minds, that the French who salute the statue of Joan and who march on the road [are going to meet] one of them, who waits, a Breton named Jean-Marie Le Pen, in whom they recognize themselves . . . Charles Péguy called these French the "piétaille" [the infantry] . . . they advance side by side with "the little girl hope" . . . I think that if, although impossible, Jean-Marie was attacked by lassitude, it would be enough for him to look at those children, those women, those men who march toward the statue of Joan. (Monnier 1994, 154–56)

A Moral Community. In fact, when Le Pen addresses the militants of the National Front he puts special emphasis on the emotional values that bind the community together. *Sacrifice* is prime among these. In order to reach the goal of saving France, the community of patriots goes through enormous sacrifices. "We think," he noted, "that the spirit of devotion and sacrifice is an integral part of our doctrine of action [and that] the homeland is not constituted only by those who are alive but also those who died as heroes, those who sacrifice themselves for the defense of their freedom" (Marcilly 1984, 188). Le Pen asked his militants at a meeting, "Don't you feel a little bit of happiness for coming here?" He added, "Don't you feel already rewarded, being so close to each other, for all the sacrifices we have to make? (1992a, 145). According to Le Pen, "the militants of the National Front are the civic elite of the nation, the soul of its continuity . . . if there is still a chance of renaissance for France we can say that it is due to them, to their devotion, to their sacrifices, their enthusiasm" (*National-Hebdo,* August 25–31, 1994).

Furthermore Le Pen often describes the National Front as a community of *love.* Le Pen has always presented himself as a "patriot of love" (Buisson and Renault 1984, 26). In a speech he noted, "in the France in which we call all French to fight for . . . the criterion [for joining the fight] is love, the criterion of the service of France" (1992a, 286). To him, "[when] we love our compatriots, the ideal entity that they represent, in time and space, we construct and develop in our hearts and souls the love for the homeland" (1992a, 19). In fact, when Le Pen addresses his militants, he repeatedly stresses the fact that they are gathered together "in the same love for the homeland" (2003b). The virtue of *hope* is also dominant in Le Pen's discourse. At a meeting he asked, "What will the future look like? Only God knows. But we have . . . the imperious duty of trying to discern its shape, evaluating the dangers but also the promises, because men need hope to live" (2003d). Le Pen declared at one of the Blue-White-Red celebrations, "As long as there are men who love France and devote themselves to her, as long as there is a French people, conscious of being French, there is a serious hope of victory" (2001b). "For the people we offer . . . a future of hope, conscious that the people will build a future of hope with us" (1992a, 286).

In the discourse of Le Pen the community of the remaining patriots is bound by *faith*. He stresses that it is this faith that makes them overcome all the obstacles in their road to save France. "We know that the main enemy is inside of us," observed Le Pen; "it is doubt, the renunciation of effort and of independence, discouragement, and despair" (2003b). Faith, however, is the answer to man's weaknesses:

> Sometimes people ask me, "Facing such adversity, aren't you discouraged, desperate?" I confess that sometimes doubt comes to me like it has come to the minds of the greatest saints. It's true, our forces apparently are so feeble compared to those of our opponents or enemies, at a time when a torrent of moral, political, and social decadence seems to push the world irresistibly toward unknown apocalypses . . . It is necessary then to study in doubt, but to act in faith. There is only one cure to doubt: It is prayer. Well, the prayer of the militant is political action. (1999d)

Le Pen has repeatedly described the work of the militants in terms of faith. Political action is neither a minor nor an expedient activity, but a way that the militants give meaning to their lives and fulfill their faith in the mission of salvation of France. Le Pen emphasized the faith-based character of the National Front militancy many times, and in different ways. The internal dynamics of the National Front's militancy, according to Le Pen, correspond to those of a pious group that is united by a common faith and devoted to a common cause. "The church [of the militant]," said Le Pen at one event, "is the National Front" (2003d). In this way it is not surprising that Le Pen discusses political propaganda in a proselytizing manner. The ultimate goal of the militant is not simply to convince but to *convert* others. In the campaign against the Maastricht treaty, Le Pen made this appeal to his militants: "Everyone of you, every conscious citizen must see yourself as a missionary . . . in order to snatch the undecided, those who don't know or haven't already understood, or those who make excuses" (1992b). "Joining the National Front is a solemn act of engagement," he said at another occasion." "It represents a promise of action . . . [the militant] has to recruit others who in turn recruit others in order to make a snowball that will end up to be the majority" (1992a, 316). At meetings he regularly thanks the militants for "testifying" with their presence their faith in the National Front (1991, 110). At the end of a speech in Dions, Le Pen thanked his audience "for making an effort to come here" and added that "I believe that one day you will be proud to say: 'I was in Dions, me too, to testify for the National Front'" (1991, 67). "Thank you all of you" he opened his solemn speech at one of the Blue-White-Red celebrations, "who came from the most remote areas of France to find your friends and compatriots, and testify to the vitality and ardor of the National Front" (1995). The militants become witnesses to the spreading, in the words of Le Pen, of *"la bonne parole"* (the good word) (2003d).

The rituals promoted by the National Front increase this dynamic of integration into an alter world where the community of believers, who go through great tribulations in order to reach their salvific mission, is set apart from ordinary reality and celebrates their collective identity as the "Elect." The former president of the National Front Youth (2001–5) describes these meetings in specifically religious terms. According to Louis-Armand de Béjarry,

> As in religions, the great gatherings keep alive the "faith" of the militants: they notice that they are not alone in having their ideas, that the National Front is powerful, organized, gatherer. The speeches, in front of thousands of people, serve to give the watchwords, slogans that the militants will use to persuade people. It is exactly the same function as the Sunday Mass: The communion to bind together the believers, and the sermon to give instructions or explain some details of the doctrine . . . [The militants] can also personally meet the officials, shake their hands, and talk to them. For them it is a sort of reward. These gatherings give courage and the will to fight to the militants, who go home highly motivated. (Béjarry 2004, e-mail interview, July 5)

This internal process of integration is coupled with an external dynamic of integration. Several studies have shown that a person who joins the National Front experiences a gradual process of stigmatization from the rest of society. On one hand, the National Front promotes an alternative world; on the other, the party is often perceived as a dangerous pariah by members of the "other France." This dynamic of outsiderhood is essential to an understanding of the missionary nature of the community of true believers of the National Front. They see themselves as different and set apart not only from militants of other parties but also from that "passive France," still resistant to the Front's message yet whom the militants are duty-bound to convert. The following words of Eric Domard attest to this notion, deep rooted among the militants, of being a community under siege that endures pain, sacrifices, and persecutions in order to realize their mission:

> It is difficult today to be a militant of the National Front. To belong to and defend the ideas of a party constantly demonized, vilified, put in the dock of society, may be difficult to live [through] and endure. To be a militant of the National Front demands a surplus of courage, determination that we do not find anywhere else. Through the adversity and the hostile environment in which they live, the militants of the National Front bind themselves into a moral force and [develop] a capacity to take blows. It is this supplement of motivation that illustrates the difference between the militants of the National Front and those of other parties. (Domard 2004, e-mail interview, May 25)

From its beginning the National Front has been the target of protests and counter-manifestations, and there have been confrontations and aggressions with anti-Front groups, such as Ras Le Front, which, in the name of "anti-fascism," pledges to disrupt the meetings and fight the militants of the National Front across French territory.[16] The National Front media registers every attack on its militants and constantly accuses the authorities of complacency (see, for example, *Les Français d'Abord!*, March 3, 2004). This perception of being constantly under physical threat and danger fuels the

---

16. The group has its own magazine and has published a "Manual of Combat against the National Front." See <www.raslfront.org>.

integration process of the militants of the party. As noted by Patrick Binder, "differently from other militants, those of the National Front are regularly assaulted, verbally or physically, every time they engage in militant action (holding signs, postering, etc.)" (Binder 2004, e-mail interview, July 2). The following words of Louis-Armand de Béjarry offer a powerful testimony of a community that feels besieged.

> The militants of the National Front are different from other militants. Their degree of engagement is truly superior: they put up posters at night and many times are attacked. They distribute leaflets on the streets, many times under insults. The militants of the National Front never trigger the indifference of people, contrary to the militants of other parties. They often trigger hostility, which creates among them a particular mentality, a sentiment of being apart, of having almost the entire world against them, which makes them bind together [even more] closely. The militants form a true community. (Béjarry 2004, e-mail interview, June 4)

In this scenario in which political action is not partial but all-consuming and full of sacrifices and risks, Le Pen, in the eyes of the militants, appears as a true authentic leader. His life story, his role as the founder of the party, and all the perceived campaign of hatred against him dramatically bolster his leadership credentials. In their eyes, Le Pen, constantly demonized and persecuted, embodies all the tribulations that the militants have to go through. He offers a powerful example to follow and to emulate, of someone who—under trying circumstances—never wavered in his commitment to the mission of saving France. According to Dominique Martin, "Jean-Marie Le Pen gives us the desire, the taste, the courage, the pride . . . of fighting for France, for their elders and their children (Martin 2004, e-mail interview, May 22). In this manner, the leader also assumes the function of first militant of the group. In fact, Le Pen has even hinted that he could eventually pay the highest price—his life as a martyr for the national resistance against the full frontal assault of hostile forces—for his commitment to the cause (see, for example, Jouve and Magoudi 1988, 110–20). Naturally, a cult of the fallen, of those patriots who devoted or even gave their lives for the completion of the National Front's mission, serves as the highest standard of militancy.[17] "Maybe the militants see Jean-Marie Le Pen [as] a militant like themselves," commented Béjarry, who added that

> [i]t cannot be forgotten that before he became an elected official for the FN, in 1984, for almost twenty years he had been in politics almost alone, leading a minuscule party. He has been very obstinate and always believed in his chances. All of that cannot but seduce the militants. In fact, Jean-Marie Le Pen is more a militant than a politician. He has the mentality of one who gives everything without expecting anything in return, he has the plain-spokenness and the comradeship of a militant. He is like a *primus inter pares*, the first of the militants of the National Front. (2004, e-mail interview, June 4)

This personal attachment between the militant and the leader is a crucial aspect of Le Pen's image. Le Pen incessantly tours France, and participates with militants from local sections in such occasions and gatherings as breakfast-debates, dinner-debates, festivals, or picnics in the countryside. During the Big Schism of the late nineties, Le Pen embarked on what the party called "patriotic meetings," sometimes held twice a week all over the country, intended to reinforce the militants' commitment to his person. In this manner Le Pen gives his followers an opportunity to recognize publicly their leader and to testify to their loyalty. On these occasions, as with the series of patriotic banquets held during electoral times, the militants see, hear, talk to, and sing "La Marseillaise" together with their leader (*Le Monde*, January 17–18, 1999; see also *Libération*, October 6, 2006). At a time when party militancy in France and in Europe in general is on the wane, the militancy of the National Front remains strong and mobilized. Militants actively participate in the rallies, parades, and meetings of the party. A recent study has

17. In 1994, during the eulogy at the funeral of André Dufraisse, a long-time member of the National Front, Le Pen addressed his dead colleague, telling him, "your friends will continue your combat." "Now," continued Le Pen, "you march with the angels, with your friends already gone." He paid tribute to those who, like Dufraisse, had "dedicated their lives to serving their country, to the national, popular, and social cause." Among others Le Pen mentioned François [Duprat] and Jean-Pierre [Stirbois] (see *Le Monde*, March 12, 1994).

shown that the militants of the National Front are the most active and visible cybernauts in Internet discussion groups (Datops 2004). Also, the electoral support that they give in each election to the FN is consistently high. In contrast, militants of other parties vote for their parties in much lower numbers. The typical FN militant is a loyal voter and a dedicated party worker (Mayer 2002, 207). Valérie Lafont sees the National Front as a "total institution, similar to a religious sect revealing the world . . . by an ideological discourse that wants to change history . . . offering in the first place the dream and hope in a different future, a better future" (Lafont 2001, 195). Le Pen acts as the guiding prophet who empowers his followers by elucidating for them who they are, who the "others" opposing them are, and what their collective mission is. The leader gives them a sense of purpose and potency, a sense of participation in history.

Charisma. Le Pen's popular level of charisma has undoubtedly helped the party. He is a powerful speaker, and his interventions are full of formulas and sound bites that captivate the media. In today's visual media-oriented elections, Le Pen has the ability to put on a good show. Le Pen is an entertainer. "He is at ease," wrote Nonna Mayer. "He provides formulas, counter-arguments . . . each of his appearances constitutes a show" (Mayer 2002, 186). However, Le Pen's main asset within the National Front is his capacity to develop a missionary level of charisma that makes him the avatar of the aspirations of the entire community of patriots. Throughout his leadership, the charisma of Le Pen has been maintained by the incessant work of what I call the "Le Pen industry," and by the development of powerful religious rites and symbols of integration.

Succession to the Charismatic Leader

Finally, and particularly since the beginning of this decade, Le Pen (born in 1928) has been preparing a post–National Front without his leadership and working actively to raise the status of his own daughter, Marine Le Pen (born in 1968), within the party. A lawyer in her second marriage and with three children, Marine is telegenic and well spoken. She appeals not only to the media but also to the female electorate that over the years has showed itself to be more resistant to the National Front. She has taken on her shoulders the task, in her words, of "de-demonizing" the party's hardline image (*New York Times*, April 27, 2003). Le Pen has said that "she has the material to become, one day, the president of the Front" (*Le Monde*, August 23, 2003). She gained increasing visibility in the media and influence within the party—and was put in charge of her father's strategy for the 2007 presidential campaign—although there are veterans within the party who do not seem comfortable with the prospect of seeing Marine Le Pen as the future leader.

The ascension of Marine Le Pen seems to be a natural corollary of the personal charismatic leadership of the National Front. Le Pen has always given prominent party roles to family members, from his son-in-law Samuel Maréchal to his wife and daughters. This favoritism has caused some to accuse Le Pen of nepotism. In the words of Mégret, "Le Pen always favors his family, his 'clan' [and] even wanted to put his wife as the head of the list to the European elections of 1999, although she's never been involved in politics. The National Front is a family enterprise" (Mégret 2004, e-mail interview, July 2). Le Pen's eldest daughter, Marie-Caroline, observed, "there are dynasties in the movie world, why shouldn't we have political dynasties?" (*Le Parisien*, October 24, 2006). Mégret sees the National Front as being too intricately linked with its leader: "The National Front lives by and for Le Pen," which will undermine its future when the moment of replacement of leadership comes (Mégret 2004, e-mail interview, June 28). There is an anti–Marine Le Pen wing in the National Front led, among others, by Jacques Bompard, the National Front mayor of Orange (who was excluded from the political committee of the party), and Bernard Antony, the founder of Chrétienté Solidarité, a Christian group close to the party (see, for example, *Le Monde*, September 9, 2005). Marine Le Pen is accused of trying to lead the party down the dangerous path of "normalization." In the spirit of taking the National Front out of the "Extreme-Right ghetto," she has been active in appealing to the *beuer* vote (Arab immigrants or Arabs with French citizenship) (*Le Monde*, June 25, 2006). More traditionalist voices accuse her of being too soft on such issues as immigration, abortion, and gay rights (*Le Figaro*, August 23, 2004). She has found some support among such long-time party members as Jean-Claude Martinez, who wrote about the need for a pragmatic "revolution" in the National Front's "way of thinking."[18] To these critics' charge that her desire to approximate the party to the political mainstream is putting the Front in danger of losing its own identity as a true alternative, Marine Le Pen repeatedly states that "[w]e cannot gain power by being just rebels" (*Le Figaro,* August 23, 2004). In her autobiography she wrote that the National Front, "if one day was an extreme-right party, today is a big popular party," should welcome those who will join not "because of secondary elements of [the party's] program," but because of its most important one, "the defense of our nation and compatriots" (M. Le Pen 2006, 259). Le Pen's disappointing 2007 presidential run was perceived by a faction of the National Front as the consequence of the disastrous "banalization" of the party's message that his daughter pursued. As one of her critics said, "We let Sarkozy run on a platform that belongs to us: immigration, insecurity, national identity. Le Pen's message didn't distinguish itself: he was not perceived as the voice against the system" (*Le Monde,* April 25, 2007). Marine Le Pen was able, however, to recover ground by being the only candidate of the party who made it through to the second round in the following elections for the National Assembly. Her father hailed the "great promise" her strong electoral showing held for the future (*Le Monde,* June 19, 2007).

The fact of the matter is that Le Pen's effort in raising his own daughter's profile within the party as a "potential next leader" is part of the continuous work of maintenance and protection of his charisma that he has performed since the foundation of the National Front. However the method has its obvious risks owing to the fact that Le Pen's choice is contentious within the National Front. The party, after having been held together in large part by the charismatic domination of the founder, may well split as a result.

---

18. In face of the new challenges brought by globalization, Jean Claude Martinez argued that the time for change had arrived and that the National Front needed to broaden its appeal to different sectors of the population, including those who lived in the *banlieues.* He called for a Council of Jerusalem for the movement, and the adoption of a more universal message by the party. See Martinez 2006. In the wake of the electoral fiasco of the 2007 presidential elections, however, Martinez was one of the more scathing critics of the direction that Marine Le Pen took the campaign and accused her of promoting "media-events" to the detriment of "ideas for the future" (*Le Monde,* April 25, 2007).

THE MISSIONARY MODEL—POLITICS AS SALVATION

In the oral and symbolic discourse promulgated by Le Pen, the National Front is a movement that progresses along a path of salvation. Le Pen is persistently represented as the guide leading the National Front on the road toward the renaissance of France. A common image in the official literature of the party is that of Le Pen walking alone on a beach toward the horizon where the sky and the sea meet. The first decade of life of the National Front is commonly described as "La Traversée du Desert," or "The Crossing of the Desert" (Bariller and Timmermans 1994, introduction). The analogy of the desert is constant in the mythology of the National Front and suggests the image of a suffering people led by the prophet in the direction of the Promised Land. Addressing his followers, Le Pen once said,

> This movement has existed for ten years: The National Front! I have to say that this crossing of the desert . . . makes us proud [for we have] the pride, in the face of adversity, of continuing to mark the history of our country with a strong will to not be let down by discouragement, aggressions, calumnies, insults, as long as God gives us life. And the History of our people shows us that spectacular new developments, sensational renaissances have always been possible. (Marcilly 1984, 150)

On another occasion he thanked his followers, "all of those who have been persecuted because they wanted to remain French," for having the courage of "keeping the faith [while] in the desert" (Marcilly 1984, 205). In this way the National Front, through Le Pen, illuminates the path to salvation for the other French who have still not joined the movement (see, for example, Le Pen 2003d). In truth, Le Pen has always subscribed to a bigger conception of politics. "Everything needs to change," he declared, "because in the face of decadence everything is at stake" (*Les Français d'Abord!*, November 16, 2005). According to him,

> The government of men has the primacy above all other aspects of the life of the community. That's what is implied in the famous [statement] "Politics first," that is, politics must be not below but before all the other activities of the city. Theories, no matter how brilliant, must help people

to see. This vision is what characterizes politics. It is this vision that Max Weber demands of the politician, together with passion and sense of responsibility. They cannot be assigned to the simple manager who lacks the vision of the future and undoubtedly the passion that arises from a sense of urgency. The need for vision in politics . . . arises from situations of crisis [for] in those moments when society can be reduced to nothing or worse to slavery, it is necessary to find the supreme defender of the collective values and laws. (1989b)

Politics in a time of crisis is therefore not the domain of technocrats who see it as a judicial activity but the domain of those who, as Le Pen put it to his followers, embrace politics as a "priesthood, the service of the community understood as a disinterested devotion to the cause of natural entities: Family, City, and the corollary of everything: the Nation" (*National-Hebdo*, November 12–18, 1987). At the basis of Le Pen's philosophy is a willed, rather than a bureaucratic, conception of politics. Drawing no doubt from his heroic vision of history, Le Pen emphasizes the power of human will to fight resignation and change the course of events. "We are voluntarists," he said at a press conference. "That is, we believe that men can act on their destiny" (1991, 82). In the vision of Le Pen, France has been immobilized and lies at the mercy of the destructive forces of internationalism. Mainstream politicians, because of their technocratic nature, have resigned themselves to an irreversible fusion of France in the "euro-internationalist magma." The following excerpt reveals the voluntaristic nature of Le Pen's philosophy.

> We think that as long as there are men with willpower, there will be a better path, [that] France will remain! Events are unpredictable today, and they will play their role, but so the will of men, especially those who are the most loyal and courageous . . . We refuse to believe that [the death of the nation] is unavoidable and that the worst is certain. Providence can act no matter how weak the light of the resistance is. But [Providence] only helps, and we know it, those who help themselves. (1999d)

Behind this grand conception of politics is Le Pen's vision of purification and renewal. The community of the Elect, led by Le Pen, is the source of this purification; and when the moment comes, the Elect will redeem the entire nation. In fact, the renaissance and recovery demanded by Le Pen is at its very basis moral and spiritual, and is undertaken in order to reverse France's fall into materialism. To Le Pen, "the National Front does not restrict its political action to some proposal of amending the constitution or to a narrow political program [but rather] [w]e know that the recovery of the country implies a *spiritual* and *moral* renaissance" (1991, 30). "Before the economy comes politics," observed Le Pen, "and before politics comes morality" (1999d). Referring to the national recovery defended by the National Front, Le Pen said, "Our country has a vital need: literally, to comply with the natural order of the world. As stated by Péguy, 'Order, and only order, creates freedom; disorder creates servitude.' Our children need to be raised in the respect of true values, in the respect of the Good, the Beautiful, and the True. That is our first duty as parents and politicians" (1997).

To Le Pen, France has been drifting away from the natural order of the world since the Enlightenment. The development of an artificial and increasingly materialistic internationalist ideology has corrupted the natural and eternal spirit of France. As maintained by the National Front's leader, "materialism, rationalism, scientism, will be defeated by a formidable aspiration for a spiritual renewal . . . a vital reaction against the programmed death of the human civilization in all its diversity" (1999d; see also National Front 2001). The spiritual degeneration of France is the most profound cause of all the other problems that afflict France. "The enemy is in you," declared Le Pen in a speech. He added, "It is in the soul of the French that deformation was made. It is at the very end of our heart, our families, our divorces, our churches, our schools, our newspapers, our courts, our books, our false ideas, our negative thinking, that we find the evil that weakens France, the Nation, the State, its survival" (Le Pen 2001b). In the eyes of Le Pen, France's future is endangered to the point of soulnessness, and only a spiritual purification can save her from extinction; when the dangers are abolished, the community can engage in a peaceful, balanced, and spiritually rich era. He described this scenario of happiness in the following manner:

> There are things that are required for human happiness, [such as] poetry, music, theatre, language, the taste of being together in these landscapes, the love for the land, the warmth of the family, of friendship, the commu-

nal and shared moral and spiritual values, the sense of God, the love for the creatures and the nature that surround us, a certain partaking of happiness. All the things that we have nurtured, developed and defended in France and which make her a model, creating a true need [for France] in the world. Yes, the world also needs France! (2004a).

Some of the French, those whom Le Pen likes to call "the most lucid and courageous," have already followed the path toward salvation. In Le Pen's vision, these true believers, bonded by love and sacrifice, have on their shoulders the collective mission of saving and redeeming the entire community. Their reward will be an ultimate recognition as pioneers of the renaissance of the French nation. In the words of Le Pen

> Those who have fought and continue to fight until the end of their strength, will look at the path covered and say, having accomplished the mission, proudly: "I was there." They advance together with all of those who, greater in number every day, see very well that they do not have any other solution than the nation, hence the National Front, [and] with eyes set on the goals of tomorrow say: "I will be there." (Bariller and Timmermans 1994, 173)

As argued by the National Front's magazine, after decades of struggle, "Our movement is ready to confront, behind its Captain, the last part of its journey, that leads to a new France, straightened out and able to fulfill its destiny" (*FDA*, January 2007).

Le Pen's development of a missionary ethos of politics involves a long and careful construction of an enclave mentality that persistently defines the primacy of Le Pen as the guide, and the identity of the group as a monolithic community led by one leader and united in a common mission of rescuing France from the forces of corruption and disintegration.

3
Umberto Bossi and the Northern League

THE CRISIS—RENUNCIATION OF THE PRESENT

The discourse of Umberto Bossi is primarily anchored in a world-rejecting mentality. The political movement initiated by him is centered in a renunciation of the world as it is. According to Bossi, the modern international system of nation-states initiated a frontal assault on the identity of communities in northern Italy, and is therefore responsible both for the present crisis and for centuries of oppression suffered by its peoples. In Bossi's vision the process of Italian unification in the nineteenth century transformed different ethnic, cultural, and economic regions into colonies within an oppressive, centralized, and bureaucratic entity called "Italy." Since the beginning of the unification process, the resources and economies of the North have been exploited and transferred to a backward and dependent South, and the North's ethnic distinctiveness has been undermined by an oppressive and artificial nation-state. As stated by a doctrinal document of the Lega Nord (Northern League), "What has entered into crisis is the modern State, based on centralism and bureaucracy. The idea of 'State' is slowly losing the importance that has marked the last three centuries of European history" (Northern League 2002a, 5). This perceived attack on the distinct identity of northern Italy constitutes the structural or historical background for the act of the renunciation of the world by Bossi's movement. The first article by Umberto Bossi in *Lombardia Autonomista*, written in 1982, identified the nation-state as the source of northern desperation:

> Today, Lombardy does not belong to the Lombards, Padania does not belong to the people of Padania. [The North] is only a geographic expression

without any political value; it is only a territory without rights and facing the invasion of others. Its people is one mass deprived of political identity, anonymously incorporated into a failed nation-state that drags down [the North] in its endless and hopeless crisis. (*Lombardia Autonomista,* March 1982)

This perception of a deep-rooted crisis has both fueled the discourse of the leader and served as a powerful bond to cement the identity of the group. According to Bossi, since the 1950s a corrupt system of cartel politics (on the emergence of the Cartel Party see Katz and Mair 1995) made the exercise of government an oligarchic affair between the same old parties, and the judicial investigation of the early 1990s (known popularly as "Clean Hands") unveiled the mask of favoritism, illegality, and corruption of the old party system that were the symptoms, not the causes, of a long-simmering crisis dating back to the formation of the Italian state.

The initial political program of the Lombard League has as its first point the goal of "the self-government of Lombardy, overtaking the centralized State with a modern federal State that knows how to respect all the peoples that constitute it" (*Lombardia Autonomista,* June 1983). Since the outset Umberto Bossi has advanced a framework that identifies the group he has led as a true vanguard of northerners conscious of their identity and united in the mission of liberating the entire community from the subjugation of the centralist and tyrannical Italian state. In order to illustrate this mission, I will first demonstrate how Umberto Bossi reinforces the identity of his group as a revolutionary force that is at the vanguard of history.

THE GROUP AS THE VANGUARD

Historical Continuity

Umberto Bossi and his acolytes have made a relentless effort to link the ethnic and cultural roots of northern Italy to a distinct branch of Indo-European tribes that populated the continent of Europe in the early Middle Ages. The Lombard and Celtic peoples are hailed in the discourse and literature of the Northern League as the glorious ancestors of the "Padania," the term chosen by Bossi to describe the area north of the Po River Valley in the central-northern regions of the country. "The Padania," observed Bossi in an interview, "is a full-fledged country, a Celtic country." He added, "Nothing in history unites Latinos and Padani" (*La Padania*, July 31, 1998). According to Bossi,

> The Padania has roots and traditions that go far back in the darkness of time, if we observe events without ideological glasses. All the peoples of Padania, in fact, descend from the same original peoples . . . the last group is represented by the Goths, the Lombards, and all the Germanic populations stationed in these lands with the fall of the Roman Empire. They influence the physical traits of the Padani and have left us the heritage of attachment to local autonomies and the undying aspiration to freedom. [Those who live in the South] are in fact heirs to the Etruscan, Greek, and Italian populations stationed first in the Mediterranean basin and then in the coasts of the peninsula. So-called [united] "Italy" is therefore cut into two ethnic roots. (Bossi and Vimercati 1998, 33–34)

Bossi's intent is to bond the community with the traditions and history of central Europe. The Padania is often described by Bossi as part of Mitteleuropa, the regions of central Europe once part of the Austro-Hungarian Empire. According to Bossi, the area of Mitteleuropa "is the natural market of our area [and has] common traditions, cultures, and mentalities" (*La Padania*, June 17, 1998). In Bossi's view the Padania has more affinities with countries such as Hungary, Austria, and Slovenia than with southern Italy.

In order to emphasize the autonomist tradition of northern Italy, Umberto Bossi makes the historical example of the first Lega Lombarda a major reference in his discourse. In 1167 the communes of the North of Italy swore in Pontida to stand together against the expansionistic intentions of the Roman-German emperor Federico Barbarossa. It became known as the Oath of Pontida. The Battle of Legnano of 1176, in which the Lega Lombarda led by Alberto da Giussano defeated Barbarossa's troops, is heralded as a pivotal example of the tradition of liberty shared by the peoples of the North. The image of this medieval warrior raising a broadsword became the symbol of the Lombard League, and later of the Northern League. The party of Bossi is commonly known as the "Carroccio," an allusion to the war wagon drawn by oxen and used by the medieval republics of Italy. The link between the two leagues pervades the literature of the movement. For example, the headline of one issue of *Lombardia Autonomista* read: "1167: Defeating the Imperial Centralism of Barbarossa Opens in Europe the Democratic Age of the Communes in Europe. 1989: Defeating the Centralism of Rome, Opens the Democratic Age of Peoples" (*Lombardia Autonomista*, July 1988). Bossi establishes constant parallels between the struggle of the first historical union of the peoples of the North and the struggle of his contemporary movement:

> Eight hundred years have passed since the great battle of Legnano, which Hegel regarded as crucial for the history of Europe. In Legnano the emperor and his imperialism were defeated, and the communes of Europe were able to stand up. Almost a millennium has passed, and it is as if it were yesterday. Also, today the peoples of the North unite to hunt the Barbarossa that is in Rome. The new League recovers its origins and is committed to the final battle at the end of which there will be no prisoners: The Padania or the Roman State—one of the two will succumb. (Bossi 1996, 125)

The movement led by Bossi wants to have the same historical impact in Europe as the movement led by Alberto da Giussano. The first Lega Lombarda, as Bossi declared in a speech,

> signaled the birth, with the spirit of Padania, of the first liberal civilization. It signaled the birth of the communes, a revolutionary institution that the *Lega* knew how to defend from the emperor, who did not get what he wanted but instead went down to a defeat that marked the end of feudalism. That is why the Padania is a historical force, because it is the catalyst of the new federal era as it was in the past when it invented the modern world. (2002)

In Bossi's discourse, the tradition of freedom in the communities of the North was undercut in the nineteenth century by Italy's unification, a process that became known as *Risorgimento*. "The nation that has never existed is not the Padania, but Italy," observed Bossi. For the leader of the Northern League, "The division of Italy, therefore, is not the exception but the rule, and only a dishonest historiography can find in the past any justification for the present borders of the Roman State. The truth is that the unified State post-*Risorgimento* was a military construction at the expense of old territorial entities that were based on centuries-old autonomies and freedoms" (Bossi and Vimercati 1998, 31–33). The League refused to participate in the official celebration of the 200th anniversary of Giuseppe Garibaldi's birth and instead accused this "mason without scruples" and "enemy of the Church" of being one of the architects of a unification of Italy that has borne disastrous consequences for the North and the South (*La Padania,* July 4, 2007).

The centralist tradition brought by the *Risorgimento* has persisted through time, and has remained untouched by different political systems and regimes. The Italian Republic of post–World War II Europe was in essence not different from the Fascist regime of Mussolini. As stated by Bossi to his biographer Daniele Vimercati,

> This is not a Republic born from the resistance [against fascism] as stated in the official rhetoric; This is the same old State, untouched from the *Risorgimento* to the liberal period, and from fascism to the Republic. I don't see any fractures in this history . . . The State, our centralist State, has never truly overcome fascism. It is the same logic of continuity from the bureaucracy to the magistrates that has absolutely not changed [and] we of the League will try to break, for the first time, this continuity. (Bossi and Vimercati 1992, 128)

Prominent in the Northern League's pantheon of heroes is Carlo Cattaneo. In the nineteenth century he was one of the main supporters of Italy as a confederation of republics rather than a united republic. A Lombard, Cattaneo included the formation of an autonomous Lombardy-Veneto regional entity within his confederalist project. Bossi regularly quotes Cattaneo along with nineteenth-century federalists in drawing a historical continuity between the federalist project of the nineteenth century and the fight of the Northern League for a "federal" Italy. In party literature, Cattaneo is called the "noble father of federalism" and, because of the insistence of the Northern League, a bust of the philosopher was inaugurated in the Montecitorio, the Italian Parliament (*La Padania,* June 18, 2003). The non-adoption of Cattaneo's project is viewed by Bossi as "treason" against the desire for freedom of northern Italy. But, in Bossi's words, "after the betrayal of hope in the *Risorgimento,* the Lega Nord, the popular movement, has finally opened the possibility of federalism"

(Bossi and Vimercati 1992, 197). The leader of the Northern League has even organized what was described by the party's official newspaper as a "pilgrimage" to Lugano, the Swiss town where the exiled Cattaneo spent his last days. Bossi addressed his followers from one of the windows, and was heralded in the party's magazine as the "political heir of Cattaneo" for, after all, "Carlo and Umberto are paladins of freedom" (*Il Federalismo,* March 15, 2005).

Umberto Bossi puts the Northern League at the receiving end of a positive historical tradition fighting against all of those forces that represent an oppressive, artificial, and evil historical tradition. The side embodied by the Northern League "is the heir to the Italian traditions of the Renaissance, to the communal multiformity and freedoms, that favored arts, literature and the wealth of the city." The other side, instead, "originates from the habits and social order of the papal, House of Savoy and Bourbon courts, sucking new blood from the unified Centralist State" (Bossi and Vimercati 1993, 207). Bossi identifies the Northern League as the embodiment of centuries-old aspiration that can finally be achieved.

The Definition of the Group

Those who join the struggle of the Northern League adhere to a revolutionary movement of men and women who, Bossi promises, are at the forefront of the battle to put an end to the "subjugation" imposed by Rome, and to "liberate" the peoples of the North. The Northern League is the harbinger of a new period in time, the "creative factor, the catalyst of a new era, that will be federalism" (Bossi 1996, 67). Allies can change, policies can shift, the movement led by Bossi can be either in opposition to or support of the central government; the sense of the Northern League's dispensation as a revolutionary force of grand proportions, however, remains unchanged from the very beginning both in Bossi's discourse and in the party's literature. Bossi wrote, "It must be clear, for those who have forgotten: If the League has any reason to exist [it] is to bring federalism to Italy, to liberate the peoples of the peninsula—and Europe—from the yoke of the State . . . For this it was born, for this it has grown and fights without mercy against its eternal enemies. If successful, it wins its historical battle. If not, it fails. There is no middle ground" (1995, 175).

Those who join this movement of liberation are a vanguard of courageous people conscious of their history and roots. They represent the foremost position of the peoples of the North. Because they are conscious, aware of their place in history, they have the responsibility of stimulating and awakening the dormant and passive sectors of the northern population who have still not joined this historical struggle. In Bossi's words, "Courage is the first great gift that the League has brought to the Italians. The courage to challenge the corrupts, to remember the roots of history. The courage to confront the old and surpassed ideologies . . . the courage to denounce the bad government in the *Mezzogiorno* [South] and to be amongst the people and to listen to the people. The League has brought hope for a better future" (1995, 203).

"The true problem that we have," declared Bossi in a speech at a party convention in the Italian Alps town of Ponte di Legno, "is that so many people who do not vote for us would if only they understood the Padania, the project" (1998c). The supporters and militants of the Northern League have a higher historical consciousness. Those who still do not support the Northern League lack that consciousness. The party has to work hard to help them regain it: "The problem, is how to clarify them, how to remove their ideologies, their fears, their false consciences, their superstitions. This is the problem" (1998c).

The goal of the Northern League, a revolutionary elite, is thus to spread the word among the population in order to raise them from their slumber. In Bossi's eyes, the self-government of Padania

> is also an ethno-cultural demand more and more felt by the population that is achieving self-consciousness step-by-step. We know that the origins of a nation are irrefutable religious, cultural, ethnic, and socio-economic homogeneities; but it is above all the self-consciousness of itself, limited at the beginning to some elites and gradually extended to the entire population. In this first phase we find the Padania, whose homogeneity . . . is being gradually recognized by the people who, as each day goes by, understand the colonial mechanism that made them a victim for decades. (1996, 163)

The electoral failures of the Northern League are periodically interpreted in terms of lack of conscience or courage. "It is a problem of our people's maturity," declared Bossi in a speech. "They continue to vote more for continuity than for change. We should not try to find the reason why we do not have the freedom that we want somewhere else [because] the problem is ours, it's internal [to] our peoples who have not yet acquired full conscience" (2000a). In fact, Bossi sees that a process of "brainwashing" has been executed for decades by the propaganda of the North's enemies, which has buried the conscience of its population. One of the earliest and most persistent goals of the party has been the development of its own media in order to stop this "manipulation" of a gullible public. "Soon we'll have Padanian television," observed Bossi once. "We'll develop information that is no longer a carbon copy of the regime. That way, even those Padani who are still 'chickens,' who don't understand our battle for freedom, can realize what is happening" (*La Padania,* July 19, 1998). "To read our daily newspaper," said Bossi on another occasion, "is to have self-consciousness, to want the change that our battle represents" (*La Padania,* December 3, 1998). The militants of the Northern League refuse the alienation and submission promoted by the regime and, because they are no longer "cowards," are less prone "to kneel down before Italian oppression" (Bossi 1997). Society in itself promotes a culture—particularly through the visual media—that encourages passivity and indifference. "Now people seem to be accustomed to the superficial," says Bossi, "to the image of the politicians, not to the content" (*La Padania,* December 3, 1998). Detached from the "essential," the people have forborne to assert their own identity. If the people of northern Italy were not controlled by the propaganda of the regime, Bossi argues, their historical conscience would rise, and they would actively participate in the liberation of the North.

Umberto Bossi uses a metanarrative that reinforces the identity of the Padani as a chosen group whose importance assumes world historical proportions. By linking the past with the present, Bossi identifies the Padani as the heirs of a combative tradition of freedom in the North. Bossi further joins their activity in the present to a glorious future that will open "a new chapter in history" (Bossi and Vimercati 1992, 204). In order to effect this change, the vanguard of the Northern League has had to reach out to the rest of the population. The peoples of the North have been oppressed for such a long time that many of them do not realize their subjugated condition, and have forgotten about their true roots. As Bossi declares, "The League aims at the recognition of the inalienable right to self-determination of our peoples. This is an ambitious goal, I recognize that, also because decades of Roman slavery have clouded the ability of our people to understand and [to] react. We have only one goal that is profoundly different from those of all other parties that have occupied the seats of Roman power: We aim at the Padania" (Bossi and Vimercati, 1998, 40).

It is up to the vanguard of men and women led by Bossi to take the lead in the battle for liberation, the battle to save the North from the bondage of oppressive, centralist Rome. The goal is to redeem the community and its people from their "enslavement." The mission of the vanguard is therefore total in the sense that it aims at the salvation of a specific group, in this case the communities of the North of Italy.

The Group Is under Siege

Umberto Bossi has never missed an occasion to stress the fact that, owing to its disruptive and revolutionary force, his movement has from the very beginning been the target of relentless attacks by the forces of Rome. Bossi's narrative constantly highlights the notion that the vanguard of northerners under his leadership has always been under siege, surrounded by powerful forces determined to destroy them. In his words,

> If the delivery [of Lombard League] was difficult, the childhood of this populist and popular movement was even more complicated. Being a diverse organism of those parties who occupied the State, by this time reduced to a committee of affairs and detached partially or totally from their ideological labels—socialist, Christian, communist, liberal—the League has been from the beginning the target of a furious and encompassing attack. The partitocratic powers and not only those—occasionally some sectors of the Vatican and international finance have contributed—have hurled against this new and democratic political entity . . . physical threats, psychological blackmail, economic pressure: Nothing has been spared to stop the advance of the first great federalist party of the history of Italy. (1995, 114)

Bossi said in a later interview, "Our challenge was unthinkable to the system of the time [which] used all of its weapons to annihilate us, in particular the mass media" (*La Padania,* March 3, 2002).

Both Bossi's discourse and the narrative of the party assert that the centralist forces of Rome launched two powerful weapons against the advance of the outsider Northern League: electoral reform and the work of the judicial system. "The majority system was made to prevent us from winning," said Bossi. "With a proportional system, we would have all the mayors in the towns of the north" (1998c). At the same time Bossi accuses the judges of the "Clean Hands" operation of helping to preserve the old balance of power of the Italian state. The fact that they also accused the League of taking bribes proved that they were interested in undermining the *only* "true force of change" (Bossi and Vimercati 1998, 124). Another episode regularly recounted in the discourse of Bossi and in the party literature is the search conducted in the party headquarters and in houses of militants, by order of a public prosecutor, during the Northern League's secessionist period. At the time the regime "put [public prosecutor] Papalia into action [by instituting] trials for freedom of speech [and] invad[ing the] offices and houses of militants and of all of those who were suspected of supporting a democratic secession." The regime's tentacles spread deeply, for "all of the machine of the print and electronic journalistic system, all of the famous journalists were put at the service of repression" (2003a). In the League's narrative, these episodes are telling examples of the persecutory nature of the Italian state. "As the Hebrews remembered their persecutors," said Bossi in a speech at a Northern League's congress in Milan, "we should not forget any of the crimes perpetrated against the Padani patriots" (1998a). This narrative serves to strengthen the group's self-identity as a besieged community surrounded by hostile forces.

The construction of a group identity necessitates a definition of the "other" (in this case, what "the North" is not; what "the North" is against: the "enemies"), a definition that plays a steamroller function. Bossi warned that "an impressive alliance was mobilized against the League, composed from a variety of forces and hostile to each other only in appearance" (1995, 177). "It is pointless to hide it, brothers," declared Bossi at a rally. "The enemies are many. They are hidden enemies—if they were visible, the enemies would not succeed, the people would win immediately, [the people] would have already won" (2000b). Above all, the enemies of Bossi's group have always wanted to preserve the centralist and oppressive Roman state at the expense of the North. As Bossi declared in one of his first writings, "As in all the [historical] periods where the demand for freedom was prominent, today the enemy to defeat is the centralism of political power. After the 'continental centralism of Vienna', after the 'nationalist centralism of Fascism' today it is indispensable to overcome the 'partitocratic' centralism" (*Lombardia Autonomista,* March 1982).

The forces that maintain the system are allied in what Bossi calls *Partitocrazia* (partitocracy), "the inextricable bond between the media, big economic groups, and political parties" (Bossi and Vimercati 1992, 103). Partitocracy maintained the failed centralistic system that transferred resources from the most dynamic and productive party of the country (the North) to the most backward (the South), creating a culture of dependency in return for electoral support in the South. Through his career Bossi has denounced this system and has used different expressions to describe the forces that keep it together. They suffer from "Italian nationalism," "a violent and antidemocratic monster . . . born of the necessity of creating the myth of the nation because there was no nation when the Italian State emerged" (*La Padania,* March 29, 1998). These forces follow from a totalitarian belief system that Bossi calls "the *meridionalista* [southern] ideology, which [is even] a kind of religion" (*La Padania,* September 8, 1998). Centralism, and the political parties and the media and economic groups that support it, have a permanent place on the League's enemies list. The media is always perceived as the instrument of the regime. "Big Capital" is still interested in hijacking the productive forces of Italy in order to destroy the small and middle enterprises. The names of the political parties that are among the enemies of the League may change, depending on the circumstances. Forza Italia has changed status several times. The same can be said about the center-left parties. However, at least one group of parties is always singled out as the representatives of a rotten system: the voices of "Rome," the Anti-League.

Another permanent group in the field of enemies of the League comprises all of those perceived to be undermining the roots and traditions of the communities of Northern Italy. Although the intensity of anti-immigration sentiment may vary over time, it has always been an issue in the discourse of Umberto Bossi. Particularly in the early period, anti-southern sentiment helped to consolidate the identity of the group. Southerners were usually described as *terroni*, a pejorative term for people from the South. They were described as agents of the colonization of the North imposed by Rome who brought with them the "laziness" of the South in contrast to the northern enterprising virtues of vigor, drive, and competition. According to Bossi, until World War II,

> [t]he ethnic integrity in Lombardy and in almost all of the nations of the North of Italy was preserved. One who really knows our land is aware that entire cities, entire valleys, had not been affected by migratory fluxes . . . and what matters most, our work ethic—a curious mixing of Calvinism and Catholic morality—has not been changed, [the work ethic] represents, I think, the shared patrimony, together with individualism, liberal democracy, and municipality of our peoples from the north of Italy. (Bossi and Vimercati 1992, 160)

The denunciation of immigration from regions outside of the European Community—the *extracomunitari*—has gained increasing relevance since the late eighties. Bossi declared at a rally, "We are tired, tired of being a land of invasion, first from the South and now from the Third World" (1990). The League was one of the most outspoken voices against the Martelli immigration law of 1990, which it viewed as too soft regarding foreigners and immigrations. "There is no political will to prevent immigration," observed Bossi.

> The goal is to transform our country into a multiracial, multiethnic, and multireligious society. We are getting there: We already have one million "legal" immigrants, plus one million who are clandestine. The American model is advancing; we will all live in an immense cosmopolitan metropolis where there will be no trace of the traditions and culture of our people. But I don't think this should be inevitable . . . I think we should revolt against this "inevitability" [because a] multiracial society is closer to hell than [to] paradise. (1990)

In the late nineties the League also led the campaign against a new immigration law, the Turco-Napolitano, proposed by the center-left government. "With the Martelli law, although confusedly, the borders were open," noted Bossi. "With the *Turco-Napolitano*, which we want to cancel, the goal is to construct in a scientific way an aberrant and failed multiracial society" (*La Padania*, May 15 1999). To stop the advance of this multiracial society, the Northern League, together with its allies in government, created a tougher immigration law, called the "Law Bossi-Fini," that set up quotas for migrants of Italian origin, established a new stricter policy on issuing entry visas and a more repressive policy toward illegal migrants (*Bossi-Fini*, 2002).

To an increasing degree, the discourse of the Northern League focuses on immigration from Muslim nations, and the party stresses the "millenarian struggle" between Christianity and Islam. Historical battles are reinterpreted in the light of the steady inflow of Muslim immigration to Europe. For instance, the headline of an issue of the party daily read "From Poitiers to the Crusades and Lepanto, Padania has been the arm of freedom against Islam" (*La Padania*, February 23, 2003).[1] Historical figures that distinguished themselves in fighting Islamic forces are brought to center stage. Parliamentarians of the Northern League drafted a proposal to establish Marco D'Aviano,[2] a priest who rallied Christian resistance to the Ottoman siege of Vienna in the seventeenth century, as the "patron saint of Europe" (*La Padania*, January 15, 2003). The party's newspaper

---

1. The 1571 naval battle of Lepanto, in which the Ottoman fleet was defeated by the Christians, has become a reference in the anti-Islamic discourse of the Northern League. See, for instance, the article "Lo spirito di Lepanto per difendersi dall' Islam" (The spirit of Lepanto for the defense against Islam), (*La Padania*, April 9, 2004).

2. One of the Northern's League parliamentarians who drafted the proposal was Edouard Ballaman, who wrote a short book about Islam, titled *La Piccola Guida alla Cultura Islamica* (A Short Guide to Islamic Culture) (2005), published by the Northern League, written to debunk the myths about the "genuine desire of integration" of Muslims in European culture, and to warn about the risks presented by Islam to "our society and civilization." This guide became a reference for the party and it was part of the League's electoral propaganda for the 2006 national elections. Ballaman organized a screening tour of Theo Van Gogh's film *Submission* and showed it in the Italian parliament. *La Padania* reported that, because of this

ran a four-part series on the life of this Capuchin friar, whom it branded as the man who "saved Europe from Islam" (*La Padania,* "La Storia di Marco D'Aviano," online). The League has been active in its opposition to the construction of mosques in Italy (*La Padania,* May 21, 2004), and the party led a campaign to close Italy's first bilingual Arabic school in Milan, warning against the dangers of violent indoctrination in a "Koranic school" (*La Padania,* October 10, 2006). The threat of Islamic terrorism has led some members of the party to request the closing of all mosques in the Lombard region. "Until now, the necessary severity and firmness against these centers of terror have been missing," said one of the officials of the party (*La Padania,* August 4, 2004). A Northern League official, Roberto Calderoli, decrying the West's abjuration of "our Christian roots, identity and culture," argued in the party's newspaper for the launch of "crusades of Western peoples, who still remember the battle of Lepanto," against Islam, which should be "declared illegal until Islamists renounce violence" (*La Padania,* July 8, 2005).[3]

The fear of Islamization has become deeply ingrained in party discourse. Not surprisingly, in the campaign for the European elections of 2004, a dominant theme as stated in a campaign pamphlet was a resounding "NO to the Islamic invasion," with the refusal of Turkey's entry into the European Union as a main goal. A document of the party for the election emphasized this point further:

> Turkey, historically and culturally, is not European—it has been in Europe (Ottoman military occupation of the Balkans till the siege of Vienna), but it is not Europe . . . If it would become a member of the European Union, almost 100 million Turks, in the vast majority Islamic, would automatically obtain European citizenship, electing in this way a number of members of the European Parliament greater than those of Germany. (Northern League 2004, 9)

---

tour, Ballaman received many death threats and was forced to live under security restrictions. (See *La Padania,* July 27, 2005).

3. Roberto Calderoli was forced to resign as reform minister in Berlusconi's government, after wearing on a TV news program a T-shirt with a satirical cartoon of Muhammad. See BBC News, February 18, 2006, online.

Raising the specter of a "true Islamic invasion of Europe" in case of Turkey's membership in the European Union, the Northern League has been continually campaigning for a popular referendum that "will allow all citizens to have their say on a historical issue that will seal the destiny of our peoples" (*La Padania*, March 1, 2005; see also *Lega Nord Flash* 2004).

The dominant role of honor-shame mentalities and practices in Muslim communities is presented by the League's media outlets as bulletproof evidence of the impossibility of successful integration between Western civil societies and Islam. The highly reported honor killing of a Pakistani woman by her family near the city of Brescia became, in the party narrative, a repeatedly cited symbol of the "increasing refusal of integration by Islamic communities" (*Lega Nord Flash* 2006). Further, under the heading "Islamic Party," the League warned about the danger that owing to their "demographic growth," Muslims "will create powerful lobbies," capable of irrevocably changing Italian politics, laws, and foreign policy (*Lega Nord Flash* 2006). Under the headline "News from Eurabia," the regional office of the Northern League in Piedmont reported that ritual circumcision was made available at a pediatric hospital in the city of Turin on a trial basis, a project sponsored by the center-left and intended to "build bridges" with the city's Muslim community. The regional leader of the party argued that it would be only a small step for the government to start financing infibulation (*Lega Nord Piemonte* 2006; see also *Il Corriere della Sera,* October 13, 2006). Petitions and calls to ban the burka have also been a dominant feature in the League's discourse, and a European member of parliament for the Northern League declared at a street protest against the clothing worn by Muslim women that "Islam is a dangerous virus, and we must stop it from spreading, because Padania must remain Christian" (*AGI,* October 2, 2006). The party has welcomed, promoted, and defended the positions of such figures as journalist and novelist Oriana Fallaci and film director Renzo Martinelli, who had come under attack for their blunt views on Islam and whose only faults were, according to the League, not being proponents of what are deemed "Islamically correct" points of view.[4] Asked about

---

4. After an article regarding the "myth" of moderate Islam and the "suicidal" transformation of Europe into "Eurabia," by Oriana Fallaci in the newspaper *Corriere della Sera, La Padania* announced that the Northern League "stands side by side with Fallaci." Roberto

the advance in parliament of a new law aimed at broaden religious freedom in the country, Bossi replied, "We are becoming a Muslim country. This situation with immigrants will split the country, it's an outrage we need to rebel against.... It's time to say *Basta* [enough]!" (*La Padania,* July 5, 2007).

Among the enemies of the Northern League are also all of those who are said to promote an internationalist ideology that is bent on erasing diversity and imposing a homogeneous way of life on the rest of humanity. Because it threatens to disrupt the roots and traditions of the North of Italy, Bossi targets the international system of globalization as one of the main enemies of the Northern League. This theme has been particularly prominent in Bossi's discourse since the late eighties. Originally, Bossi's criticism of globalization was mainly linked to a criticism of massive immigration and the ideology of the "melting pot." As Bossi observed in 1991, "The multiethnic and multiracial society is one that, by its nature, is against man [and is] destroying the process of ethnic identity" (1991a). Gradually, Bossi's criticism of globalization evolved into a robust defense of the distinct ethnicity of the populations in northern Italy. In his narrative the league becomes a shield that protects the "natural" ethnicity of the North against the "artificial" order imposed by the globalizers. In the words of Bossi,

> Today the capitalist system brings the immigrants here to favor the birth of a multiracial society, of identical men with the same ambitions and without traditions. In sum, the big consumer, fat from hamburgers and drowned in a sea of Coca-Cola. Economic internationalism and Catholic universalism, in a way, speak the same language and aim at the same result: a world society in which all consume the same things and worship the same God. Agnelli [the founder and owner of Fiat] and the pope have the same perspective,

---

Maroni, official of the Northern League and then Italian minister for welfare, was quoted as saying, "generally I subscribe to everything that Fallaci writes ... she vocalizes a general sentiment among the people." (See *La Padania,* July 17, 2005). Renzo Martinelli's 2006 movie *Il Mercante di Pietre* (English title: The Stone Merchant) was accused by the Italian Islamic Anti-Defamation League of portraying Muslims in the same way that Nazis portrayed Jews, comparing the movie to Veit Harlan's anti-Semitic movie *Jud Süss* (1940). *La Padania* described these attacks as one more stage in the "Islamic offensive against the freedom of expression in the West." See *La Padania,* September 29, 2006.

both want the multiracial society, because none of them gives any value to the differences . . . It is not only an economic problem, [The League] wants to stop globalization and to prevent that everything is made into a commodity. [That] man is reduced to a thing, always the same, *homo economicus*, without soul and identity. (Bossi and Vimercati 1998, 13–14)

For Bossi, the very logic of globalization is rooted in the utopian fervor of the Enlightenment. The globalizers "imagine earthly paradises without noticing that earthly paradises, in practice, turn into hell . . . we refuse to bend over to the dictatorship of homogenization, to the [dictatorship] of the cancellation of peoples" (2000b). According to Bossi,

The Enlightenment, that 200 years ago brought rights to men, the possibility of taking into their own hands their own lives, now wants to take [those rights] away. No one can have their own society, their own history; on the contrary, history has ended for the globalizers. In reality there is a mistake in this world turned upside down, because the Enlightenment is not the Western World, but only one of the doctrines of the West which is, [along with] ideas, made of real things: of peoples, that is, history, men of flesh and bones, that is [the West is made] of us, of our work that is made in our land that is not for sale. The true problem is that behind the ideas there is a system of interests that wants the West to be more virtual than real. (2003b)

In Bossi's view, the consistent effort to weaken and dismantle the family as an institution is a crucial part of this full-fledged assault by the globalizers on the true nature of the peoples. The events of 1968 marked the beginning of this assault, and the Northern League was in government to put an end to this attack. As stated by Bossi in an interview,

The iconoclast period, initiated in '68 is ending. [In this period] all the rules were thrown away and modern publicity was born: they used this system to substitute for reality the artificial, the image that creates reality. The world was turned around. The last time there was such a difficult period was with the French revolution, which turned around all the existent rules . . . these iconoclastic periods are distinguished by the reversal of all the rules, by the unhinging of all traditions. Tradition means family especially. Napoleon used a system to disrupt the family that is still vigorous today: prostitution . . . '68 used the same system. Prostitution becomes a model, the last act to destroy the family, the bulwark of traditions. (*La Padania,* February 2, 2003)

The spreading of pornography is an important component of this alleged planned destruction of the family. If prostitution represents "the sexual alternative to the wife" (*La Padania,* May 1 2002), pornography "when it is taken to its extreme is transformed into obvious pedophilia and homosexuality. We will fight until the end against these deviants, from the Left but not exclusive [to the Left], who talk about human rights and freedom of expression only to hide their filthy interests" (Northern League 2002b, 6–7). Adoption of children by gay couples is rejected on the same basis of defending what is "natural" against imposed artificialities. "We don't have anything against homosexuals; anyone is free to do what they want in bed," declared Bossi at a rally. "However we must be clear [about the fact] that the laws cannot give what nature cannot give. [The League defends] natural families, natural children . . . [a]gainst what is corrupt and artificial" (2000b). In Bossi's narrative the ideologues of internationalism, through massive immigration and the disruption of traditional lives and mores, use globalization to hack away the roots of centuries-old cultures like that of Padania.

The vision of Europe in the discourse of Bossi constitutes further evidence that the field of enemies of the Northern League is not static but is always evolving. At the beginning, the process of European unification was seen as a positive development for Padania owing to the fact that it seemed to weaken the sovereignty of nation-states and promote micro-nationalisms across the continent. "Why not substitute the centralism of the unified States with a more articulate system, characterized by a plurality of institutional sites, each one with its competences?" asked Bossi in the early nineties, adding that this tendency "is already at work with the process of the European unification" (Bossi and Vimercati 1992, 162–63). But the increased power of a centralized structure in the European Union led the Northern League to an increased hostility toward the European Union (EU). Bossi accused the EU of favoring the same "Jacobin" system of globalization, the imposition of an artificial order on peoples:

The legislative excesses of Brussels sometimes can make us laugh, like the standard for the length of peas or carrots. However, behind these things it lays a lethal design for the future and the freedom of peoples: the birth of a European Superstate, according to a Stalinist idea. I call it the Soviet Union of the West and I'm not wrong to define it like that . . . we want a confederationist Europe because, without the Nation-state, democracy dies. Without States we will have a USSR of the West, dominated by technocrats, and the stateless bureaucracy of Brussels, elected by no one. Democracy is at stake. (*La Padania*, March 3, 2002)

Bossi further explained that "there are two distinct models of Europe: the one of the Superstate of a Neo-Jacobin type that we are against, [and] the model of a Union of States which is the model of the peoples, the model of a society balanced between the global and the local" (*La Padania*, July 2, 2003). Bossi has been particularly adamant against such measures as the EU-wide arrest warrant that, according to him, only demonstrates the dictatorial nature of the European Union. "This arrest warrant makes me think that this Europe is the synthesis between the French Revolution and the Bolshevik Revolution, inventing a European community law that will cancel the residual autonomy of the States," he said in an interview. "It is necessary to oppose this Nazi madness with maximum strength" (*La Padania*, October 23, 2003). Bossi interpreted the French rejection of the European Constitution as "the end of [a conception] of Europe that was created against the people" (*Il Giornale*, May 31, 2005). From this perspective, the community of Padani, as a source of popular resistance and independence, is the endless target of a despotic and dangerous European Union.

Old enemies can also become friends. The Catholic Church was initially defined as a natural enemy of the freedom of the North, because it had been colluding with the oppressive centralist forces since the process of unification of the Italian state. The Vatican and the ecclesiastical hierarchies in particular were denounced as reactionary forces and enemies of northern liberation. "Catholicism—not Christianity—is at the origins of our evils," said Bossi. "One God, one pope, one king. One, one, one . . . Catholic absolutism has created absolutist and anti-democratic states" (1995, 196). "Catholicism is a lower sect of Christianity," said Bossi on another occasion, "that believes it must have temporal power in order to take care of the souls" (*Lega Nord–Padania Independente*, November 25, 1996). The Vatican was also attacked for actively promoting the policies of open borders in order to increase the number of the faithful in the West. But Bossi's discourse has gradually come to view the Church and the pope in a more positive light, in sync with the League's gradual emphasis on Christian and traditional values as a response to the dynamics of globalization and the threat of "Islamization." To him,

> This pope is a great [man], he is the first [pope] for one hundred years who does not retreat in front of the masonry and anti-Christian doctrines . . . I thought that the Church was over, that [it] had sold out, instead I must recognize that what John Paul II has been doing for a long time is on the side of Man. His defense of the family, of procreation, of values, have been always part of our own battle . . . the position of the Pope is commendable, the Church is starting to wake up. (*La Stampa*, February 7, 2000)

When the center-left government announced plans that would grant legal status to gay couples, Bossi remarked that the overarching goal was to attack "the Church and Christianity" (*La Padania*, December 10, 2006). For Bossi there are two clashing sociocultural models that fight each other in today's Europe: "The Neo-Jacobin model, of the universal and multiracial society, standardized by the market . . . and the Christian model of the peoples; of a society balanced between present, future, and past; between local and global; between new forces that exert pressure from the outside, and historical values rooted in tradition. This is the side of the League" (2003a). In the ongoing battle against Islamization the Northern League does not miss an occasion to remind everyone of the endangered Christian roots of Europe. As stated in the Electoral Program of the Northern League for the European elections of 2004, "The people of Padania want instead a Europe founded on common values, prime among them the Christian value: Just when Islamic terrorism is manifesting itself on a global scale, in all the gruesomeness that distinguishes it, it is fundamental to strongly emphasize the identity of Europe, which is founded on that value" (Northern League 2004, 1).

In this new context, one should find it unsurprising that the League became one of the greatest defenders of Pope Benedict XVI after he fell under heavy criticism for remarks about Islam and violence. Bossi commented that the episode only reinforced the cultural incommensurability between the West and Islam. "We are two different cultures," he proclaimed. "Our society comes from Christianity," Bossi added, and then stated that "Islamists attack the Pope in order to attack all of the West" (*La Padania,* September 18, 2006).

Thus the Church was transformed from enemy to friend of the Northern League. But some enemies remain constant. The United States of America has always occupied a place in the group of favorite targets of the Northern League. From the beginning, the American "melting pot" model of society has been derided as the antithesis of the ethnic model of society defended by the Northern League. This vision has not changed. An official Northern League document regarding the issue of immigration is clear in its rejection of this aspect of American society. "Those who fight to preserve the survival of their nations," it reads, "represent the field of diversity of cultures, of true tolerance and freedom, while the neo-American multiculturalism represents [the field] of uniformity, rootedness and subjugation." Patriotism is viewed as "the last obstacle to the progression of the universal American and Islamic empires" (Northern League, 2002c, 21). More recently, particularly since the Northern League became a member of Berlusconi's government coalition (2001–6), the rhetoric against the United States was somewhat toned down. This was particularly visible during the American intervention and occupation of Iraq. Italy is an ally of the United States, and the reaction of the Northern League and its newspaper to the Iraq war favored the Bush administration. This position was radically different from that held in the Kosovo war of 1999, which the League derided as just one more imperialist projection of power and influence. It should also be noted that, particularly after the terrorist attacks of September 11, the League has focused primarily on the "Islamic war" against the West, and the rejection of America has taken a secondary place in the party's discourse. The American model of society and its perceived attempt to export it to the rest of the world, however, remain firmly in the imagination of the Northern League as a mortal enemy.

A powerful device employed by Bossi to increase his followers' perception of being beleaguered is the pervading use of a logic of conspiracy. For Bossi, powerful enemies, who are regularly portrayed as united in a shadowy network that shelters the anti-League alliance, constantly persecute the vanguard of men and women he leads. The idea of conspiracy becomes a uniting force for the vanguard. The leader regularly blames Freemasonry for the evils that afflict the group. The discovery of documents from the Masonic Lodge Propaganda Due (P2) that alluded to a hegemonic plan to control the Italian state has a central place in the discourse of Bossi as proof of the powerful role that "occult worlds" and "secret societies" play in Italy. In the past he regularly established a link between the plan of P2 and the creation of Forza Italia by Silvio Berlusconi. "[Like] the P2 Lodge," observed Bossi, "the party of Berlusconi [Forza Italia] is not born, as people say, from the people, from social-political forces that come from below. It is an invention of powerful men, a creature constructed in a lab, and put forward through the private monopoly of television" (1995, 31–32). He accused both Berlusconi and Gianfranco Fini, the leader of the National Alliance, of "pursuing a similar project to the one of democratic recovery conceived by the Great Master of the P2 Lodge . . . 'True power resides in the hands of those who hold the mass-media' declared the venerable Gelli, leader of P2, the Masonic lodge of which Berlusconi has member card no. 1816: These are things that must be remembered! . . . The League has opposed this anti-democratic project" (1996, 91–92). In fact events from the past and present are interpreted in a conspiratorial manner. The "hidden hand" of the Freemasonry has its fingers everywhere. Explaining the reform of the electoral system, Bossi remembered that "the Masonic logic of the Roman Parliament proposed the change of the electoral system from proportional to majority so that all the parties of the Roman oppression could rally against the League and the freedom of the north" (*La Padania,* July 23, 1998). Regarding the attacks of a newspaper against the League, Bossi asserted that "the *Gazzettino* is the front-rank of attack against the League. Behind it are some small businessmen and Masonic milieus that do not want Northern unity and, therefore, try to break the Northern League" (*La Padania,* September 20, 1998).

Of the many occult forces that push the international system of globalization, Bossi highlights Freemasonry's prime role. In fact, globalization is essentially a Masonic project aimed at establishing Masonic ideals everywhere. In Bossi's view,

> Mass immigration appeals to Rome because it floods Padania; and by giving immigrants the right to vote it manages to transform Padania into

a permanent colony. Moreover, the ideologues of globalization are allied with international bankers [and] want to reduce the man to a microbe, alone in front of globalization, without links, without traditions, without a sense of belonging to a community. In sum, the project of the Masonry: "without family, without house, without God, without religion, without children." You can see very well that behind the "turco-napolitano" law is the work of shady figures, well hidden, faraway, but also very close. (*La Padania*, May 15, 1999)

The Masonic nature of globalization permeates Bossi's discourse. As he said in an interview, "Masonry is the instrument through which globalization acts at an ideological-cultural level, in support of economic decisions . . . The idea of the traditional family, is in radical contrast to the vision of the American Masonry [and is an obstacle] to the attempt of this octopus to take control of the world though globalization" (*La Padania*, February 6, 1999). The danger posed by Masonic globalization is eminently spiritual because "[a]ccording to the Masons, there is a need to destroy the family and to blend religions, so that the only God left, a single God for everyone, is money" (*La Padania*, February 6, 1999). The project of the European Union has been increasingly regarded as a tool for the Masonic domination of world affairs. An article published in the party daily described in detail the dynamics of Jean Monnet's "Masonic plan" (*La Padania*, September 25, 2002) at the origins of the European Union. The European superstate is usually derided as the "Europe of the Masons." According to Bossi,

> When we took hold of the government of our country the "monster" [the Nice treaty that furthers European integration] was already in flight. The band of the Masons, Amato [former socialist prime-minister] and his ilk, have been already in Nice and it is difficult to stop the "monster" when it is flying . . . now we have to stop the "offence of racism" [the European legislation that criminalizes racist comments], which only serves to put those who are opposed to the project of destruction of peoples pushed forward by Masonic fundamentalism in jail. (*La Padania*, October 27, 2002)

America is in the center of the collusion of forces that push globalization in order to destroy humankind as we know it. Globalization, according to Bossi, is a monstrous tool created and guided by America to impose its multicultural model of society on the world. To accomplish this end, they use sycophantic European elites, who serve as their lackeys. "Ah America," observed Bossi, "these masters of ours, where everything is controlled by money . . . the diplomacy of the dollar cancels our cultural identity and our historical dignity. The European intelligentsia is reduced to identifying the Promised Land in the rootless civilization on the other side of the ocean" (1999, 111). Explaining the American project, Bossi said,

> The design of the masters of the world, those who through international economic power want to create a unique race and throw the world back to the Middle Ages of the papacy-empire is clear and lethal: [to] destroy the roots of peoples in order to subjugate them politically . . . Unfortunately with the fall of the Soviet empire, the winner was not the desire for freedom and democracy, but the more terrible face of globalism, under American guidance. In the Middle Ages, the empire of Acquisgrana [the Holy Roman Empire] dominated; today the turn goes to [another empire] whose royal palace is in Washington. America wants to impose its vision of the world: mercantilist, consumerist, and advocate of the disastrous "melting pot," the multiracial society that has failed everywhere. We Padani, together with so many other peoples, refuse this project of utter cultural and ethnic destruction, in the name of the values of democracy and freedom. (*La Padania*, July 19, 1998).

Bossi sees the hand of America behind the massive immigration to Europe in the last decades. The goal, he says, is to eradicate ethnic attachments in Europe and, particularly through Islamic immigration, to destabilize Europe in order to weaken its potential economic and political rivalry with the United States. "It is clear," noted Bossi, "that if the European economy is hit by millions of immigrants, it will be so overburdened that America could regain again its primacy over the economy. This is their objective" (*La Padania*, January 21, 1999). Behind this project is the work of "invisible Masonic powers, the Trilateral, the Bilderberg, the tools of the big American bankers" (*La Padania*, January 21, 1999). Further, and particularly during the nineties, the Northern League has denounced the American project of "Islamization" of Europe. The party daily gave great prominence to authors who defended this thesis, particularly the French intellectual Alexandre del Valle.[5] For Bossi, the Kosovo war was the result of the economic interests of American corporations, and was intended to reinforce the Islamic presence in Europe. According to the leader of the Northern League,

> Obviously, for a long time, Washington has had in mind the creation of an Islamic spine [in Europe] and now they are close to accomplishing this plan ... in putting together all the "vertebrae," the Americans will create the Muslim "spinal column" that will serve to prevent the birth of a political Europe ... using the pretext of the expulsion of the Kosovars, Clinton has created the conditions to hide the project of an "Islamic spinal column" [that was] planned by the global corporations from the eyes of the people ... [As part of this plan] corporations want to open Europe to Turkey and all the 170 million Muslims which would annihilate Christianity and above all Catholicism. (*La Padania*, April 7, 1999)

Bossi says that in Italy the parties of the Left, Big Capital, and the Church have also taken part in the alliance to destroy Europe through their support for relaxed immigration policies. The Left "searches for a new sub-proletariat that can vote for her," the Church "tries to fill its empty seminaries with religious people who it now only finds in the Third World," and Big Capital "unloads on the citizens the costs of its own development through the immigration from the Third World" (Bossi 1991a). A 2002 Northern League document dedicated to immigration denounces a similar alliance of different forces. It reads,

> The orphans of Marxism and of the dictatorship of the proletariat in a *cattocomunista* ["catholicism" and "communism"] mix, followers of

---

5. See, for example, "Islam–Stati Uniti, quella strana alleanza" (Islam–United States, the strange alliance, *La Padania*, November 26, 1998). On Alexandre del Valle's argument, see *Islamisme et Etats-Unis, une Alliance Contre l'Europe* (Islamism and the United States, An Alliance against Europe) (Valle 1997). In this book Valle describes the establishment of a "real collaboration" between two "conquering civilizations," the American and the Islamic. In the new world to come, Europe, decadent and debased morally and culturally by the "americanization of spirits and values," will be an easy prey to revengeful and expansionist Islamic designs (see especially 257–87).

internationalism, carry on in this way [approving the Turco-Napolitano immigration law], their subtle work of destruction of European civilization using immigration as a picklock and future element of destabilization and chaos; but in their road they have found the Northern League . . . the multiracial society is mostly supported by an alliance between the global finance and the international Left, based on common economic and ideological reasons. (Northern League 2002c, 11–12)

Time and again this conspiracy element reappears in the discourse of Bossi. Powerful elites—often described as "The Illuminati" (see, for example, *La Padania*, September 18, 2001)—work together against the people, hide their secret plans from the masses in order to continue a self-serving project of world domination. This conspiracy element increases the Northern League's self-perception of being surrounded by hostile and evil forces. The hidden hand is larger than life and omnipresent; those who recognize its dark powers must combat it at every step.[6]

In order to increase group mobilization against this evil, Bossi's rhetoric relies on cataclysmic imagery. Here are just a few examples.

The Centralist State

The alternative in Europe and even in the world at this stage, is truly between the explosion of ethnic or racial conflicts, and complete federalism. (Bossi 1991a)

The League is engaged in a fight without truces that can only have one of the following outcomes: the destruction of the League and the incarceration of its officials starting with the [federal] secretary, or the collapse of the State and the start of a liberal revolution based upon the principles of self-determination. (Bossi and Vimercati 1998, 105)

---

6. Though anti-Semitism is absent from Bossi's and other Northern League officials' discourse, it should be noted that the party is not immune to ideas of a "Jewish international plot" to dominate the world. Specifically, *The Protocols of the Elders of Zion* has been reportedly sold at party gatherings in Pontida (see Scaliati 2006, 98).

[Federalism] is the only alternative to the system, to the centralist dictatorship. Pay attention, citizens who love freedom; if the League lowered down the standard or, even worse, [if the League] disappeared, an abyss would open in front of the peoples of the North. (Bossi and Vimercati 1992, 88)

Immigration

Be aware that we are facing an apocalyptic invasion, not just a few hundred people. There has been talk about thirteen million immigrants falling upon us in the next ten years. (*La Padania,* May 15, 1999).

Think about what may happen if there are no limits, no confines. The entire world would rain upon our European countries. And this situation will not bring development, will not give benefits, but will lead to the collapse of our society. It will lead to a crash and, therefore, to the end of democracy. (*La Padania,* January 14, 2001)

Immigration has to be stopped . . . at stake is our existence, our future . . . either we manage to regain the sanity and love for our future, or we will all be dead. (*La Padania,* September 29, 2002)

European Union

The United States has supported the birth of the Fourth Reich [the European Union] because it serves them to start uniting the European States. Afterwards, they will open Europe to the Islamists, and the French-German axis will find it difficult to maintain the control of the Fourth Reich. [When this happens] only America, "the chosen people," will lead the world. (*La Padania,* November 28, 1999)

The way the project [the European Union] is emerging should give everyone the creeps. So many peoples, each with a different language, forced to be together by a higher power. Something like this has already happened in history, when the Soviet Union was created, with the results that we all know for democracy. (*La Padania,* December 11, 2001)

Regarding Europe we do not want a Neo-Jacobin structure, standardized by the market and dissolving the nation-state . . . the Neo-Jacobin Masons want to give us a new slavery. But the peoples will not let themselves be crushed, and a decisive confrontation will happen. (*La Padania*, July 2, 2003)

Globalization

If we don't want man reduced to dust, to a "microbe" addicted to consumerism and materialism, and not in charge of his own future, it is necessary that peoples organize and enter directly into politics. (*La Padania*, November 20, 1998)

[Globalization] is an enterprise of massification and worldwide de-personalization that threatens to extinguish ethnic cultures and nations . . . it is evident that a system that destroys each cultural past is not a civilization but on the contrary is a system that makes everything the same like the cells of a malign cancer. (Bossi 2002)

The mystics of the market economy assure us that in the future we will all be richer, but I fear that in the meantime we will be all dead. (Bossi 2003a)

Bossi's rhetoric to the besieged community is sustained and permeated by a sense of impending ruin, of cataclysmic events in the waiting. It is filled with images of "death," "destruction," "collapse," "extinction," and "abysmal future," that suggest a scenario in which the end of the world is a strong possibility. The use of biological imagery serves to augment the power of the message of doom. As Bossi has said, "If Padania remains in Italy, Padania dies" (*La Padania*, April 28, 1998). Bossi often associates enemies of the group with diseases. "Nationalism," declared Bossi, "is a symptom of a mortal disease" (*La Padania*, March 29, 1998). "If there's no democracy," said Bossi about the situation in Italy, "there's the diffusion of a mechanism of impunity that affects the elites and then, like a cancer, the entire social body" (Bossi and Vimercati 1998, 41). His images suggest vivid images of degeneration and putrefaction. On one occasion he said, "We are trapped in the cadaver of a society swarming with worms" (1999, 119–20). A typical manner in which Bossi describes the destructive effects of globalization on human society is with a comparison of man to a defenseless "microbe" swept away by forces outside of his control (see, for example, *La Padania,* May 15, 1999).

No matter what the subject, a sense of doom is present throughout Bossi's discourse. Issues such as centralism, the European Union, and globalization are described in a way that portends disasters on the horizon. "What will be the way out?" asked Bossi about the situation of Italy. "Great reform, restoration, armed confrontation? I don't know; it has not been decided yet. For now, we from the League have managed to keep the anxiety of change from degenerating toward armed revolution. But at the next crisis what will happen?" (Bossi 1995, 205). At another occasion Bossi pronounced that "the time of change has come: it can be like a steady wind that turns the pages of the Italian book or like a storm that will sweep it away" (1998a). Writing about the situation of Padania in Italy, Bossi said that

> [w]hen there is not a basis of common historical roots or a common ethnocultural matrix, or when this basis is thin ... then problems arise, and there are two solutions: Either the State accepts the plurality of regional cultural traditions and makes them contribute to the Nation, in a way that all the cultures contribute in making the rules of the system, or [the State] tries to liquidate them, if they let themselves be liquidated. (*La Padania,* January 27, 2004)

"After the fall of the Berlin wall," Bossi declared at a rally, "a new historical phase was opened, simultaneously wonderful and terrible." It was terrible because "the era of 2000 has been opened, full of hopes but also of great unknowns for Italy, which the way it is now is not ready to enter the new era" (Bossi 1996, 30). "Give us this freedom," said Bossi on another occasion, "before it is too late" (*La Padania,* March 31, 1998). As Bossi stated at a 2002 meeting,

> Only a cataclysm provoked by extreme revolutionary violence (as happened in France in 1789 or in Russia in 1917) can extirpate the *nomenclatura* at the roots and open a new historical time. But also, authentic democracy can become a revolutionary force capable of setting off a completely new epoch with federalism. When I'm having serious difficulty

advancing federalist reform I will call upon you to shake the palaces of pharisaic falsity, of aversion against our peoples; I will give you the names of the racists who fake bonhomie and democracy but who, in reality, are against the people, especially our people and its freedom. (2002)

Bossi's discourse is aimed toward ultimate ends and "final battles." As he observed, "Today our land is engaged in a mortal battle for independence" (Bossi and Vimercati 1998, 45). This ominous mentality is visible in the way that Bossi interprets globalization and all side effects he sees associated with it. "It is not only federalism that matters," observed Bossi at a rally. "There are epochal changes that we know we must contribute to. It may be a question of life and death" (2003a). Because globalization corresponds to an "artificial" perversion that corrupts the nature of man and society, there is a sense of urgency in stopping this process. "History is not dead," observed Bossi. "Men will play a role again; but it needs to be soon, because the enemy destroys at a great speed" (*La Padania*, December 2, 1999). According to Bossi, "Internationalism is losing ground [in this battle] because those who wanted it to win have not managed to cancel the identity of peoples. However to win this battle [the peoples] need to be supported with even more strength" (*La Padania*, October 10, 2002). The League's criticism of the European Union is also viewed in terms of a final confrontation between those who favor the "Jacobin and centralist dictatorship" of a European Superstate and those who side with a "Europe of the peoples." The end of this battle will bring either democracy's death or its victory.

The League's Exceptionality

Bossi's discourse is characterized by a constant polarization that simplifies realities and focuses his group on what separates the Northern League from its enemies. This polarization is applied to national or to international contexts. In the Italian political system, the pole of the Northern League (whether in coalition or not) is always defined as the last resource available against an antagonistic pole at which all the other parties and forces are lumped together. Bossi described what was at stake in the national elections of 1994 in the following way: "There is a virtual pole constituted by three groups: the fascists, the Christian democrats and communism. They support the welfare policies that have ruined Italy [and] want a centralized state. Against them is the new, represented by the Northern League" (1993). In 1998, lumped at one pole was "Italian nationalism," representing the old forces of centralism: the Vatican, the parties of the left, the former neofascist National Alliance, the big financiers, and the Mafia. They incarnated the centuries-old forces of centralism. On the opposite pole was the "Padani patriotism" of the Northern League, constituted by those who "have united their forces to fight the beautiful battle of freedom" (1998a). In 2002, Bossi saw the political system divided in two blocks: "The block that we represent is indeed 'small enterprises,' federalism, the power that comes from below [the people]. It is very different from the [other] block, 'Left, Big Capital'" (*La Padania*, April 16, 2002).

This polarizing technique can also be seen in the way Bossi describes the function and role of the Northern League in the international system. The European Union is always described in an either-or manner. "We have to ask ourselves," said Bossi at a rally, "what kind of Europe we want: the one of the peoples, that we defend, or the one wanted by the Jacobins, where some thirty so-called illuminati want to command 360 million citizens imposing [on] them a unique model" (*La Padania*, September 18, 2001). Bossi sees the struggle against the international system of globalization in a similar manner: "Enterprises, peoples, identity against virtual finance and rootlessness . . . these are the terms of the political dialectic that is progressing. One time in Europe it was Atheism against Christianity; now it is materialism against identity" (*La Padania*, November 14, 1999). In Bossi's discourse the League is always portrayed as being on one side of the spectrum while all the others are lumped on an opposite, hostile side—including Americans and Muslims, capitalists and communists.

At the same time this use of polarization reinforces the group's self-perception of the Northern League as a unique movement, an exceptional force different from all the others. In the discourse of Bossi, the League is the *only* movement to which the peoples of the North can look when they feel their cultural and ethnic traditions to be in jeopardy. The vanguard of men and women led by Bossi is the only hope for the North. As Bossi stated at a rally,

> We have defeated the centralist counterrevolution because we [unlike all the other political forces] are not [founded] in a palace feud but are a force of nature that has shattered the basis of partitocracy and influenced the political life of the last twenty years. The League uses power to put ideas capable of transforming society in place . . . without us our land would be without identity [but would be a land] plowed by invaders. (*La Padania,* June 25, 2002)

It is not surprising, then, that Bossi has proclaimed that "the vote for the League has more value than other votes [for other parties]. The League has the honesty and the courage to transform into projects the ideas of the people. With the League politics is indeed the only instrument that the people have in order to matter" (*La Padania,* May 5, 2002).

I have so far showed how, through his discourse, Bossi strengthens the identity of his group, which he characterizes as a vanguard of men and women who are conscious of their history and under siege by powerful and demonized enemies. Bossi's use of conspiracy, catastrophic imagery, and repeated polarization serves to mobilize and increase the focus of the group. The mission of defending the North from those hostile forces—be they the dictatorship of centralism or the tyrannies of the European Union and globalization—rests on the shoulders of the vanguard elite who are engaged in a final battle and, therefore, are the last hope of the peoples of the North of Italy. In my next section I will demonstrate how the discourse of the Northern League idolizes Bossi as a savior and messianic guide of the vanguard mission to save the communities of Northern Italy.

BOSSI THE SAVIOR

The Bossi Industry

Since the early days of the Lombard League, and on through its solidification in the Italian political and social landscape, the official literature of the party, coupled with the narrative of the leader himself and his strong personalized hold on the party, have contributed to a process of mythologization of Umberto Bossi. I refer to this process as the "Bossi industry." To outline this industry, I will first look at the role played by the inner circle in mythologizing the figure of Bossi. This examination includes reviewing party literature, interviews, and public interventions by Bossi's closest collaborators, parliamentarians, or those who occupy public offices as members of the party.

The Inner Circle. Bossi's inner circle goes to great lengths to emphasize the role played by the leader in the formation and development of the party. The successes of the Northern League—and of its ancestor, the Lombard League—are characterized above all as the work of Bossi. The preface to a compilation of writings by Bossi about the history of the Northern League, written by a one-time director of *La Padania,* offers an illuminating example of lionization of the leader among the party faithful:

> This tale, if seen in its totality and slow fluidity, manifests all the characteristics of an extraordinary authenticity. Because, without hiding torments and mistakes, it outlines first hand the faithful itinerary of a lonely intuition [of Bossi's] that becomes, step by step, a valuation of local culture and therefore an ideal of liberation till it expands to an identification with a full fledged political project. (Baiocchi 1999, 6)

Christina Malaguti and Stefania Piazzo describe the early days of the movement in the following manner: "In this way, the strength of an idea [and] the genius of a man became the idea and the strength of all the peoples of the North, in a 'ferment of recovery and revival'" (*Lega Nord–Padania Indipendente,* December 9, 1996). As asserted by a contributor (under the pseudonym "Camisa Verde" [Green Shirt]) to the party daily, the advent of the Northern League represented "a formidable union of freemen launched with determination by Umberto Bossi to gain the independence of their lands" (*La Padania,* April 28, 1998). And another contributor writes, "Umberto Bossi [is] the father-brother . . . father of a movement created for us and brother in all the battles, victories, and defeats" (*La Padania,* July 27, 1999). Roberto Maroni, longtime party official, emphasized the indispensable role played by Umberto Bossi: "At the beginning, in the League, it was practically only Umberto Bossi who had ideas. Without him we wouldn't even exist because a movement that hasn't tradition, a common history, cannot survive without a strong leadership" (Maroni 1994, 143).

This trailblazing function of Umberto Bossi in the early days of the movement is commonly stressed. "[The militants] must remember the immense debt of recognition," said Senator Pagliarini, "that all of us have and always will have to Umberto Bossi and those few people who had the courage of founding the movement, and the strength to make it grow, against everyone else" (Caravita 1993, 54). According to Giuseppe Leoni, founder of the Lombard League together with Bossi, its enemies knew of the primal role of Bossi for the movement, which is why they concentrated their attacks on him. As Leoni wrote in the party organ of the eighties,

> [These attacks] are naturally focused on senator Bossi, National Secretary of the Lombard League, because he represents the turning key of our movement. However, the end result of these attacks had the opposite reaction [to that] hoped for by the perpetrators: [The attacks] have contributed to bind instead of separate the militants of the movement around their *great leader* who because of his capacity, determination, culture, and also because of his honesty and unselfish idealism, has few equals. (*Lombardia Autonomista*, July 1988)

In the testimony of those close to him, the leader is a man with a spellbinding personality. "From the first time that I listened to him," remembered parliamentarian Elisabetta Bertotti, "all my doubts ceased to exist. I sleep two hours at night, I dedicate all my time to the League" (Ottaviani and Canteri 1992, 15). "What impression has he made on me?" asked Maroni. "[That of] a man of a very strong personality, fascinating. We could listen to him for hours without getting bored. He was prepared [to discuss] any subject" (Zanzi 1994, 47–48). Maroni puts the "bewitching" power of Bossi's personality at the center of the group. In his words,

> We were all bewitched more by this great personality than by the project. He was a sort of Hindu Holy Man who enchanted not so much by what he said but by what he did, because Bossi knew how to be always in the front line, the general that guides the assault with the bayonets . . . I have been in the League for so many years because of this strange, unusual relationship that tied all of us to Bossi, almost like a psychological hook that

forced you to put part of your time committed to this insane, unachievable project. (Maroni 1994, 144)

Franco Rocchetta, one-time president of the Northern League, noted that one of the determining factors of the party was that it was led by a "man with a strong, exceptional personality" (Ottaviani and Canteri 1992, 25). Longtime loyalist Giovanni Meo Zilio sees the spellbinding nature of Bossi as the driving force of the Northern League. As he wrote in *La Padania*,

> We should ask ourselves why it is that the League, notwithstanding everything [schisms, mistakes] survives. As always in political phenomena, and in human phenomena in general, the reason is not univocal, but rests on a conflation of factors. There are, however, prevalent factors. In this case it is general opinion that the prevalent, even determinant, factor *rests on the personal charisma of the leader* . . . [which] represents an emblematic case in the recent history of our politicians and would deserve to be studied by political scientists and experts in political psychology. The fact is that Bossi, independent of his stature as a statesman (with all its lights and shadows: in truth more lights than shadows), not only drags the masses along with him and is the only political man who manages today to summon 50,000 people, but also exerts "political fascination" even on us, men of science used to critical evaluation, objectivity, reality. This is a very telling thing. (*La Padania*, January 4, 2000)

His acolytes repeatedly describe Bossi as a unique man with rare qualities. Among those qualities praised by those close to him is his *clairvoyance*. He is depicted as someone who sheds light before the group, the person who can see what others cannot. Current events are interpreted as a proof of Bossi's prophetic ability. According to Senator Carlo Pisati, "Bossi, long before the fall of the Berlin [wall], had foreseen everything and said that left and right were dead, and that the Christian Democrats would follow communism in its fall" (Ottaviani and Canteri 1992, 37). In the view of one of the national secretaries of the Northern League, "It is enough to read what Bossi said five, six, seven years ago. We find exactly everything that is happening today. You don't believe it? Go and check it" (*La Padania*, December 6, 2000). Roberto Cota, one of the national secretaries of the Northern League, noted that "more than seven years ago some accused Bossi of lunacy, saying that federalism in Italy was impossible. Today no one has the courage anymore to call himself anti-federalist" (*La Padania,* September 17, 2002). In an interview with *La Padania,* Leoni hints at Bossi's almost supernatural capacity to predict events as he reflects about "the confine that exists between the free will of man and Providence, which makes impossible paths feasible. I'm thinking about my battles alongside Umberto, when I was beside him from the birth of the League, and the goals reached [by him] with strategy, anticipating all the signs of the political world" (*La Padania,* March 14, 2004).

Bossi is repeatedly portrayed as a man with rare foresight. Official documents of the Northern League emphasize this quality. A party document of the history of the movement refers to Bossi's "formidable political intuition" in the eighties, when he "understood that the first thing to do was to initiate a fight without mercy to combat the political situation" (Fassini 1998, 29). Bossi "intuited very early that a solely ethnic claim would not have led to concrete results" (Fassini 1998, 32). "Suffice it to say," the same document states, "that Bossi has once again foretold the political turn that the League must undertake" (Fassini 1998, 49). In the words of Senator Staglieno, "[The project of] federalism is the future of Europe and, I would say, of the entire world. This has been the splendid intuition of Bossi, who has updated the federalist doctrine of Cattaneo" (Ottaviani and Canteri 1992, 52). According to Camisa Verde, "Our leader is not right *a priori* [but] the facts tell us that he has never made a mistake. Thank goodness, because if it depended on some of us, the Padania would remain an unachievable mirage" (*La Padania,* April 8, 1998).

Unlike all other self-serving and elitist politicians, the leader of the Northern League is celebrated as an ordinary man who understands and serves the true interests of the people because he comes from the people. "His human qualities, above all the fact the he is someone from the people, and is not a politicker like the others," notes one of his collaborators, Filippo Pozzi, "serve as an example for the people of Padania who reclaim the freedom to decide their future without the interference of the Roman palaces." Pozzi added that Bossi "speaks with the language of the people, not [the language] from the palaces" (e-mail interview, May 13, 2004). Giancarlo Giorgetti, the national secretary of the Lombard League, emphasizes the popular nature of Bossi as a crucial element of his relationship with the militants: "Party militants see him as truly being one of the people. He has a very informal style and avoids being perceived as a man of power." Giorgetti also notes that Bossi "speaks the language of the people, to the people, about the problems faced by the people" (e-mail interview, May 19, 2004).

It is therefore not strange that Bossi is perceived as someone who has always honored his duty to fight for the people, and has never been in politics for personal gain or naked ambition. "He doesn't think about power [for the sake of power]," noted a former director of *La Padania*, Gigi Moncalvo. "His goal is not to [sit] in comfortable armchairs, but to fight for the dignity and the pride of his people, against Rome." Bossi, notes Moncalvo, "has always showed and continues to show that honesty and honest words are the most important thing for a political man, for a representative of the people" (e-mail interview, May 31, 2004)

There is a natural tendency of the party's inner core to associate Bossi with the Northern League itself. Particularly in times of crisis, especially those owing to internal schisms or electoral defeats, Bossi is hailed as both the incarnation of the party and the only leader that can point the way out of the crisis. In 1993, after the League was hit by accusations of corruption and internal dissension, longtime loyalist Giuseppe Babbini declared in an interview that "[t]he League is Bossi. Bossi is the only leader: There's no one else. Lord forgive me, but I feel like saying the following: There will not be another [savior] for me." (*Il Corriere della Sera*, December 11, 1993). In that period, the parliamentary group of the Northern League made known its loyalty to Bossi by this press release:

> If anyone believes that Umberto Bossi does not represent any more the genius-like and unquestioned leader of the League in the fight for the triumph of a fulfilled democracy, a State of rights and federalism, it is better that they disillusion themselves immediately . . . [T]he sword of Alberto da Giussano is firmly in the hands of Bossi, and the armies of the *Carroccio* are united today as they were yesterday, and more. (*Il Corriere della Sera*, December 11, 1993)

The inner core's testimony that Bossi is the personalization of the party and its goals is repeated over and over. During a period of internal divisions and

4. Umberto Bossi delivers a speech to militants at the annual Northern League rally in Venice, September 15, 2002. Courtesy of *La Padania*.

eroding electoral support in 1999, another wave of declarations of faith in the leader emerged. Stefano Stefani, then president of the Northern League, declared that "Bossi represents and incarnates the project of the Northern League, for which our Movement was born and has fought for years" (*La Padania*, June 23, 1999). Another member of the League apparatus noted that "if the Senator [Bossi] leaves, the League will fragment into pieces in ten days" (*La Padania*, July 2, 1999). After the disappointing results of the party in the national elections of 2001, a longtime official of the Northern League, Senator Tabladini, proposed the creation of a "Reformed League." Although very critical, he did not cast Bossi's primacy into doubt. And his proposal specifically stated that "the figure of Bossi is not under discussion, not so much because he hasn't made mistakes but because [he is] the only glue powerful enough to prevent the dissolution of the party in one week" (Tabladini 2003, 19). In the accounts of his acolytes, Bossi is often pictured not only as someone who is the face of the party, but also as a leader who *is* the Northern League.

In the narrative put forward by those close to him, the leader emerges as someone who will leave an indelible mark on history. Bossi belongs to the category of "Great Men." In a photo book dedicated to the early years of the Northern League, a full-page picture of Bossi is subtitled with the following caption: "The true director of the political revolution of the last years in Italy. He hasn't finished yet" (Caravita 1993, 201). To a local official of the Northern League, "Bossi is one of those men who write the story of a country, a true charismatic leader. Everyone recognizes it, even from other parties" (*La Padania*, June 2, 2004). In the writings of longtime party official Giovanni Meo Zilio, Bossi is praised as one of those uncommon leaders destined for a permanent place in history as a hero.

> Umberto cannot be regarded as a normal man. But a "monster" (in the etymological sense), in the same way that all of those who left a mark in history were monsters ... characters who feel that they bear an imperative and ineludible mission, to which they dedicate their lives in a superhuman manner, with a perseverance that is so opposed to the philosophy of "quietism" that [it] should be defined as "heroic." They don't withdraw in the face of obstacles, they don't know physical tiredness, and they are above all "ruthless" with themselves, refusing relaxation, comfort and wealth. [The leader gives] everything in order to achieve the ideal, for which the leader of the League has declared more than once (and he was not kidding) he was ready to pay, if necessary, the ultimate price. When we hear him repeating that the League "is a force that comes out of nature," we cannot avoid thinking that, first of all, the force that broke out of nature was him; and that it is the League that grows in [Bossi's] "image and likeness." (*La Padania*, December 12, 2000)

Followers acclaim Bossi as a visionary committed in a missionary manner to a project that will transform history. "There are men to whom we owe the changing of our way of imagining the world," writes *La Padania*. "One of those men is certainly Umberto Bossi" (*La Padania*, March 16, 2004). "Umberto Bossi is the only, truly enlightened political man that Europe has had in the last three centuries," noted longtime friend and colleague Erminio Boso, who placed Bossi "side by side with Cavour, Metternich, Churchill, De Gaulle" (Stella 1996, 48). One-time parliamentarian Simonetta Faverio sees in Bossi the harbinger of "a revolution of poets": Bossi set off "a revolution of great dreamers. And the greatest dreamers are those who fulfill their dreams, or at least they try hard with all their strengths" (*La Padania,* September 23, 1998). Paolo Grimoldi, the federal coordinator of Padania Youth, stresses the missionary commitment of Bossi to his project as an important aspect of his appeal. "Umberto Bossi is important for several reasons," he says in an interview, "above all by his clear political ability. But it is not only political; [It is] charisma, constant presence in the territories [of Padania], personal sacrifice, perseverance" (e-mail interview, April 14, 2004). Giovanni Meo Zilio expresses a similar view that "the psychophysical strength, the idealistic tension and the objective charisma of the Senator can be connected, *mutatis mutandis,* (but the fabric is the same) to those of [Garibaldi] and so many other 'monsters' in a positive way" (*La Padania,* December 12, 2000). As we can see in the narrative of the leader's inner circle, Bossi is continuously and consistently portrayed as someone with the missionizing, charismatic qualities necessary to save the North of Italy and create a new reality. To the inner circle, these qualities testify to the salvationist nature of the leader.

The Leader's Discourse. Umberto Bossi's discourse also plays a powerful role in the development and consolidation of images that portray him as a missionizing savior figure. Whether in books, speeches, or public interventions, Bossi assumes a prime position as the sole guide of the vanguard. Bossi repeatedly emphasizes the fact that the movement is in essence the fruit of his missionary commitment and vision. He regularly traces back the origins of his calling to the meeting with the autonomist Bruno Salvadori. Drawing an analogy between himself and the apostle Paul, Bossi noted in one of his books, "I thought I was on my way to a good professional career when Salvadori opened a new world in front of my eyes, made of political and social commitment in the service of a great idea. For me it was like ending up on the road to Damascus: Something had released the vocation of the apostle in me" (Bossi and Vimercati 1993, 87).

In Bossi's personal discourse the creation and development of his movement take the shape of a quest in which he himself plays the role of the heroic leader. In a compelling example of missionizing rhetoric, he writes,

> Fifteen years ago, in the heartland of Lombardy, something happened that recalls the sagas of Brittany. A fairytale began: A man of the people has

extracted the sword from the rock and used it to defeat adversaries that looked invincible. In the open field the League has always triumphed . . . at the end of the battle, in any case, the blade will return to the rock. And the man who had gripped it, who is a man of the people, will return to the people. (1995, 208)

Bossi always identifies fervor for the cause as the driving force for his entrance into politics. He often portrays his motives as profoundly unselfish and pure. "I created the League because I followed [the advice] of my father who once told me that there was a need to defend the interests of the North, to give voice to those who didn't have the courage to speak," he expressed in an interview (*Panorama,* December 21, 2006). In his own account, power is not an end in itself. It only matters as long as it is a means to an end: to the cause, the ideal. As he observed, "I'm not ambitious. I feel like a father who helps his son [the League] to grow. If a father is a good one, after having brought up his son, he goes to the sidelines and lets him walk by himself, with his own legs. I will do the same with the movement: When it will be in a position to walk by itself, I will retire. Power is of interest to me only if it serves the cause" (Vimercati, 1990, 118).

Bossi's self-representation as a leader who is driven not by a thirst for power but by a grand ideal is a permanent feature of his rhetoric. He has always expressed his willingness to step down as leader as "proof" of his selflessness. "Power does not interest me," he said in an interview in 1993. "[W]hen I was elected I signed my resignation and put it in a safe. Whoever wants it can present himself to the League, and I'll be ready to be an infantry soldier" (*Il Corriere della Sera,* December 3, 1993). In 2003, while minister of reforms of the Italian government, he expressed a similar sentiment: "I have never wanted and I don't want to make a career. I have decided to be the minister not as an end but as a means: to make reforms, to change things" (*La Padania,* June 18, 2003).

At the same time, because of the fact that the League is above all his creation, Bossi expresses through his discourse a sense that he is entitled to decide its destiny. "I am the League," he said in an interview, "the League is a gigantic machine that I operate, nobody else" (La Repubblica, March 18, 1993). Bossi has remarked that he "created [the League] from nothing, I had to provide for everything: recruitment, organization, and also the political platform" (Bossi and Vimercati 1993, 16–17). "I founded the movement," he also said; "I have watched it grow, and I know all the officials" (Bossi and Vimercati 1998, 106). Bossi juxtaposes his biography with that of the movement: The life-narrative of Umberto Bossi and that of the Northern League are one. As he wrote in the preface for a compilation of his writings,

> The League and its Secretary have not changed; they have just grown in the conscience of the people, and they have given birth, with hard work but also with joy, to the first true political class of the North. This book tells, without mediation, through original documents and therefore incontrovertibly, the story of a long political march. If one day, many years from now, an historian wants to know how the idea of Padania was born, he will have in this book a useful tool. (1996, XI)

Bossi also portrays himself as someone who has the necessary qualities to lead the vanguard. Underscoring his uniqueness as a politician who is driven not by mundane motives like personal wealth or prestige and is therefore free of self-interest, Bossi casts himself as a simple person, with everyman qualities. His discourse emphasizes the unpretentiousness of his life. He said in 1990, "I did not become rich; I have not taken any advantage from my political life. I could have sold myself for a good price, that's for sure. I have not done it and I will never will. I still live in the periphery of Varese, with my wife and son, in a two-floor apartment. I drive an old Citroen. I'm usually dressed in the same old clothes. I earn almost ten million as a parliamentarian, but I give half to the League" (Vimercati 1990, 118).

On another occasion Bossi commented on the fact that "my house is very modest, [a typical] working class house" (1995, 198). "I am someone who comes from the people and to the people I will return," he noted in an interview (*Il Corriere della Sera*, December 7, 1993). In order to underscore both his popular image and the gap separating the League from the other political parties, Bossi has always prided himself on speaking in plain, everyday language. Particularly in its initial stages, the political discourse of the League was a direct rejection of *politichese*, the "political cant" of the other parties, which was full of grandiloquence, euphemisms, and abstractions that were totally unintelligible to the average citizen (see, for example,

McCarthy 1997). Therefore, as a man of the people, Bossi swears and is not inhibited about casting himself as a macho man, especially through the use of sexual references. This sexist attitude became part of the identity of the party—usually referred to as *celodurismo*—after Bossi's intervention at the conclusion of the First Congress of the Northern League, when he yelled that "the political parties will not cheat us because *la Lega Ce l'ha duro!* [The League has a hard-on!]." In an interview he jokingly said that his announcement "increased the popularity of the Lega among the female voters" (Bossi and Vimercati 1992, 70). On another occasion, when a female socialist politician accused the League of getting ready for an armed secession, Bossi, at a political rally, told the *"cara bonassa* [dear hottie]" not to worry. The only weapon that the League had, said Bossi, while making the gesture of an erection, was "the *manico* [broomstick]" (Iacopini and Bianchi 1994, 54). "In order to make revolutions," he said at another meeting, "[w]e need to have balls and not to let ourselves be influenced by the opinionated" (*La Padania,* April 21, 1998). Such vulgar language has been a permanent feature of the "tell-it-like-it-is" populist style of communication that Bossi adopted early.

In his discourse the Northern League appears as a reflection of the populism of its leader. The party is unrelentingly characterized as being "of the people, and for the people," as the leader declared in the 1994 party congress in Bologna (Bossi 1994). Bossi has compared the League to the Greek mythical figure of Antaeus, "a giant who drew his immense force from the earth, because the earth was his mother. In the same way, the explosive charge of the League comes from below, because [the League] takes its strength from popular sovereignty, of which it is the most direct and qualified interpreter" (*Lombardia Autonomista,* May 1992). The League is "an authentic popular and revolutionary force [that works for] the advent of a federalist democracy. We don't fear the people because we are their tool!" (Bossi 2003a).

Intimately linked with the popular nature of the party is the depiction of its discourse as an extension of common sense, of what is self-evident. In an interview Bossi assailed the elites for being purposefully aloof from the people. "Those beautiful types," said Bossi, "say that we speak a language [that is spoken] in taverns. They don't know the compliment they pay us for saying that! Because we say the things that the people think, we are on the side of the people" (*La Padania,* July 2, 2003). Whether in opposition or in power, Bossi's emphasis on the intrinsic, commonsensical nature of the party remains unchanged. The way Umberto Bossi explains the League's opposition to what he calls "immigration-invasion" exemplifies his populist approach. "We are in government to stimulate," he said in an interview. "We are a popular party, and we go around holding rallies to listen to the people. And when the people see the arrival of thousands of immigrants, all at the same time, *si incazza* [they get mad]." The solution to this situation is not related "to money, it is about having the balls to do it, which is a different thing" (*La Padania,* June 27, 2003). In another interview Bossi declared, "The people don't want millions of illegal immigrants—you just have to walk around to know what the citizens think. It is a very simple thing, just listen . . . I am a leader, and in general a leader must mediate; however, a leader cannot betray the people. Therefore he must be able to make the voice of the people heard inside the palace. That is why, once in a while, the voice [of the people] must be raised [by Bossi]" (*La Padania,* June 18, 2003).

Bossi presents himself as the medium through which the people speak. But they often do not know what to say since their native good judgment has been anesthetized and undermined for years by the destructive propaganda of the enemies of the people. That is why the vanguard led by Bossi has the role of reminding the people of its roots. As noted before, the vanguard plays the role of vigilantes protecting the natural identity of the people. The League, Bossi vowed, "must commit itself to reminding the people [of] Padani of their history and how their slavery started, not by the work of the Romans, but by ourselves" (1997).

Among the necessary qualities that Bossi claims to have in order to lead the group, his power of prescience, which I discussed previously in relation to his inner circle, occupies a central role. Bossi constantly interprets both historical and contemporary events to provide evidence of his clairvoyance. According to Bossi, he understood the path of history long before others. "[T]his is a discovery that goes back many years," said Bossi, "even before international events showed how right my intuition was, we could say that the pendulum of history, after having moved for more than a century in the direction of justice, has inverted its oscillation and now moves towards the pole of freedom" (Bossi and Vimercati 1993, 15). As he stated in an interview, "When I told you [about a revolution in Italy] six months ago, you [journalists] got all scared. Then, after foreign journalists came and said the same, it became trendy [to talk about a revolution]. We, instead, have understood for years now that it would be like this, that a moment would arrive in which idealistic philosophies would replace materialistic philosophies and would give birth to a cultural and political revolution" (*La Repubblica*, March 5, 1993).

"In 1991, when many, including [many in] the League, were convinced that the worst was behind us," said Bossi, "I warned [our] officials: Be ready, now [against us] the most insidious reaction of the regime will be unleashed . . . I was a good prophet" (1996, 154).

At the same time, Bossi highlights his resilience, his suffering, and his capacity to endure hardships in order to fulfill the mission. The image of sacrifice is dominant in Bossi's discourse. As he wrote, "The League has cost me so much, in all kind of ways" (1999, 38–39). He often tells the story of how one day his mother found him cooking for one of the political parties of the League: "[She said] 'Look at you, from a doctor to a cook!' This disturbed me," Bossi said, "but there was no other way if we wanted Lombardy and the North to become free of Roman tyranny one day" (1999, 39). As he declared at a political rally, "I know how to distinguish creation from property. I know that the League is yours, even if it has cost innumerable sacrifices to some people, especially me. And, let it be known, that in so many years the League has given me not even one lira" (1996, 73). In developing the narrative of himself as the savior, Bossi has played the character of the self-sacrificing son of Padania many times. "I think that the base of the League sees the right reference point only in me. They know I don't betray," he said in an interview. "However the Romans are also aware of this, and that is why they massacre my image and hit me in all possible ways, because I represent the glue of the united North against Roma *ladrona* [Rome the thief] and its parties" (*La Padania*, July 11, 1999).

Victimization abounds in the leader's narrative. He has repeatedly stressed his persecution by Rome. "Personally, I have had in my life hundreds of judicial warnings, many unjust and pre-ordained sentences, creations of Roman nationalism. We have to resist [by] smiling" (*La Padania*, August 1, 1999). In addition, he claims that his unconditional defense of the group has put his own life in danger: "Yes, in order to stop Bossi there is a very quick way, but the ideal, *that* cannot be stopped by anyone" (Vimercati 1990, 117). "I could tell you about the threats, the so-called suggestions, the blackmails," he said at a press conference. "I know very well that I'm surrounded, I know that they want me" (*Il Corriere della Sera,* December 7, 1993).

In a meeting with his militants Bossi declared, "I can even become a persecuted, a prisoner for life, a Mandela of Padania; but the North wants federalism, reforms, and [that] cannot be stopped" (*Il Corriere della Sera,* August 21, 1995). Images of sacrifice and martyrdom in Bossi's narrative are a dynamic part of the missionary dimension of his leadership. The savior goes through great hardships, and is ready to die, in order to redeem the entire community.

Bossi's self-depiction, through his discourse, as a missionizing figure plays an important part in the development and consolidation of the Bossi industry. I will consider now how the hierarchical structure of the party reinforces and legitimates his primacy as the leader of the vanguard.

The Personalized Party. The centralized structure of the Northern League plays a significant role in the identification of the party with its leader, Federal Secretary Umberto Bossi. There are five organizational sections: federal, national, provincial, district, and communal. At the top of the hierarchy are the federal secretary, who is elected by a federal congress, and the Federal Council, which is composed of the secretaries of the national sections and a dozen other members elected by the congress. The Federal Council has the right to dissolve the national sections of the party if they "act in clear contrast with the political, moral and administrative line established by the Federal Congress of the Northern League" (Biorcio 1997, 219). The federal secretary has a say in all federal organs. He coordinates the directives of the Federal Congress and chairs the Federal Council. Furthermore, the statutes of the party establish that the federal secretary represents, at a political and legal level, the unity of the movement. At the same time, the organizational structure encourages militancy. Membership is conditioned by the time (sometimes years) that a member has spent working for the party and proving his loyalty to the movement. The Northern League makes a strong distinction between old and new members. Only older members have rights and duties within the organization. There are no institutionalized criteria for promotion or career, which could have the risk of transferring loyalty from the leadership to the organization. Only Bossi's word leads to promotion.

Umberto Bossi has always justified the primacy of the leader within the Northern League as a necessity. Because enemies loom everywhere and try to infiltrate the group, the survival of the movement demands strong leadership. As Bossi has argued, "It is better to suffer accusations of hierarchization, or even worse of dictatorial management of the movement, than to allow the diffusion of immoral behavior" (Bossi and Vimercati 1993, 170). "The Lombard League—and afterwards the Northern League—has been protected in many ways," Bossi said, "in order to prevent disloyal officials from ruining the structure" (1995, 115).

"There's only one thing that I will never accept," explained Bossi in an interview; "to have a vice [deputy] or an alter ego." He added, "there needs to be clarity about who is in command" (*Il Giornale,* November 27, 2006). The primacy of the leader is accepted naturally by other officials, as the following words of Giancarlo Giorgetti reveal: "He is not just the current leader of the party: He *is* the party. He has an extremely charismatic influence over party members, and controls the party entirely by himself. Anyone seen to challenge his authority is expelled" (e-mail interview, May 19, 2004).

Bossi sees the Northern League as a true example of direct democracy. So far, he has always been reelected by acclamation, without a formal ballot. With a strong public mandate from the party congress, Bossi always sets the agenda of the organization. As he once declared,

> The delegates have become conscious of the need to put on the road a car with one driver at the wheel. When the car drives at 150 miles an hour, the driver must be left alone . . . I am at the top of the League with a precise mandate: to prevent the horses from stopping at the manger of the regime, so that they become fat and let themselves be ridden by our enemies. I cannot admit that the strategy of the movement is put under discussion at every curve. I am the guarantor of this strategy. I intend to respect the mandate of congress. (Bossi and Vimercati 1992, 89–90)

The Federal Council is, in essence, an instrument of Bossi's power. A former member of the Federal Council, Senator Tabladini, describes the absolute dominance of Bossi in these meetings in the following way: "The term

'Council' might give the wrong impression. Everyone went there to listen to the Secretary [Bossi] who was always mildly angry, who didn't care about any agenda, who would distribute epithets to anyone. [The other members] do not even contradict him because that would be the guillotine, but would nod [like robots] . . . It was in practice a long monologue only interrupted by the ring of his cell phone" (Tabladini 2003, 69).

The creation in 1998 of a new section in the party—the Segretaria Politica (Political Committee)—testifies to the complete sway that Bossi holds over the structure of the party. Bossi appointed its members, and its goal was to provide "support and consultancy for Bossi" (*La Padania*, December 23, 1998). The party paper explained the rationale for this new organ by saying that "the fight of the League relates to many sectors of society and, therefore, it must be conducted, within the intents of Bossi, in an effective way" (*La Padania*, December 23, 1998). This section is typical of the hierarchical and personalized structure of the Northern League. All components of the party ultimately relate to Bossi and follow his personal guidelines. The uniting force is absolute loyalty to the leader.

In an organization that gives complete primacy to the leader and in which personal allegiance to the leader and his mission plays a crucial role, dissent is invariably perceived as an act of personal betrayal and lack of commitment to the cause. Therefore, in the vocabulary of the Northern League, dissension is synonymous with treason. According to Bossi,

> I have had no regrets when I had to get rid of the men who had not respected their commitment. The consensus of the base is the measure of all of my choices . . . They left no trace, neither among the people nor inside the party. They sold a great idea in the pursuit of their personal ambitions. Without them the League is richer . . . It is not a coincidence that those gentlemen end up nowhere or survive in a pathetic way, like the former president of the Chamber of Deputies [Irene Pivetti]. The one who betrays the people is condemned by the people to the most terrible punishment for ambition: oblivion. (Bossi and Vimercati 1998, 107)

Time and again, Bossi warns against the enemy within. Those who leave the League are invariably characterized as agents infiltrated by the League's enemies, whose purpose is to divide and ultimately destroy the group. The need to expunge internal spies is a recurrent theme in Bossi's discourse. As he stated to his followers at a party congress in Varese (in the province where he was born in Lombardy), "There is always someone who, every four years, ends up involved with Rome and clinging to the enemies of the North and of the 'Northern Question.' It's like the Olympics of those who side with the Romans: In 1991 it was Castellazzi, in 1994–95 those who followed Berlusconi; Now [1999] we have the same types, climbers that always side with the wealthy" (*La Padania*, July 26, 1999).

Bossi has repeatedly referred to the expelling of dissidents as a necessary "cleansing" (*La Padania*, July 6, 1999). Dissension is described as if it were a disease that weakens and corrupts the body of the party. During one of these periods of "purification," Bossi said that "it is necessary that the 'fifth columns' internal to our movement crumble; it is necessary to squeeze the pus out of the League" (*La Padania*, July 26, 1999). In the discourse of the Northern League, betrayal is not only always possible, but probable, and this perception maintains the tension and mobilization within the group at high levels. Personal doubt could be the beginning of betrayal. Therefore, any member's qualms regarding the ultimate cause of the group and the abilities of the leader must be put aside. As Bossi stated, "We have to be aware of the resistance that we will find in the decisive battle. To combat until the end we need to know that the greatest enemy is inside us, between ourselves: It is division, doubt regarding the final goal" (Bossi and Vimercati 1998, 180).

So far, I have demonstrated that both the personalized nature of the party and the promotion of a cohesive and compact organization are important ingredients in the consolidation of the leader's missionary leadership. I have shown how these attributes coincide with a polarized view of reality, a sense of imminent catastrophe, and a near deification of the leader, who is regarded and who presents himself as a man of superhuman prescience and political ability. In addition I have shown how internal betrayal and purging of the disloyal is a constant theme in Bossi's discourse. Now I will look at the role of symbolism and ritual in binding the close knit-community of the League.

Political-Religious Symbolism

Rhetoric. Umberto Bossi has always defended the lay nature of his movement. "The League is secular," Bossi stated; "it is perhaps the first Italian political force authentically secular" (1996, 196). As noted by Bossi in an interview, "The Church has always taken a position against us. I don't know why. I'm a layperson, I don't follow these things very closely, but I know that there are priests close to us, to our people who have understood that the process [freedom for Padania] is unstoppable" (*Famiglia Cristiana*, June 11, 1997). Although his party is indeed not a confessional movement, Bossi has repeatedly used Christian images to describe the threats to his community and has adopted a good-versus-evil backdrop for his denunciation, for example, of globalization. The final goal of his vanguard should be to vanquish evil.

In Bossi's eschatology a gigantic final battle is going on in the world. Either a new era of freedom and prosperity will arise from this battle, or the outcome will spell the end of democracy, and the end of cultural and ethnic diversity. As noted, Bossi's discourse proclaims the coming epochal confrontation between two different visions of the world that corresponds to a battle between good and evil: "The vision of 'Lucifer,' of the Jacobins and Masons that have worked on finance in order to impose their 'business community,' the power of elites over the citizens, and [the vision] of the League, according to which the economy, like power, must come from [the people] below" (*La Padania*, September 19, 2002). On another occasion Bossi referred to the increasing danger that "materialism, that is, evil, erases the spiritual dimension of Man. The confrontation that has taken place today concerns, closely, Christianity" (*La Stampa*, October 19, 1999). "The struggle pits local Identity against the evil empire that is globalization. If we take action soon, evil can be stopped immediately," Bossi said in an interview (*La Padania*, November 14, 1999).

Ritual. In order to legitimate the strategy of renunciation and redemption of the world that is the basis of the movement, the Northern League has provided its supporters with a vision of an alternative world. Specifically, it has provided them with a new collective identity that defines the peoples of the North of Italy as a specific historical group united by shared traditions and values. Ritual has at all times been an essential facet of the symbolic construction of this alternative world by the Northern League. These repetitive and standardized actions have had the purpose of reinforcing the solidarity within the group while at the same time augmenting the emotional investment in Umberto Bossi as the standard-bearer of the mission. Among the mass events organized by the Northern League, two occupy a central place in this process: the annual rally, inaugurated in 1990 at Pontida (in the province of Bergamo, Lombardy), where in April 1167 the communes of the North vowed to resist Emperor Barbarossa; and the annual rally in Venice, where the Padani celebrate the independence of Padania, announced by Bossi in 1996.

These annual rallies sacralize both the ultimate goal of the Northern League—freedom for Padania—and the members' allegiance and commitment to the mission. The first great manifestation in Pontida was convened in 1990, where newly elected members of the party swore loyalty to the movement. From that moment on, as is written in one of the party biographies, "nothing must distract them from the task that . . . has been given to them: That is, to be the loyal tools of the Lombard League in the fight for Lombardy" (Fassini 1998, 48). The text of the oath, which was aimed at establishing a parallel between the oath taken by the defenders of the region in the twelfth century and its contemporary defenders, declared:

> Today in Pontida, our commitment is bound to the sacrifices of our ancestors who chose this place to swear their commitment to the defense of freedom. I, who have decided to join in the lists of *Lega Lombarda–Lega Nord* to become an active standard-bearer in the fight for the autonomy of the people from Lombardy, Veneto, Piemontese, Ligure, Emiliano, Romagnolo and Toscano, unite my oath with that of our ancestors. **I swear loyalty to the cause of the autonomy and freedom of our peoples, which today,** as it was a thousand years ago, is incarnated in the *Lega Lombarda* and its democratically elected officials." (*Lega Nord* 1988–95, 9; bold in original)

The party paper at the time, *Lombardia Autonomista*, announced that "an oath, a big Lombard party, 8,000 militants of the Lombard League celebrating in Pontida. Sunday, May 20, 1990, will remain a historical day for our movement and for Lombardy." It added, "After 800 years, History with a capital 'H' repeats itself, notwithstanding those who say that history has ended" (*Lombardia Autonomista*, May 1990). This claim of Pontida's sacred aura has continued in the imagination of the Northern League. Within this narrative, Pontida stands for uncompromising loyalty and devotion to the all-consuming, sacred mission of liberating Padania from oppressive forces. Referring to the 1990 oath, the party daily *La Padania* observed that "[in] this way a long story of loyalty was initiated, [the oath] has been repeated for thirteen years . . . the unstoppable history of a movement that has unhinged the apparently immutable rules of old politics" (*La Padania*, April 30, 2003).

The high point of the annual rallies in Pontida is a solemn speech by Umberto Bossi. In these speeches, Bossi announces the steps that the movement must take in order to fulfill its mission. As ritual events, these speeches have a standard form. Bossi explains, in an instructive manner, the realities facing Italy and the world, and then unveils the path forward for the movement. He announces new decisions and asks for the approval of the people, which is invariably given. This rite of the legitimation of Bossi as the guide for the group happens every year at what *La Padania* calls the "Sacred Ground of Pontida" (*La Padania*, May 15, 2004), where Bossi plays the role of the prophet who interprets the present and points the way toward the future. The group expects the leader to play this role. As written in *La Padania*,

> Every time that Bossi calls for the gathering of the men and women of the North in Pontida, a new page of political history is opened. We go to Pontida to understand what will happen in Rome, to reason about politics, because change comes from the North. It was like that also in April 7, 1167, when men who wanted to be the masters of their houses again subscribed to a pact of loyalty against Barbarossa, in the same Pontida of the historical abbey . . . The present and the future of this redemption from centralism continues to come from the meadow of Pontida with the words of Bossi to accelerate the reforms. (*La Padania*, April 29, 2003)

The following excerpt by Gigi Moncalvo epitomizes the trust in Bossi as the guide who, in Pontida, sheds light on the path to the future. According to Moncalvo,

5. In Pontida, standing before a large banner depicting the medieval warrior Alberto da Giussano, symbol of the party, Umberto Bossi addresses his followers, May 4, 2003. Courtesy of *La Padania*.

> We are ready one more time to follow the battles, the indications, the political line outlined by Bossi. And today in Pontida the people of the League will show [that] to everyone, one more time . . . We believe, [we] think, and know that Bossi has all the elements to know what to do and how to do it. And today, [Bossi] first on the stage and then in the middle of the crowd, looking in the eyes [of] the People of Pontida, the flags, the faces, the smiles of our militants, seeing that unique spectacle in the world and listening to the cry that comes from Pontida—the "Freedom for Padania" from thousands of people—our secretary will have one more element, important and emotional, democratic and binding, to establish what are the most just decisions, the path in which we'll walk, the ways to get closer to the final goal. The road is still long, it's not easy . . . Bossi knows all of this very well. (*La Padania*, May 4, 2003)

Pontida symbolizes the periodic renewal of trust between the leader and his followers. It is also the place where the leader goes every time he wants to test the loyalty of the group toward him. After the disappointing results in the European election of 1999, which risked undermining Bossi's leadership, he announced that he would submit his resignation as federal secretary at a rally in Pontida. There the followers of the Northern League would have to vote for or against Bossi's continuation as head of the movement. "I put myself at stake," declared Bossi, "for a cultural revolution, to wake up the conscience of the people of the North from its dormant state" (*La Padania*, June 17, 1999). Bossi wanted to make sure that the militants were firmly behind him. What followed was a collective and public testament of loyalty from all sectors of the party, from longtime officials to simple militants. The president of the Northern League, Stefano Stefani, made it clear that "although we can discuss many things, only one thing is not in discussion: the irreplaceable nature of Umberto Bossi as the guide of the Northern League" (*La Padania*, June 19, 1999).

The "Letters to the Editor" section of *La Padania* was swamped with emotional comments from its readers about Bossi's intention to resign. These letters, in which the leader was overwhelmingly referred to by first name, exude both personal devotion and a sense of intimate connection to him. Here are a few examples:

> Dear Umberto . . . Non si Lasciare! [Do not leave us!]
>
> Umberto, you have made us dream. You are always in our hearts as our unique guide, polar star of the north!
>
> Umberto, wake up from the nightmare . . . if you resign, "they" have won.
>
> Umberto, without you there is neither Padania, nor future . . . Do not abandon us, otherwise we will all leave.
>
> Umberto, please, don't give in.
>
> Dear Umberto, we are disturbed by your declaration. You cannot abandon your people! Without you there is no future for us.
>
> Dear Umberto, you cannot leave us now, you cannot abandon your children . . . I'll be in Pontida . . . to yell out loud how much all of us love you.
>
> I'm telling you: without you never, *you are* the League and we are your extension. (*La Padania*, June 16–22, 1999)

In Pontida, the commitment of the followers to their leader was reinforced, and the militants voted overwhelmingly for Bossi to stay on. Under the suggestive headline "Il nostro Condottiero non si tocca" (No one touches our leader), *La Padania* asserted that "[t]he battle of the League begins anew. It will one more time be guided by Bossi" (*La Padania*, June 22, 1999). The loyalty of the followers to Bossi had been tested in the sacred place of Pontida, and they had passed the test. The leader remained, with increased legitimacy, as the guide of the vanguard.

Another major symbolic event for the Northern League is the annual rally in Venice. In September 1996, in solemn ceremony, Bossi took water from the source of the Po River and initiated a pilgrimage that took him and his entourage to Venice, where the water from the Po River was poured by a nine-year-old girl, symbolizing the new republic, into the city's lagoon. The pouring of water was described by the party organ as "an act of purification" indicating the "refusal of subordination to Rome" by the peoples of Padania (*Lega Nord–Padania Indipendente*, September 16, 1996). This ceremony was intended to symbolize the birth of Padania, and constituted a crucial moment in three days of rallies of the militants and sympathizers of the Northern League, from the source of the river in Monviso to Venice. During this period an oath was taken for the "Declaration of Independence and Sovereignty of Padania." It read,

> We, the people of Padania, assembled in the great Po River . . . From immemorial times we have lived, worked, protected and loved these lands, passed on to us by our ancestors . . . Here we have developed an original way of life, of developing the arts and work. We belong to a historical area, the Padania, that is strongly integrated internally under [the same] socio-economic profile . . . We constitute a national, cultural, and socio-economic community founded on a shared patrimony of values, culture, and history and on homogeneous social, moral, and economic conditions . . . The History of the Italian State, instead, is a history of colonial oppression, of economic exploitation and moral violence. Over time, through its bureaucracy, the Italian State has systematically occupied the social and economic system of Padania . . . These are the reasons why: We firmly believe that the continuation of Padania under the Italian State would mean that any hope of rebirth would die out [and] we firmly believe that a free and independent Padania will become a political and institutional reference for the construction of the Europe of regions and Europe of peoples . . . We, people of Padania; because the courage and the faith of those who fought for the freedom of peoples are our inspiration and must lead us to take our own destiny . . . In the name and with the authority that comes from the Natural Right for self-determination into our hands . . . We, peoples of Padania solemnly proclaim: The Padania is a federal republic, independent and sovereign. (*Lega Nord* 1996–98, 12–14)

During this historical episode, described as a "sacred moment" (*Lega Nord–Padania Indipendente*, July 29, 1996), the Northern League publicly proclaimed a provisional constitution and a "Bill of Rights of the Citizens of Padania" (*Lega Nord* 1996–98, 14–16).

Every year the rite commonly known as the "Ceremony of the Water" is reenacted in Venice. As in Pontida, the mass rally culminates with a solemn speech by Umberto Bossi. Like that at Pontida, this ritual serves as a symbolic representation of the group's sacred mission, and a representation of freedom for Padania. The League's position in Italy's political landscape has not affected the celebration of the ritual. "Yesterday a journalist asked me why the League is still pouring water of the Po River in the lagoon of Venice now that we are heading toward governing," Bossi said at one of the rallies in Venice. "'Isn't that a symbol of secession?' [she asked]. I told her that it is much bigger than that—It is the symbol of our identity" (*La Padania,* September 20, 2001). In the party literature this event is characterized as "the birth of Padania" (*La Padania,* April 29, 2003). It is to such "sacred" places that the leader makes significant return trips during setbacks or periods of reflection on the direction or the future of the party. In September 2006—in the year where the party's coalition lost the national elections, and a party-backed referendum on constitutional change to advance regional autonomy was rejected by the general public—Bossi led the Ceremony of the Water and held a typical missionizing speech in which he declared that the path to freedom and the "end of slavery" required only a united and mobilized people, with the leader vowing to stay with them "until the end" (*Il Corriere della Sera,* September 18, 2006; *Lega Nord* 2006a).

The rituals of Pontida and Venice both serve to consolidate the alternative world promoted by the Northern League. Alongside these two major mass rallies, the party regularly organizes rallies, conventions, conferences, and "Padania Days" in different parts of the North (see, for example, *La Padania,* January 16, 2000). The creation of specific "Padania" groups and associations is part of this strategy of cementing the image of Padania in the rank and file's collective imagination. It has created such organizations as a special security guard called Guardia Nazionale Padana (Padania National Guard), Sport Padano (Padania Sports), Movimento Giovani Padani (Padania Youth), Donne Padane (Padania Women), Cattolici Padani (Padania Catholics), and Scuola Padana (Padania School). Each gathering of the "people of Padania," whether in Pontida or Venice, spawns an atmosphere that resembles a festival, with a playful dimension constituted by organized games and musical events. At the same time, all associations close to the movement make themselves visible at their own stands. In the words of one of the organizers,

> Everything in Pontida emanates history and myth. Emanates autonomy from central powers, in the past from Germany, in the present from Rome. The meeting in Pontida is also a true festival, like the one in Lorien. There are 300 to 400 stands of associations, movements, groups. They sell everything: stamps, bumper stickers, craftsmanship. There are the motorcyclists, truck drivers, fishermen, linguistic and cultural associations, [people] play[ing] the *baghet* (Lombard bagpipe). Every nation of Padania has its stand, with their own typical products to drink and eat [and] the night before [the end of the rally], we, the Padania Youth have our own meeting, we play Celtic or Irish music, and [we] have our own groups who speak in our local languages. (Paolo Grimoldi, e-mail interview, May 24, 2004)

At the same time the party has launched such annual beauty contests as "Miss Padania," "Miss 'Green Shirt,'" and "Miss Sun of the Alps." Bossi always attends these contests (see, for example, *La Repubblica,* April 2, 2004).

The intense symbolic production of the Northern League can also be seen in the adoption of the *Sole delle Alpi* (Sun of the Alps)—a green, six-rayed Celtic symbol—as the logo of the party, and in the chromatic adoption of green as the color of the movement. These are all part of the attempt to reinforce the alternative history of the Padani. In the choreography of the party's congresses and rallies, the color green is dominant. An article in *La Padania* refers to green as "our totemic color," and adds that, because of the Northern League, "the Green Sun of recovery and awakening shines in the North" (*La Padania,* February 13, 2000). Bossi often dresses in green because, "in order to succeed in persuading the others, we have to give visible examples. We have, and I have already decided personally, to wear green shirts more often" (1997).

The development of its own media network, including Telepadania (Padania Television), Radio Padania Libera (Radio Padania Free), *La Padania* (*Padania,* a daily newspaper), and a website, serves as a way of strengthening the identity of the group by releasing information and programs that are free from the perceived bias of the regime. The following description by Stefania Piazzo of the role played by the party periodicals testifies to the importance that the party gives to their media: "*Lega Nord* [party weekly] is and remains our pride ... because it has carried the ideas that have raise[d] from the earth a people who dozed, almost resigned; it has sowed the conscience of an identity" (*Lega Nord–Padania Indipendiente,* December 9, 1996). Every rally of the Northern League culminates with the playing of the piece "Va Pensiero," from Giuseppe Verdi's opera *Nabucco,* which was adopted as the "national anthem" of the Northern League (*Lega Nord* 1996–98, 14).

A Moral Community. This ongoing construction of a symbolic reality increases in the followers the perception of the Northern League's exceptional nature, and expands their own self-perception of being a unique community integrated by an alternative set of historical roots and values. An official of the Northern League observed that "some commentators, showing all their ignorance and materialism, speak in a superficial way or ridicule our celebration [and] despise what they don't know, what they don't feel to be 'their thing,' because they are strangers to popular culture." He added, "We instead are proud of this day in Monviso [the Ceremony of the Water], because behind those peaks we celebrate an important appointment to recover the identity of the north" (*La Padania,* September 11, 1998). "One who has never been in this meeting of the people [Pontida]," emphasized a *La Padania* editorial, "does not know what its meaning is" (*La Padania,* June 15, 1999).

In the alternative world created by the Northern League, gatherings of the party are interpreted not as mere political meetings but as a testimony of faith in the members' collective mission. In the words of a movement official, "Pontida remains the party [as in "festival"] of the League, which a militant, a Padani, a supporter cannot in any way miss. Beyond anything else Pontida is a pilgrimage that must be accomplished at least once a year" (*La Padania,* June 20, 2002). The federal coordinator of Padania Youth expresses a similar sense of destiny about the community assembled in Pontida as follows: "It is amazing how a political movement manages to bring together thousands of people in the name of our identity, and to take an oath about the freedom of our peoples. Sometimes we don't think about it, we are used to it; but if we reflect we become aware of the importance of the event. This is the sign that our movement is a movement destined to change the history of the country" (*La Padania,* June 19, 2002).

The militants, those who have undergone the path of integration into the alternative world of the party, are a community of true believers united in their sense of collective mission and profoundly devoted to the leader. A former official of the Northern League, Francesco Tabladini, sees in the pool of voters for the Northern League two kinds of people. In his words,

> In practice, the crowd that flocks to our meetings is always the same: It grows or diminishes according to the appeal of the demonstration, but we are always talking about tens of thousands. To make a practical example of the voters of the League, it is necessary to imagine two containers of different proportions that have scarce connections between them, if any. In the smaller one are the *"movimentisti"* [activists]; they are those who go to Pontida, to Venice, to [the river] Po and wherever Bossi calls them. This container augments and diminishes in negligible ways . . . they seem many and in reality they are many, but they are always the same ones. Then there is the other container, with bigger capacity, that determines the electoral results without making noise. They don't go to Pontida or Venice . . . this is the container that was filled in April 1996, and that now is emptying inexorably. (Tabladini 2003, 121)[7]

The attachment of the militants toward the leader is of a different nature than that of the attachment of the general voter. The leader puts forward an account that encourages the inner core to see itself as a community of belief. Bossi repeatedly stresses the emotional values uniting those who belong to this community. In the discourse of Bossi, the Northern League is a community bonded by *love*. In his own words,

---

7. There has always been a tension within the Northern League between the activist and the more moderate forces. In 1998, writing in *Quaderni Padani*, Brenno lamented the "unresolved ambiguity" between "the League of struggle and the League of government, that is, between those who want the independence of Padania and those who are satisfied with governing [Padania] only slightly better than previous [governments]" (*Quaderni Padani*, May–June 1998). Bossi has tried to bridge the gap between these two dimensions of his movements and in a 1998 "letter to the militants" warned that the party members "must understand that the [Northern League] official who is close to the institutions is not a traitor but a brother who is trying to find a better position [to fight for Padania]" (1998b). Bossi has made similar statements regularly, particularly when the League enters into coalition governments. On the tension between the League as a social movement and an "institutional actor," see, for example, Ruzza 2005, 65–84.

I say often that the League is like a baby; it is the result of love. I am convinced that this movement is the result of the generous work of thousands of men and women who feel strongly toward each other, who feel strong about the city they live in, about the nation that they belong to. The baby has grown, has started to walk with its legs. But there's still work to do so that it becomes an adult and fulfils its ambitions. (Bossi and Vimercati 1992, 92)

"Our patriotism is the love for our Padania," posited Bossi in one of the League's congresses, "the love for our peoples, who have united their forces to fight the beautiful battle of Freedom" (*La Padania*, March 29, 1998). "To love something means to hug it, not to repel it," said Bossi regarding those who "sold" the ideals of the League for their own self-interest, "Padania is really the only thing that we have" (1998d). According to Bossi, "Our love, dear Padania, brought you back to life. Not as an ordinary country but as our Fatherland" (*La Padania*, January 27, 2004).

In the narrative of the leader of the Northern League, there is an investment of *faith* at the very basis of the movement. This faith-based nature of the League's politics is a recurrent theme. A messianic certitude about the success of the movement can be seen in the following words of Bossi:

Without faith it is not possible to make politics, and my faith is the certainty that the good right of the North to be free sooner or later will prevail over Roman colonialism. I have never doubted, since the League was formed by just a few militants, that in the end we will be free of Rome. I have always thought that if [the goal] wasn't reached by my generation and me it would be reached by my children and, after them, the children of my children. (1999, 95)

Addressing the League's parliamentarians, Bossi stated that "any one of you, perhaps without a total understanding but with the strength of faith, of that faith that moves mountains, has done your part in this grand design (*La Padania*, July 14, 1998). "The master of the League is the people," announced Bossi at a rally in Pontida, "the people who are looked after by the faith of Pontida: a civil and lay faith in the common good of freedom" (*La Padania*, May 1, 2003). Time and again, in order to keep the levels of mobilization of the militancy high, Bossi warns against the dangers of the weakening of faith. At one of these moments he said,

> We can say that it is a problem of conscience that sometimes can weaken, [a problem of] weak faith, we can say. And weak faith leads to a reduced willingness to sacrifice. And without faith, as we know it, the faith that moves mountains, without [faith] Padania cannot appear. This you all know, I'm certain; [without faith] we cannot do anything other than settle and go for careers, [materialistic] things . . . and God forbid that this kind of people would [belong to our movement]. (1998c)

Faith sets the militants apart from ordinary people and gives them strength in moments of doubt regarding the project. "The lack of faith is unbearable," declared Bossi at a congress in the city of Brescia in Lombardy. "Do not despair, because it is despair that destroys the world, because it is easier to dominate those who do not believe in anything" (1998d).

In Bossi's discourse, the Northern League's political action is always framed in terms of an *ideal*. For him, the rise of the League brought with it the return of ideals to political life. "[The other parties] didn't understand that the League was winning because the materialistic philosophy that had won in the post-war was in crisis and that new idealist horizons were being opened . . . they didn't understand that the League was somewhere else. It was impossible to damage it because it belonged to another world [the world] of the great ideals" (1996, 56).

"Federalism, [and] freedom," declared Bossi at a Pontida rally, "are like oxygen for us. They are a dream: Either we'll achieve it or we'll die because of it. They are great ideals, great love" (*La Padania,* May 6, 2003.) As Bossi warned at a rally in Venice, the battle for federalism would be a "very tough battle. But we from the League are not soldiers of fortune. We are not mercenaries. We are idealists ready for any clash" (2002). In the narrative of Bossi the word *dream* is interchangeable with the ultimate ideal goal of the group. In his words, "The base [of militants] is strongly characterized by the [power of] dream, and by dream we mean the tension toward the transformation of society, a dream that is worthwhile to fight for, which in our case is the freedom of the Padani peoples. There cannot be a lack of dream otherwise we would lose the base of the party, and a party without a base cannot achieve any change" (*La Padania*, August 5, 1998).

Bossi's language is purposefully belligerent, and in the continuing battle for the concretization of the project Bossi puts a high premium on *courage*. "The League is a force of courage," he said to his militants. "We can confront any adversity" (1998c). As he stated in a speech, "Courage is the first great gift that the League has brought to the Italians. The courage to confront the corrupt and to remember the roots of our own history" (1996, 202–3). The *sacrifice* of the militancy is an imperative in order to fulfill the collective mission of the group. "The hope of the peoples is a shining aurora but the dawn is still far away," said Bossi. "The battle will be long and difficult" (Bossi and Vimercati 1992, 85).

In the narrative of the leader there is an all-consuming sense of mission that binds the group together and transforms it into a pious community. "Until we reach our goal," declared Bossi, "any man of the League must have only one concern: to work toward a politics aimed at the transformation of Italy in a federal State. One goal to be achieved no matter what the cost" (1995, 176). All suffering and sacrifices can be endured by the community because they are part of a wider story, a wider order that offers an ultimate goal that lies in the future. As long as there is a final goal that offers salvation, suffering can and should be endured by hard-core believers in the Northern League. The militants see themselves as a righteous community of people bound by the same idealist fervor for, commitment to, and belief in the justice and goodness of the mission. "The militant [from the Northern League] has not only a political idea, but almost a faith," notes Matteo Salvini, official of the Northern League and director of Radio Padania. "[The militant] does not have an ideology but has absolute confidence in Bossi and in the idea of federalism and freedom of the North, which makes him dedicate hours and days, voluntarily, to political activities and more" (Salvini, e-mail interview, July 6, 2004). Viviana, a member of Padania Youth, sees in the "belief in an ideal, the Padania" the reason why the militants of the Northern League are fundamentally different from all other militants. "The initiatives of the Northern League are carried out by the militants because they believe in them and not because they are being paid as happens in other political parties" (Viviana, e-mail interview, June 15, 2004).

The following words of the provincial secretary of Como testify to this deep-rooted self-perception of the uniqueness of the members of the community:

> The first requisite of a militant is the faith in the ideal that, supported by enthusiasm and courage, can surmount and overwhelm any obstacle and fear . . . From the iron discipline of courage arises the free civic consciousness and the moral sense from which originate the balance, coherence and finally the strength to carry out a great mission . . . *like the soldier who faces the extreme sacrifice—and wins the "saintly battle"—after the captain reminds him of the suffering endured, the courage showed and the recompense of the supreme redemption: it is like that for the true militant who gives everything and does not asks for anything else than to serve the just cause* . . . The League has always known how awaken the courage, the enthusiasm, the brotherly union, and the faith in the ideal that have shaped the only real Militant: our Militant. (*La Padania,* January 10, 2001 [emphasis mine])

The messianic character of the vanguard may be seen in the way a parliamentarian, Simonetta Faverio, described the *ultimate goodness* of the Northern League. According to her,

> We have believed and still believe that the citizens have the right and the duty of making history by writing a new pact between themselves. *We are those who think we have ideas to offer not only to Italy but also to all men.* We are those who have renounced the small tricks and conveniences of the usual habit of compromise [in order] to think big and, like poets, we have constructed our model of the world, our model of social cohabitation. We try to impose the idea that we love, as do honest and defenseless people: working hard to persuade others of the goodness of our project. We know that the one who claims its dignity and wants to change things will have a difficult life and many cruel enemies. (*La Padania,* September 23, 1998 [emphasis mine])

Given this redemptionist message, it is not surprising that the community interprets dissension as a moral failure. The dissenter did not live up to the high standard of the group. "The men of the League," noted Bossi at a rally in Pontida, "have the moral, rather than political, duty to remain compact and deaf to the sirens of the regime" (1991b). As declared by

Bossi, "Betrayals—because *they are* betrayals—sadden me, but they don't surprise me. I know very well that men easily give up to temptation" (Bossi and Vimercati 1992, 85).

Periods of difficulty are seen as tests of the loyalty of the individual to the community. The following words of one of the provincial secretaries of the Northern League reveal the elitist high-mindedness of the group. In his view, "The moments of crisis in such profoundly idealistic movements as the Northern League for the independence of Padania, also have positive aspects; in fact they test the loyalty and the ideal *[sic]* of the men, causing a beneficial 'natural selection' that keeps away the rotten apples, the opportunists" (*La Padania,* July 9, 1999).

Evidently recruitment into the community is not an ordinary process based on simple persuasion. It is a process based on the conversion of others to an all-consuming project. Ordinary political parties demand a minimum participation from their supporters; at best theirs is a partial involvement. The Northern League, however, demands maximum participation, and the involvement required is total. A writer close to the party complained that "its activists are subject to an excess of activism: A day does not go by without being called to a manifestation, [whether it is] collecting signatures, joining an association, attending a course, show or conference" (*Quaderni Padani,* May–June 1998, 3). The demanding nature of Northern League militancy can be seen in the following words of longtime official Gilberto Oneto:

> In order to strengthen its tactical maneuvers (whatever they might be) the Federal Secretary needs to have obedient people, [needs] a disciplined troop, of militants of a movement, not of a party . . . our militants must not distract themselves with sordid games of power but [they] must convince, convert, and create consensus. Every militant must be a propagandist, a preacher, an enlister: Like a small seed [the militant] must concentrate in itself all the genes of the big tree of freedom . . . when a commander of an army brings his men to battle, he needs obedient soldiers who hate the enemy (and even some of the momentary allies). (*La Padania,* January 9, 2000)

Referring to the recruitment of others to join the Northern League, Bossi declared, "I trust, my Padani brothers [that] all of us must commit ourselves in a true work of evangelization" (1997). This evangelical call is typical of a close-knit community that seeks expansion through *conversion*. In this process of evangelization, from the League's inception Bossi set the example. He is the itinerant preacher going from town to town to spread the gospel of the League. Bossi has always encouraged regular rallies, which he personally attends. "I like to be in the middle of the crowd," he says, "those simple meetings with my people, with the children who ask for autographs and want to take a picture with me. I'm not divine, mind you. But in me the people see a hope, the dream of change. I'm happy if they love me, because in reality they love the idea that I represent. As long as the people are with me, I will have the strength to fight the mafia of Rome" (Bossi and Vimercati 1992, 67).

In fact this regular presence of Bossi in the middle of "his people" is a crucial driving force in the development of dynamics of personal devotion between the leader and the followers. "Umberto Bossi is charismatic," notes Filippo Pozzi, "because first of all he does not spare efforts in the work for the freedom of Padania." "As a consequence," Pozzi added, "he is the first to give the example to his militants and to the people of Padania" (e-mail interview, May 13, 2004). In an interview, the federal coordinator of Padania Youth, Paolo Grimoldi, referred to these ceaseless personal contacts between Bossi and the militants as a crucial feature of the leader's charisma. According to Grimoldi,

> The militants love him because after every rally he spends hours and hours giving autographs, taking photos, speaking with every single voter or any bystander who walks by him. Two hours after the rally, and after being two hours in the middle of the people, he finally goes eating with the militants of the place, and entertains himself speaking about politics, the structure of the party, and even frivolities with all the militants of the province. I have to tell you that he is very friendly, and loves speaking about everything. Around four A.M. he goes back home, sometimes with hours of trip in front of him . . . Almost every night he is in a different corner of Padania at rallies: He doesn't go only to big cities, but [to] even the small and very small villages. (Grimoldi, e-mail interview, April 14, 2004)

A similar view is expressed by Matteo Salvini:

> Umberto Bossi does politics, in the middle of the people, for a long time, touring markets, cities, festivals, dining until the early hours of the day side

by side with the young and the elderly. I don't know any other leader, men, not to mention ministers, who stay up until three A.M. talking about what goes on in Rome with people who until that moment were perfect strangers . . . Because of this, I think that between Bossi and "his people" there is a unique relationship, formed during years after years of personal relations and not invented by the television. (Salvini, e-mail interview, July 6, 2004)

Along with making a physical connection to his followers, Bossi's regular presence in the midst of the people testifies to his personal commitment and sacrifice to the community. In the eyes of his followers he personifies the all-encompassing mission that he demands of all members of the vanguard. This aspect of Bossi's leadership is emphasized in the literature of the party. As written in *La Padania,*

Two and a half million kilometers. This is [the number of kilometers] traveled by Bossi since he started in politics. And they keep increasing because even in these days the word "vacation" does not belong to his vocabulary; the agenda of the secretary of the Northern League is full of appointments all over the four corners of Padania. Conventions, meetings, but mostly rallies at the festivals of the Carroccio [Northern League]. (*La Padania,* August 1, 2002)

In this manner the leader sets the standard for militancy within the Northern League.

Charisma. As I have shown, within the narrative and imagination of the Northern League, Umberto Bossi is a salvationist leader who has through the years developed a charismatic missionary aura. He presents himself, and is perceived by the vanguard, as the messianic leader of a mission of redemption. His level of charisma is more deeply rooted than the more common and superficial "popular" level. It is intimately linked with an enclave mentality that Bossi has been able to inculcate within his militants. Although the general electoral support for the Northern League has dwindled in recent years, the devotional support of the core militancy has remained stable. No matter what the tactical changes are, they follow Bossi's guidance. This chapter has focused exclusively on his charismatic missionary relationship with this core militancy. In order to remain at a high level, this type of charisma demands constant work to maintain and preserve. The work of what I have called the "Bossi industry," coupled with the constant ritualization of the movement, has played and continues to play a fundamental role in keeping the loyalty of the core of militants, who remain devoted to their leader despite any setbacks or changes in party policy.

The Succession of the Charismatic Leader

Succession, as Weber noted, is always the test of the strength of a charismatic organization, which, by definition, relies on the personality of its leader for its cohesion. The Northern League is no exception. For a long time Bossi (born in 1941) had never anointed a successor, although after being reelected by acclamation as federal secretary in the 2002 Federal Congress of the Northern League, Bossi expressed his desire to step down as a leader after the mandate. In March 2004, he suffered a heart attack followed by a series of strokes and remained in drug-induced coma for a considerable period (*La Repubblica,* March 11, 2004). The reaction of the militants and officials of the party to Bossi's absence represents one more testimony to Bossi's absolute centrality for the community of men and women that he has led for the last two decades. The Group Catholics of Padania organized a prayer session in the abbey of Pontida, where the militants prayed for the recovery of the "Capo" (*La Padania,* March 14, 2004).

All of the officials of the party professed their allegiance to the absent leader. Giampaolo Gobbo, a Northern League member of the European Parliament, declared at a rally that Bossi was an all-but-impossible leader to follow, and declared, "We must only follow his teaching." He added, "There are no triumvirates or quadriumvirates: After Bossi there is only Bossi" (*La Stampa,* March 13, 2004). Significantly, Bossi's health problems were interpreted as the direct consequence of his total and unconditional commitment to the Northern League. As written by Gigi Moncalvo, Bossi uses "his own energy and power not for himself but for the idealistic battle in which he believes," because "he only looks at the good of the League [and] never his own good, even putting at risk his own health as recent events showed" (*La Padania,* May 30, 2004). In an open letter to Bossi, longtime Northern League official Stefano Stefani said,

Not even the strongest of men is able to make tens of rallies in a month, which last hour after hour, and which only end after you spend even more hours in the middle of the militants until late night. You put up with kilometers after kilometers crossing Italy in order to be always in contact with the people, with your people . . . I'll tell you another thing, one more time: You cannot, after tiring hours of work in the parliament, stay up at night working and writing . . . even the strongest of men is not, unfortunately, indestructible. Come back soon to us because, as everybody knows, you are the League." (*La Padania,* March 12, 2004)

The reaction of the rank and file to the problems of the leader offers a powerful example of their emotional attachment to the leader. Here are a few examples taken from the party daily:

Good Easter *condottiere,* who lays in the bed of an hospital, there is no one like you in the confines of Italy, like Christ who resuscitated from the sepulcher, you, reinvigorated, will guide us in the fight against all the troubles spread among us by Islam.

You will manage to win this tough battle and you will come back stronger to guide us towards the Freedom of Yours [sic] and Ours [sic] Padania.

Get well soon our great condottiere to guide us toward Padania, free at last. (La Padania, March 12–April 11, 2004)

One of the readers of *La Padania* compared Bossi to a "Gandhi who for years has enlightened our common path" (*La Padania,* October 5, 2004).

At the same time, and as a strong indication of the authority of the messianic figure of Bossi, Northern League officials promised to follow scrupulously the guidelines of the movement that Bossi traced before he fell ill. Roberto Castelli, Northern League minister of justice, observed that Bossi had "as usual . . . established the course for the movement among very precise coordinates [and that] all we have to do is to follow coherently those coordinates in the expectation of his return" (*La Padania,* March 28, 2004). Senator Calderoli even noted that Bossi would be proud of the performance of the officials in his absence: "[Bossi] has always warned us about some of the surprises and traps that might come from some allies, he has prepared us . . . he has delineated different scenarios. I have to say that when he returns, he will be satisfied with the degree of maturity of the executive class of the League" (*La Padania*, April 2, 2004). Although doubts about his full recovery remained, Bossi was placed at the top of the Northern League slate for the European Parliamentary elections of June 2004 (*La Repubblica*, May 1, 2004). After these elections, because of his ailing health, Bossi resigned as minister of reforms and assumed the seat he won in the European Parliament; he was replaced by another League official, Roberto Calderoli. It is noteworthy that, during his health-related absence, Bossi maintained contacts with his followers: Although physically impaired, he addressed meetings of *leghisti* through phone calls that invariably met an emotional response from the audience (*La Stampa*, August 2, 2004). Further, the party gave the followers the leader's address in order to promote an epistolary relationship between Bossi and his militants. The leader even managed to return to Pontida and address his followers, after being given this introduction upon arrival: "Since that dramatic day, which the people of Padania experienced with fear and hope, anxiety and prayers, we have waited for him for more than a year. He is our guide, our hope of freedom, our hero, our leader, our federal secretary, [he is] the man who descends from Alberto da Giussano and who is awakening the pride of the people of Padania" (*La Padania*, June 22, 2005).

In an atmosphere in which, as reported by the party newspaper, "everyone has tears in their eyes," silence fell in anticipation of Bossi's arrival. "The almost unreal silence of the city of the Oath became jubilee, party, screams, applause, and commotion." As the League journalist joyfully announced, "the link that unites Bossi to his people is reestablished." From the stage, the one described by the party faithful as "our warrior" saluted his followers by proclaiming that "this [Pontida and the followers] is my story" (*La Padania*, June 22, 2005). In an interview the leader of the Northern League acknowledged that his health ordeals changed him. "Before, I was like a machine," Bossi recounts. "I could stay [up] without sleeping for a week. I traveled all over Northern Italy, without stopping [and] in election times I used to write the newspaper by myself in two days. I cannot do these things anymore" (*Il Corriere Della Sera*, May 16, 2007). Yet he reassured his followers that he had not mellowed: "I am always a warrior!" (*Gente*, July 12, 2007).

6. On September 17, 2005, after a period of absence owing to heart failure, a frail-looking Umberto Bossi returns to one of the sacred places of the movement. Here he observes one of its rituals by holding a flask of water that he took from the source of the Po River in Crissolo, northern Italy. Photograph by Luca Bruno, courtesy of AP Images.

Giancarlo Giorgetti declared that the Northern League could survive without Bossi's leadership, though "it would lose its current importance in the political arena. There is no leader charismatic enough who could substitute [for] Bossi in the party" (e-mail interview, May 19, 2004). This episode serves to demonstrate yet again how strong the dependence of the movement is upon Umberto Bossi's charismatic leadership. The fact of the matter is that—especially since his strokes and in typical, charismatic fashion—Bossi began to give a more preeminent role in the party to his sons. At his first rally with his followers since he fell ill, Bossi introduced his son Renzo to his followers.[8] In an interview, Bossi was straightforward about

8. Riccardo, Bossi's eldest son from his first marriage, stated in an interview that he is also in line to succeed his father, despite what the media reported about the leader of the Northern League's presenting Riccardo's half-brother Renzo to the crowd. "I'm very close to my

this gesture: "It was a clear signal about who is coming after me. I don't know when that will happen . . . but my family will remain at the service of the League" (*Il Corriere della Sera,* March 12, 2005). His succession and its consequences, however, remain an open question for the Northern League's future.

THE MISSIONARY MODEL—POLITICS AS SALVATION

In his political life, Umberto Bossi has emphasized his rejection of generalized or state-sponsored salvationist projects for humankind. He has always referred to them as "Jacobin utopias." At their basis is what he sees as immoderate optimism. "It is rooted in ideological or religious utopias," he observed. "The Marxists saw in Communism a lay miracle, the creation of a new man. An obvious excess of optimism as history has demonstrated . . . [The project of] Federalism does not believe in the new man, that utopian idea that often assigns the State the task of imposing a new morality with Stalinist methods" (Bossi and Vimercati 1993, 162–63). For him, those who push globalization suffer from the same utopian "symptom," the imposition of an artificial project that seeks to redefine man's behavior and the structure of societies. Globalists are constantly derided as children of the Enlightenment.

Yet the fact of the matter is that in the discourse of the Northern League, in both its oral and symbolic modes, politics plays a salvationist role. A grand conception of politics has fuelled the action and behavior of the vanguard led by Bossi from the beginning. Politics is the sacred tool through which a new era will be opened in history. As Bossi articulated at a rally in Pontida, "After having created the Northern League, a political movement that merges in itself the autonomous will of the peoples of the North, the epoch of great politics can now be initiated, the epoch in which our Federalist ideal can spread its wings and project itself from our con-

---

father," Riccardo said; "he is a great example for me, a great teacher, I love the League, I love Padania." See *Il Corriere Della Sera,* March 16, 2005. On the dynamics of succession in the Northern League, see also Scaliati 2006, 118–19. Bossi has also raised the possibility of being succeeded in the leadership of the party by his lieutenant Roberto Maroni, "he was born as a politician in the League, and I have a lot of respect for him" (*Gente,* July 12, 2007).

sciences to those of the citizens" (*Lombardia Autonomista*, June 1991). This redemptive function of politics is present throughout the discourse of Bossi. "The League has the honesty and the courage," wrote Bossi in a letter to his militants, "to transform the ideas of the people in projects, politics through the League is indeed the only tool that people have in order to make themselves matter" (*La Padania*, May 5, 2002).

The vanguard is fuelled by the visionary project of transforming society. As stated by Bossi, "The decisive element of the revolution is not violence but the project. That is, the vision of a new order that substitutes [for] the previous one. This distinguishes the revolution from revolt, which lacks any objective" (Bossi and Vimercati 1993, 12–13). Through its radical politics, the League will inaugurate a new chapter in history. As stressed by Bossi in his book *La Rivoluzione* (The Revolution),

> It is a great revolutionary design that is proposed by the League ... It is only necessary to make an inventory of the revolutions of the last three centuries to understand that the federalist revolution is part of it. Rather, in the history of unified Italy [the League] is perhaps the most radical and decisive, because it deals with all aspects of the social, cultural, and economic life. It is not a jest. (Bossi and Vimercati 1993, 11)

Bossi has repeatedly emphasized the life-changing nature of the political project of the Northern League:

> It must be clear to everyone that the League is not a product of power or, even worse, of low politics. The League, on the contrary, not only is a formidable phenomenon of [an] historical nature but is above all a catalyst that has demonstrated itself able to accelerate time. The League can be defined, without emphasis or arrogance as a force of nature. And it has confirmed this, first by disrupting the basis of partitocracy, [and] also by opening a new chapter in history. And this chapter has one name only, the name of the greatest democratic revolution: Its name is Federalism. (2002)

The ultimate model of society for which the Northern League fights extends beyond the borders of Padania, and even of Italy. It has a universal dimension. As declared by Bossi in a speech in Pontida,

> We know that the federalist battle is not a battle for the bell tower, is not a battle for Lombardy, is not even a battle for the North, which has to do only with the north, is not even a battle solely for our country—it is a bigger battle ... Federalism is the road, the fundamental choice, the high-priority [road] for the world to have a future. The one who fights for freedom and justice fights not for a certain type of man, but for all men. Pontida represents the fight of all men for freedom and justice in the world. (*Lombardia Autonomista*, June 1993)

At the very foundation of this conception of politics as a redemptive instrument is a voluntaristic vision of history. The efforts of the loyal vanguard, galvanized by the power of Bossi's vision, can reverse trends and introduce change. Reflecting on the trend toward multiracial societies in the West, Bossi said, "I'm not convinced that this is inevitable ... I think we should rebel against this 'ineluctability'" (Bossi and Vimercati 1992, 148). As he declared at a rally in Venice,

> Some say that it is too late to save our home: Individualism, profitability, the failure of *Risorgimento* have put to death our Padania. Someone told me a few months ago at a rally, "You are right. Unfortunately today we can only lower our hats in front of the death of our land." I told him that we should not resign ourselves, that he had uttered the same sentence with which Nelson Mandela had pushed and lifted South Africa to the conquest of its own dignity and freedom ... after death, life. This is my interpretation. (2003b)

Bossi has put forward a framework in which his vanguard is on a path toward salvation. He repeatedly defines the political activity of his movement as a "long march" (see, for example, *Lombardia Autonomista*, June 1991). In the literature of the Northern League, the various interventions of Bossi over the years in Pontida, the sanctuary of the movement, are described as gradual steps on the long journey toward the "freedom of Padania" (see, for example, *La Padania*, April 30, 2003). In this long march, normal political fights are viewed as if they were harbingers of Armageddon. The community is involved in a never-ending twilight battle with powerful enemies—be they the corrupt centralist forces of Rome, the tyrannical European Union, or the materialistic forces of globalization—hell-bent on its destruction. In Bossi's narrative this apocalyptical battle is gauged on a good-evil spectrum. The moral goodness of Bossi's community is repeatedly emphasized. The vanguard is good, just, and moral. It has taken upon its shoulders the mission of salvation. It is the "natural" defender of the roots, history, and tradition of the North of Italy and, in principle, of the future of humanity. In describing the League's enemies, Bossi commonly uses images of corruption, perversion, obscurity, and subversion of what is natural and "pure."

Bossi's discourse portrays this confrontation as leading inevitably to an either-or final scenario. This has been a recurrent image in Bossi's discourse over the years: "If the League is defeated in Italy, it is the end of its European culture and the victory of the culture of mafia. Federalism is the last stand" (Bossi and Vimercati 1993, 216). "We know that either we succeed and win our grand battle, or the lights of Federalism will be spent for a long time" (2002). Therefore the political fight is incessantly framed in terms of absolutes. The battle of the Northern League against the forces of globalization is described in the same absolute way. For Bossi,

> The Northern League is the sun of the peoples who do not agree to endure the criminal design of the occult powers, those few "illuminati" who want to impose one state, one race, one government, through aberrant tools such as cloning, the rights of adoption to homosexual couples, the destruction of the natural family, and the invasion of immigrants. We stand for what is natural. The Left, the caretakers of the occult powers and of the great international economy, is sided with the artificial. (*La Padania,* September 17, 2000)

Bossi plays the role of the missionary leader of a monolithic community united around a gospel of freedom from those who seek to enslave northern Italy and humanity. No matter what the instructions of the leader may be, no matter what sacrifices he demands for the concretization of the collective mission, the vanguard follows him because it recognizes in him the missionary, charismatic leader with the necessary qualities to save the community.

4
The Missionary Model

A FRAMEWORK OF ANALYSIS

I want in this chapter to illuminate the persistence of political religions in contemporary European democracies and to demonstrate that Le Pen's and Bossi's movements are recent manifestations of sacralized politics. I both identify the different elements of sacredness in Le Pen's and Bossi's respective movements and reveal how this sacralization of politics provides a transcendent framework of meaning for individuals within the movements. This sacred framework, based on a narrative of salvation, myths, and rites, generates and galvanizes group solidarity and institutes a moral community in the Durkheimian sense. Such cultural frames structure the group and sustain the charismatic relationship between leader and followers.

ELEMENTS OF SACREDNESS

A Sacred Nation

A force propelling the respective political religions of the National Front and the Northern League is the deeply felt premise of the "sacrality" of the "nation." Very little of the literature on nationalism focuses specifically on political religion. Among the first historians who have analyzed nationalism's sacred dimension, Carlton J. H. Hayes described nationalism as "essentially a religion of modern secularism" that appealed to man's "religious sense" and offered a "substitute for, or supplement to, historic supernatural religion" (Hayes 1960, 176). In an essay from 1926 Hayes described how, since its advent in Western Europe, nationalism has had the nature of a cult with a dimension of worship including ritual processions, pilgrimages, temples, and a mythology of sacrifice "performed in the name and for the salvation of the whole community" (Hayes 1926, 105). He writes,

> Human beings do not normally and willingly give their lives for economic gain.
> The supreme sacrifice is oftenest paid in behalf of an ideal and in response to the "religious sense". And perhaps the surest proof of the religious character of modern nationalism is the zeal with which all manner of its devotees have laid down their lives on the battlefields of the last hundred years. (Hayes 1926, 114–15)

Historian George L. Mosse further developed the sacred foundations of nationalism identified by Hayes, and integrated them into his study of the "new politics" that emerged after the French revolution. At the very basis of this new politics was the concept of popular sovereignty, which evolved into a truly *secular* religion in which "the people worship[ed] themselves" (Mosse 1975, 1–2). Mosse noted that earlier studies had neglected nationalism's mythic and cultic character: The masses were primarily attached to the nation not as simple, rational, and disembodied actors but as adherents of a secular religion. In an important passage of his *The Nationalization of the Masses* Mosse wrote,

> The unity of the people was not merely cemented by the idea of common citizenship; rather, a newly awakened national consciousness performed this function . . . The nation in the eighteenth century was now said to be based upon the people themselves, [up]on their general will, and was no longer symbolized solely by allegiance to established royal dynasties. The worship of the people thus became the worship of the nation, and the new politics sought to express this unity through the creation of a political style which became, in reality, a secularized religion. (Mosse 1975, 2)

Mosse explored such crucial features of this secularized religion as the use of national myths and sacred spaces, and the development of a liturgy enabling the people themselves to be full participants in such "hours of worship" (1975, 207). Rites, festivals, myths, and symbols objectified the general will and, therefore, cemented the identity of the national community.

In a more recent study that follows Mosse's work, Anthony D. Smith locates in the "sacred foundations" of the nation *both* the primary sources of national attachments *and* a crucial reason for the durability and strength of national identities. Nationalism is "a form of culture and a type of belief-system whose object is the nation conceived as a sacred communion" (A. Smith 2003, 18). This sacred communion is "devoted to the cult of authenticity and the ideals of national autonomy, unity, and identity in a historic homeland" (2003, 254). The belief-systems of nationalisms have drawn on earlier belief-systems associated with "religion," from four particular kinds of cultural resource: "A myth of ethnic *election;* a long-standing attachment to terrains regarded as *sacred;* a yearning to recover and realize the *spirit* of one or more golden ages; a belief in the *regenerative* power of mass and individual sacrifice to ensure a glorious destiny; and the importance of commemorating and celebrating the community and its heroes" (2003, 255). These sacred sources are at the very basis of the devotion and loyalties evoked by the nation:

> Where a given community manifests a clear sense of itself as "chosen" for a task or covenant, where its members are firmly attached to homeland and soil, where they seek to emulate the virtues of past golden ages, and where their members are prepared to make personal sacrifices, if not life, then of time and effort for the future of community and the yet unborn, there we may expect to find a lively sense of national identity, one able to withstand the dangers and temptations of rapid change in a more interdependent world. (A. Smith 2003, 260)

In the context of "rapid change in a more interdependent world," both the National Front and the Northern League foster a deep attachment to a holy nation that is perceived as an original and authentic entity, with peculiar and unique characteristics and features. The nation is not only conceived as an abstract or imagined community but is *worshiped as the objectification and concrete realization of the collective will of the people.* There is a dimension of *feeling* in this attachment to the nation that should not be overlooked: In the dynamic of these movements, the nation is elevated as the authentic repository of the common destiny, territory, and unique virtues of the people, and venerated as sacred. This dimension of the "true nature" of "the nation"—forged during the centuries in a specific territory—expresses the collective will and sets the nation apart from all others. The centrality of this concept of national "authenticity"—as well as the collective emotional force and devotion it spawns—to the internal *cohesion* of these movements cannot be stressed enough. This sense is the wellspring of the sacredness with which the people—with both their dead and their yet unborn "citizens"—become invested and which they recognize in "national" figures, objects, emblems, rites, and places. One should not be surprised at the emotional dimension pervading these movements. At the very heart of the attachment that the sacred communities of France and Padania demand from their respective inhabitants, both Le Pen and Bossi put forth the idea of *filiation*, of a personal relationship grounded in and authenticated by the love that a *true* Frenchperson or Padano must invariably feel for "his or her" nation.

For Le Pen and his National Front the French people—defined as "an incomparable alchemy of Celts, Germans and Latins" (National Front 1991, 21)—are invested with unique features, from a deep-rooted sense of the sacred to a spiritual and personal attachment to the land. Bossi and his movement have consistently emphasized the Celtic roots of the Padani and have described the typical Padano as fiercely independent, with such autochthonous enterprising virtues as industry and competition. Both peoples are therefore rooted and original islands of authenticity amidst a sea of diversity.

Thus each movement formulates a geography of the sacred, of lands and places that objectify the collective memory and testify to each nation's authenticity and holiness among nations. Le Pen, as we have seen, refers to the city of Reims, the coronation place of later French kings, as the "sacred altar of the homeland." The statue of Joan of Arc in Paris and the burial places of the saints and martyrs of the nation—including the war dead, the fallen patriots to whom the "community of the true patriots" pays regular homage—are both invested with the same sacrality. These sacred sites invoke the memory of its self-sacrificial sons and daughters, and serve as testaments to the true nature of France as a Western, Christian nation.

The sacred geography of the Northern League emphasizes those sites that the League believes demonstrate "national" holiness. Thus the Lega sanctifies Pontida as the place where the autonomy and independence of the

Padani are proclaimed for the ages; the city of Legnano with its statue of the warrior Alberto da Giussano, where the autonomist troops defeated imperialism; and the Po River as the sacred geographical delimitation of the homeland. These are the sacred foundations of the homeland, the testaments to the common destiny of independence and freedom of the Padania nation.

A Sacred History

The narratives utilized by the National Front and the Northern League elevate the past to a condition of myth and consider select historical figures to be avatars of the "essence" of the respective nations. This call to a mythical history to legitimate the identity of both groups is present throughout the narratives put forward by their leaders. The premodern roots of the history of France have a prominent place in the mythology of the National Front. The Gallic past of French history and identity, and in particular the struggle of the Gallic leader Vercingétorix against the troops of the Roman Empire, serves as an important touchstone to the mythic origins of the French nation. But the main reference in the construction of this myth of origins is the historical figure of Clovis, the sixth-century king of Franks who converted himself and his nation to Christianity. This moment is heralded as marking both the birth of the French people and France's Christian roots. In fact, the city of Reims, where the baptism of Clovis occurred, is a sacred place in the imagination of the National Front. Standing before the cathedral of Reims, remember, Le Pen gave his "sermon" indicting the treaty of Maastricht for threatening France's survival. The life of French martyr Joan of Arc lent itself to a process of mythologization by the National Front. The narrative of the National Front permanently shifts the life of Joan of Arc from the level of history onto that of myth. She is above all a symbol of the independence and sovereignty of France. By serving as sacred reference points of the glorious Christian and independent nature of the French nation, both Clovis and Joan of Arc together serve as a visible image of holiness: They stand above questioning and, therefore, serve as objectifications of established truths. They are not mere images: They *are* France. Further, they are identified in party literature with the National Front, which, furthermore, is identified with the mythical narrative of France.

A similar process of mythologization of history can be seen in the narrative put forward by the Northern League. As in the case of the National Front, the League emphasizes the premodern roots of the collective. The Padania's Celtic origins are emphasized in order to distinguish the nature and character of the northern populations from the rest of Italy. This Celtic heritage of the Padani becomes a resource of symbols: The emphasis the movement places on the color green, for example, together with its adoption of the six-rayed "Sun of the Alps," a green Celtic symbol, as the logo of the party are part of this effort to mythologize the past in order to legitimize the present. At the same time, the example and achievements of the original Lega Lombarda constitute a powerful myth of origins for the contemporary Northern League led by Umberto Bossi. Alberto da Giussano, who led the communes of the Northern League to victory over the invading troops of the emperor Barbarossa, has a central place in the mythology of the group. The image of a sword-wielding Giussano has become a prominent symbol of the Northern League. Further, Pontida, where the communes swore resistance to the invaders, serves as a sacred place for the Northern League. This is the place where the group gathers periodically in order to emphasize the historical continuity between them and their twelfth-century ancestors. Pontida is also the place where the leader gives the most prominent examples of missionizing rhetoric. The Northern League has been particularly prolific in cementing the mythology of the group through the incessant production of new symbols of identity such as the Po River, where since 1996 the Padania nation has gathered in celebration.

Both groups have, therefore, holy historical and national figures whom they associate with ideas of freedom, independence, and continuity. They embody in themselves the virtue of total and unconditional commitment to the nation. In the words of Smith,

> The key to that inspiration [for the people] has been the readiness of heroes and prophets alike to sacrifice themselves for the community—not in a spirit of disinterested love, but with a passionate and all-embracing commitment. Theirs is not an act of noble renunciation; it is, on the contrary, a fervent affirmation of life and love for the community to which they belong and cherish. This is what gives their actions, and especially their

self-sacrifice, such profound meaning and consequence for the surviving members and their children. (A. Smith 2003, 42–43)

They also hold as sacred particular places, invested with "holy" significance, where the militants can demonstrate and experience their attachment both to these symbols and to the ideas associated with them. In order to emphasize the sacrality of this bond, both groups have created ceremonies in which its members solemnly swear loyalty to the identity of the French or Padania nation. Le Pen and his followers have made such an oath in the sacred place of Reims. Bossi and his followers have ritually sworn an oath of loyalty to both group and Padania in the sacred place of Pontida. Through these ceremonies, ideas become sacred, adding to their power of persuasion. Such ceremonies legitimate the passage of ideas from the condition of arguments to the condition of established and sacred truths. It is an important distinction.

Finally, both groups promote a sacralized, polarized interpretation of the history of the nation to rival the dominant, mainstream narrative. This rejection by these groups of the hegemonic and secular historical paradigm serves to delegitimize the order that has emerged from it. Such a constant reinterpretation of historical events and rehabilitation of historical figures legitimizes the alternative paradigm of history. From the perspectives of the National Front and the Northern League, there is a negative historical tradition against which each group positively defines its identity.

This negative history has also, in both cases, a myth of origins. From the perspective of the National Front, all evils currently afflicting France hearken back to the Enlightenment. According to the Front's version of history, this period marks the beginning of the erosion of the "natural" order of France and of the onslaught of the "artificial" and the "abstract." The *Siècle des Lumières* is the beginning of *la dècadence:* the uprooting of the millenarian roots of France and the French people. In the imagination of the National Front, the Enlightenment constitutes the original sin from which, in one way or another, all problems and dangers to France originate. The tradition of French Republicanism is anchored in the historical paradigm that emerged from the Enlightenment and therefore, in the eyes of Le Pen, is artificial because it is separated from the true roots, desires, and needs of the

French people. The National Front, in contrast, proposes to bridge this gap and to return France to a pristine state.

The evils plaguing the Northern League have their origins in the nineteenth-century ideology of nationalism that created "artificial" nation-states and transformed different ethnic, cultural, and economic regions into colonies within a centralized and oppressive entity. The micro-nationalist imagination of the Northern League favors an interpretation of history stressing the "traditional" autonomy of the peoples of the North spanning the fight of the communes against invaders to the federalist movement of the nineteenth century. The negative history against which the Northern League defines itself is symbolized by the idea of "Rome," a symbol of evil and oppression suffered by the peoples of the North.

It is important to stress that for both movements the dominant historical paradigm, in becoming a negative symbol, furthers the self-image of the group as a deviant, revolutionary, and morally righteous force separated from a mainstream that has been corrupted. By setting itself apart, bounded by a "forbidden" belief-system, the group acquires an outsider status that is in itself sacred. The group becomes a symbol and torchbearer of the "sacred history" that it has sworn to represent and to defend. This outsider dynamic has a crucial importance that will be revisited later in this chapter.

The Chosen Peoples

Intimately linked with the concept of an alternative history is the concept of a chosen people. The rank and file of both the National Front and the Northern League are identified as the heirs to a historical continuity hearkening back, respectively, to the beginnings of France and of the Padania. Portraying themselves as the true representatives of the good and natural traditions of their nations, party militants are untainted by the artificial, hegemonic historical paradigm. Militants of the National Front are portrayed as a "community of the elect": They constitute the remnant few, the last of the patriots. Le Pen repeatedly calls them the most "courageous and lucid" of the French people. The mission of "saving" France has been thrust upon them. Le Pen's active-passive dialectic distinguishes his "community of the elect" from the rest of the French population. What distinguishes the "active France" is its awareness of the roots and traditions of France: Because the active French are aware of their heritage, they are conscious that France is in danger and surrounded by wicked forces bent on its destruction. The "passive France," to the contrary, is unaware of or indifferent to the heritage of France because their patriotism has been weakened by the evil work of the hegemonic historical paradigm. Unlike the "remnant few" of the National Front, these passive French have lost their sense of authentic being. They have been brainwashed. They are like directionless zombies who wander in a world without meaning. In this context, it is up to the "community of the elect" to carry out the mission of the recovery and rescue of France from its decadence.

According to the myth created by the Northern League, its members constitute a "true vanguard" of men and women who are aware of their cultural autonomy. In explaining the distinctiveness of the League, Bossi employs a consciousness-unconsciousness metaphor. The "vanguard" is self-conscious of its history and its ethnic traditions and, because of this, is immune to brainwashing by outside forces. Those who have not joined the Northern League are usually described as passive, alienated, immature, and lacking the self-consciousness to understand fully that the Northern League is the *only* force that stands for truth and goodness. In this context, it is up to the vanguard to burden themselves with the mission of reminding their compatriots of their roots, of increasing their self-consciousness, of achieving a freer future for the Padania.

In this way, the militants of the National Front and of the Northern League have invested themselves with the messianic function of guiding their respective "peoples" into a better future. This is their sacred mission. Enjoined by their respective leaders to self-sacrifice for the sake of the ultimate goal, militants of each party are committed to something bigger than the sum of individuals who constitute the group: a collective and transcendent mission giving meaning to their political commitment and reinforcing group solidarity. This self-perception of being a "chosen people" exerts a powerful dynamic in each group. By raising the bar of what is at stake—the recovery and redemption of the community—the mission increases both the focus and the sense of potency that makes their members much more effective in terms of commitment and activism than the members of any mainstream organization. This sacredness of the mission of the "chosen people" maximizes their effectiveness.

Apocalypticism and the Dynamics of Salvation

Apocalypticism. The discourses of the National Front and the Northern League are anchored in an epistemological framework of salvation and redemption. In order to emphasize the need for salvation each movement advocates an idiosyncratic apocalyptic vision of the present. I will start by analyzing the motion of apocalypticism inherent in these movements and then move to an analysis of its millenarian consequences. It is worth pointing out that these movements are characterized by secularized expressions of apocalypticism, though in the case of the National Front and Le Pen the boundaries between the religious and the secular are blurred. In the discourse of both movements, four logical strands intertwine and fuel apocalyptic expectations: the logical strands of conspiracy, catastrophe, ultimacy, and urgency.

The first strand is a *logic of conspiracy.* Several studies of social psychology have emphasized the "uncertainty reduction" mechanism of conspiracy for maintaining group psychology (Hogg and Mullin 1999, 266–67). In fact, social psychologists have particularly focused on a widespread, deep-rooted sense of anxiety as the driving force of conspiracy theories. In the same way that crises pave the way for the identification between the masses and a savior, offers Franz Neumann, they create the conditions for conspiracy theories. "Just as the masses hope for their deliverance from distress through absolute oneness with a person," he writes, "so they ascribe their distress to certain persons, who have brought this distress into the world through a conspiracy." Further, "Nothing would be more incorrect than to characterize the enemies as scapegoats (as often happens in the literature) for they appear as genuine enemies whom one must extirpate" (Neumann 1957, 279). Carl F. Graumann shares a similar perspective when he notes that "a state of anxiety is more easily coped with if anxiety becomes *fear of someone* whom we can hold *responsible* for the bad shape in which we are finding ourselves" (Graumann 1987, 248).

Perhaps a deeper current that can be found in the development of conspiracy theories is a need for what Mosse called "permanent and timeless longings," namely the desire for "permanence and fixed reference points" in a changing world (Mosse 1975, 211–12). The fear of atomization and fragmentation felt by the individual, a general sense of loss of relationship with an organic whole, with a totality, being the community or the nation, spawn theories of subversive and disruptive conspiracies. Historian Raoul Girardet, in his study of political mythologies, has alluded to this longing for community at the center of the myth of conspiracy. According to him,

> [Developed from] an obscure sentiment of threat, testimony of incertitude or panic, the mythology of conspiracy appears at the same time as the negative projection of tacit aspirations, [as the] inverted expression of wishes, more or less conscious but always insatiable. The order that the "Other" is accused of wanting to establish [could it be] the antithetical equivalent of what we ourselves want to put in place? . . . That organic unity . . . that supreme will where all the particularistic wills dissipate, that absolute authority, provident, protective . . . [A]ren't they the answer to a certain type of communitarian ideal tenaciously kept alive in the deepest spot of our consciences? (Girardet 1986, 61–62)

To these psychological and communitarian approaches that attempt to explain the formation and development of conspiracy theories a teleological approach should be added. Such an approach is particularly relevant to the development of Salvationist dynamics in both the National Front and the Northern League. I focus here on conspiracy as a powerful unifying mechanism that exacerbates the dramatic moral contest between the forces of good and evil. Because both the National Front and the Northern League envision themselves as the "last guardians" of their respective nations, they believe that they face a powerful, even demonic, alliance of enemies working and conspiring together to put an end to the chosen community. In this way the logic of conspiracy gives the group the key its believers seek to understand the world and every evil afflicting the community. Revealed "conspiracies" provide anxious believers with a model of coherence and clarity. Events are neither random nor arbitrary but, like the pieces of a giant puzzle, are decipherable by those who know the "hidden truth." According to Graumann, "Only those who 'know,' namely the experts, are able to unmask, to disclose, that is, to 'see' the conspiracy and to identify the conspirator(s)." He adds, "he who 'knows' has the burden of fighting the invisible enemy, and he has a mission, namely to convince or persuade the majority that they all must learn to recognize and fight the enemy in all his or her disguises" (Graumann 1987, 248).

The "true communities" are beset by forces typically described as "demonic." Many times the leaders employ diabolical vocabulary in contrasting these "forces of darkness" with the essential goodness of the community. These forces can be reduced to two main groups. In one group are the enemies *within* the nation. They can be either an alliance of the mainstream political parties, the media, and powerful civic society groups and secret societies, or they can be the "enemy within," those who have infiltrated the community to destroy its solidarity. It should be noted that there is an element of anti-Judaic rhetoric in Le Pen, mostly in the form of innuendo about the subversive activities of Jewish groups, that is nonexistent in the rhetoric of Bossi. At the same time Bossi, particularly in earlier stages, demonized many times the institutional Church as a major co-collaborator within the conspiracy against the community. This anti-Church rhetoric is flimsy to nonexistent in the case of Le Pen. Le Pen can eventually criticize what he sees as the hostility of some bishops toward the National Front, but he has always refrained from attacking the Vatican.

In the second group are the enemies *outside* the nation. These are hellbent on pushing for a tyrannical New World Order. Because rooted ethnicities and nationalisms stand in the way of this "monstrous and gargantuan" project, they are being destroyed by policies of depopulation and massive immigration. Globalization obeys a script written by powerful, rootless cosmopolitan elites and groups, and has as its function to create a fluid, worldwide market, driven by America, with no distinctions between peoples, cultures, or ethnicities. In this conspiratorial view of globalization we found dynamics of what historian Léon Poliakov deemed "diabolic causality" (Poliakov 1980, 10–27; see also Poliakov 1992), a deterministic and systematic correlation between the calamities that torment the community and a primary cause: the malefic actions and designs of a specific group, in this case globalists. Those forces like the National Front and the Northern League who dare to challenge this project are marked for destruction.

These external enemies are, therefore, allied with the internal enemies, who are nothing more than "sycophants" of this worldwide conspiracy against the "true community." The development of New World Order conspiracy theories—which increase with a deepening globalization—elevates the struggle of these groups to a cosmic level. It gives them the perception of an apocalyptic, ongoing cosmic drama between the forces of evil and good, the forces of light and darkness. Therefore, the greater the scope of the conspiracy and evil, the greater will be apocalyptic expectations. There is a natural link between the discourses of conspiracy and apocalypse. They share a common function because, as stated by Stephen D. O'Leary, "each develops symbolic resources that enable societies to define and address the problem of evil." To him, "conspiracy strives to provide a spatial self-definition of the true community as set apart from the evils that surround us, apocalypse locates the problem of evil in time and looks forward to its imminent resolution." O'Leary concludes by noting that "[t]he story of the apocalyptic tradition is one of community building, in which human individuals and collectivities constitute their identities through shared mythic narratives that confront the problem of evil in time and history" (O'Leary 1994, 6).

In order to further the perception of apocalyptic times, the *logic of catastrophe* is dominant in the narrative of both the National Front and the Northern League. In his taxonomy of apocalyptic beliefs, medieval historian Richard Landes distinguishes between *cataclysmic* and *transformational* apocalyptic scenarios. Cataclysmic scenarios are characterized by rapid and vast devastation that precedes the advent of a new reality. Transformational scenarios are equally vast but generally slower and less violent (Landes 2004, 347). Adapting this classification to the world of contemporary politics, one discovers an "apocalyptical" distinction between the discourse of Le Pen and that of Bossi. As I have noted in chapter 2, Le Pen has many times included in his discourse "signs" announcing sudden and devastating events for France. He has often given a timetable for the "survival" of France. His apocalypticism can be considered "cataclysmic." Bossi, on the other hand, sticks with denouncing the apocalyptic consequences of policies and, therefore, promotes an apocalypticism that should be termed "transformational."

Landes also distinguishes between *passive* and *active* apocalyptic scenarios. In some apocalyptic scenarios, humans have a passive role: For example, they await God's time or some natural disaster like a comet. Other scenarios depend on human agency. In Landes's words, active apocalyptic scenarios "plac[e] the operative deeds in the hands of a redeemed community of faithful who, either as God's agents or in 'his' absence, build the millennium. Secular apocalyptic movements are almost always active" (Landes 2004, 348). Le Pen's and Bossi's movements should be positioned on the active side of the apocalyptical spectrum: They stress both the role of agency in changing history and the power of will in fighting decadence. However, Le Pen's narrative features some ambiguity between the role of man and the role of God. The possibility of God's intervention is not totally excluded in his discourse. His positioning on the active side of the apocalyptical spectrum is not as solidified as Bossi's.

The logic of catastrophe is complemented in both cases by the constant invocations of disaster images. The consequences of immigration, of the European Union, or of globalization are described using verbs that convey a sense of impending tragedy and doom. To further this logic, both Le Pen and Bossi use biological imagery to describe the threats to their communities. Images of putrefaction, diseases, and impurity abound in the discourse of both leaders. It helps to contrast the defiling nature of these dangers to the essential purity of the community. The discourse is constructed to instill fear and to shock, maximizing the power of these portents of doom.

Apocalyptical expectations are also increased by a *logic of ultimacy*. The discourse of both parties is aimed toward ultimate ends and final battles. It is a discourse of finality. By giving issues the greatest possible size and significance, an air of finality magnifies the solutions. As politics becomes interpreted in terms of "the world to come," the logic of ultimacy is intimately linked with millennial expectations. Political scientist Michael Barkun describes how "politics becomes 'millennialized'" and "ceases to be seen as an instrument for the incremental adjustment of conflicting interests and becomes instead a 'politics of ultimacy,' where ultimate issues are at stake in a once-and-for-all confrontation" (Barkun 2000, 458).

A dynamic of polarization feeds and is fed by this logic of ultimacy. They are mutually enforcing. Binary rhetoric permeates the discourse of the movements. The political landscape is clearly divided between two conflicting and contrasting poles. The "true patriots," all of those who are courageous, lucid, and incorruptible, constitute the pole on which stands the National Front. This is the side of the France Française, the "French France." Against them stands the pole of the "Anti-France." This pole is malleable and can include any party, group, or force that is perceived to be in opposition to the interests, principles, and values of the National Front. The "Padani," those who are self-conscious about their roots and traditions, are also free of corruption and immorality. The diametrically-opposing pole atop which sit the people's enemies is also malleable and includes any force perceived to be in opposition to the group. All issues are interpreted and explained in this binary manner.

At the same time, the constant use of a belligerent language generates drama for this confrontation. These movements define what for some are routine political fights as world historical "battles," and military metaphors and warriorlike images can be found throughout. Naturally this discourse of finality ends many times in an all-or-nothing scenario. Either the community engaged in these "mortal battles" will achieve its final goal or its enemies will prevail. As expressed by historian Richard Hofstadter, the spokesman of a politics of ultimacy against ubiquitous and sinister enemies "traffics in the birth and death of whole worlds . . . He is always manning the barricades of civilization. He constantly lives at a turning point: it is now or never in organizing resistance to conspiracy" (Hofstadter 1967, 29–30). In the discourse of these movements, if not always in practice, the middle ground is neither viewed nor desired as an acceptable outcome. These movements, by their nature, flirt with perfection. O'Leary expresses a similar idea when he notes that "a world seen as inherently imperfect invites discourse that makes sense of imperfection by reasserting the principle of perfection" (O'Leary 1994, 33). Finally, a *logic of urgency* is the natural corollary of the discourse of these movements. Because the community is besieged by a powerful alliance of enemies and represents the last stand against catastrophic events in the making, there is a pervading sense of the necessity for urgent action to stop these diabolical trends and to fight toward the edification of a new reality. Intimately linked with this discourse of fear, however, is a discourse of hope. In these movements, fear and hope are closely linked and fuel millennial expectations.

Millennialism. In *The Pursuit of the Millennium*, medieval historian Norman Cohn writes that millenarian sects or movements always picture salvation as:

Collective, in the sense that it is to be enjoyed by the faithful as a collectivity;

terrestrial, in the sense that it is to be realized on this earth and not in some otherworldly heaven;

imminent, in the sense that it is to come both soon and suddenly;

total, in the sense that it is utterly to transform life on earth, so that the new dispensation will be no mere improvement on the present but perfection itself; and

miraculous, in the sense that it is to be accomplished by, or with the help of, supernatural agencies.

But "even within these limits," Cohn adds, "there is of course room for infinite variety: There are countless possible ways of imagining the Millennium and the route to it" (Cohn 1970, 13–14). There has been some dispute among scholars of nationalism about whether or not nationalist and millennial movements share goals and composition (see, for example, A. Smith 1979, 14–42.) I hold the view that in the discourses of Le Pen and Bossi, the millennial imagination counterbalances and completes the apocalyptic vision. The apocalyptic dynamic of an imminent "turning point" in time triggers millennial dimensions that can be seen in both of these movements. I use the term "millennium" not in the Christian sense of a Second Coming of Christ but in the sense of a belief in a future golden age, typically positioned as an end to the existing world order, which in these cases is synonymous with the triumph of the movements' nationalist agendas.

Therefore, I employ Thomas Flanagan's definition of *political millenarianisms* as "political ideologies or movements that propose, not just to take power, but to transform the human condition, ushering in an era of peace, freedom, equality and abundance" (Flanagan 2000, 4). Where I part ways with Flanagan is when he states that, in today's world, because there is nothing "left to rebel against," political millenarianism is essentially a dead issue. As he has written, "It seems that we may be at the end of a two-century-long cycle of rebellion against the human condition. As we get ready for a new century and a new millennium, it is time to return millenarianism to the religious realm, where it belongs. Let us admit that our society, our economy, our politics do and must reflect the basic facts of human nature. Nothing is fixed; there is an indefinite prospect for piecemeal change" (Flanagan 2000, 14).

The movements under study do not share Flanagan's program: Their dynamics and rhetoric are obviously geared not toward piecemeal change but toward widespread, totalistic transformation. For these movements there is indeed still something cosmic or global to "rebel against." However, unlike Cohn's medieval cases, these contemporary movements envision salvation as neither miraculous nor needing the help of supernatural agencies in order to be inaugurated. Nevertheless, the absence of a supernatural dimension promising divine intervention is not necessarily clear-cut in the French case. Many times Le Pen gives the impression that his group basks in God's favor. The miraculous element, even if tepid compared to medieval religious millennial movements, is still present.

Landes distinguishes between restorative and progressive millennialism. While a vision of *restorative millennialism* tries to achieve a return to a golden age of original purity, *progressive millennialism* aims at constructing a new and unprecedented society (2004, 347). Based on this distinction, I include the National Front in the category of restorative millennialism and the Northern League in the category of progressive millennialism. However, this taxonomy should not be seen as based on all-or-none categories: These extremes exist on a continuum as, for example, in the case of the Nazis, who combined both notions of restoring a lost racial purity and medieval romanticism with the most advanced notions of technology and social engineering. Jeffrey Herf called this "Reactionary Modernism" (Herf 1986, 1). The Northern League, while aiming at something unprecedented in history—the creation of an autonomous Padania—bases the "society to come" on an original purity located in the past. At the same time, the National Front, while aiming at the restoration of the "natural and pure" society of the past, has strong modern dynamics, in the sense of trying to adapt the modern society of masses to a "true form" of democracy, where the sovereign people rules. Their program is not a simple return to or knee-jerk imitation of the hierarchy of the past.

We can discern similarities in both movements' notions of the "world to come." Within these millennial visions, changes in public policies are insufficient conditions for salvation. To those who testify to these visions, salvation is total in a metaphysical sense: Evil is everywhere, and within the realm of evil lie the root causes of the oppression and injustice that the chosen people suffer. Therefore, salvation implies the expunging of evil; millennialism represents the advent of a perfect age and the elimination of evil from the earth; apocalyptic prophecy warns of evil's imminent victory and thus provokes from the group the totalistic reaction that will defeat that evil.

As stated by anthropologist Mary Douglas, "a strong millennial tendency is implicit in the way of thinking of any people whose metaphysics push evil out of the world of reality" (Douglas 2002, 211). Millennium implies purification and renewal. The "true community," constituted by those who are good and just, will be rewarded while "the enemies," those who are powerful and corrupt, will be punished. This millennial tendency has been left out of many studies of Le Pen and Bossi. In the discourse of Le Pen, we clearly see this portrayal of an evil that is at once pervasive and capable of elimination, coupled with a corresponding call for a total spiritual renewal, for a "moral renaissance" of France that can destroy the evil of decadence and degeneration. Similarly, Bossi indicts globalization for "devaluating" man, and has denounced the drift toward materialism of humankind. He has described globalization as the "work of Lucifer." Members of both movements primarily portray themselves as the defenders of their own groups. However, because of the metaphysical nature of their claims, it is not surprising that they also proclaim to offer a model of salvation for Europe and, ultimately, the entire world. In some forms of millennial politics, one thinks globally by (initially) acting locally.

As they ultimately aim to vanquish both evil and all of the oppression and suffering caused by evil, both movements demonstrate a dimension of demotic millennialism. In this redemptive worldview, the millennium will tolerate no evil and despotic elites, and the faithful will live, in an egalitarian manner, within "authentic" communities based on cultural ties and belonging. This millennial vision, the basis of the profound anti-elitism of these two movements, motivates a radical egalitarianism that undergirds the calls by each for a "direct democracy" to bridge the gap between the people and the power structures wielding control. It is not surprising that the "true communities" described by Le Pen and Bossi serve as idealized models of brotherhood and fellowship in which the faithful are bound into a moral community by love for each other, for their homeland, and for their leaders. They are unified into a collectivity with a common will, common values, and shared affection. They are not mere individuals but are *members* of a moral community of the faithful and saved. This millennial vision eliminates the divide between democracy as *practice* and democracy as an *ideology*.

The attitude toward this divide among demotic thinkers defines the difference between millennial and non-millennial democratic aspirations. As noted by Giovanni Sartori at the beginning of his study on democratic theory, "The democratic ideal does not define the democratic reality and, vice versa, a real democracy is not, and cannot be, the same as an ideal one" (Sartori 1987, 8). The pure ideal of "Power to all the people" is unachievable in practice. Sartori takes his point further and highlights the temptation of a millennial turn:

> In a system of representative government the people actually exercise power (political power) by being able to *control and change* the people in power. With all of this, it is still the case that the original principle is far from being fulfilled: *The people still do not exercise power in any full or literal sense of the expression. What to do next? The temptation, and indeed the easy path, is to repropose the principle in its purity*. If so, the intermediary structures (the representative state) are no longer seen as means of implementation and appreciated for what they have achieved; they are perceived, rather, as obstacles and thereby dismissed as impediments along the path of the realization of the ideal. (Sartori 1987, 71 [emphasis mine])

For Pierre Rosanvallon the "crisis of representation" in democracies "results neither from dysfunction nor betrayal: it is consubstantial with its very object." This crisis arises from what he calls the "constitutive gap between the people as the legitimate sovereign, in its unity in principle, and the people as an existing society, in its actual complexity" (Rosanvallon 2006, 91). In the same vein, Norberto Bobbio has written about what he sees as the "broken promises" of democracy that reflect "the gap between democratic ideals and 'actually existing democracy'" (Bobbio 1987, 18). Bobbio writes that "the model of the democratic state, based on popular sovereignty, was conceived in the image of, and as analogous to, the sovereignty of the prince, and hence was a monist model of society." He added, "The real society underlying democratic government is pluralist" (1987,

28). Another major broken promise was the unfulfilled elimination of invisible power in democratic societies. The question of "Who controls the controllers?" remains as pervasive as ever: "If no adequate answer can be found to this question, democracy in the sense of visible government is lost. In this case we are dealing not so much with a broken promise but with a trend which actually contradicts the basic premises of democracy, a trend not towards the greatest possible control of those in power by the citizens, but towards the greatest control of the subjects by those in power" (Bobbio 1987, 34–35; on this issue, see also Rosanvallon 2006, 235–52).

Democratic politics works in a complex manner: Full of intricacies and procedures, it creates institutions that, while formed to mediate between a people and power, end up alienating "the people" unable, in the words of Margaret Canovan, to "form a picture of the location of power or to trace a clear path through the maze" (2002, 26). These problems of alienation and anxiety intensify in periods when there is an irresistible perception that the will of the people has been neglected or repressed in a modern liberal democracy (lack of public debate or denying of popular say in issues like immigration, or the transfer of sovereignty to European institutions). This vortex of resentment is aggravated in times of globalization, which has among its features the increased influence of transnational bodies and corporations who appear aloof from and even contemptuous of "the people," and out of popular control or reach. In this context where either the elites do not seem to know what to do (and hence the voters do not know whom to choose), or the information coming from the elites (spokesmen, media, intellectuals) appears, at best inaccurate, and most likely and deliberately deceptive, movements that claim to represent "the people" against "the powerful" thrive.

At such times, democracies can generate their own millennial movements. I am in agreement with those democratic theorists who contend that behind the rise of movements such as the National Front and the Northern League lies an attempt to "reassert popular sovereignty as the essence of democracy" (Panizza 2005, 27). This process is not necessarily "civil," and is often based on a construction of exclusionist and conspiratorial outlooks; nevertheless, this is part of an old ambition (one as old as democracy itself), to recreate the popular will: to bridge the gap between democracy as *ideal* and *reality*, and thus to "force" democracy to live up to its (ever-unfulfilling) promises.[1]

Le Pen and Bossi offer in their discourses a vision of a "true democracy" that eliminates distant, venal, self-serving elites and, by identifying the leader with the community, provides a clear mental picture of what democracy *really* is. In so doing, these movements combine transparency with popular empowerment. Why else would both the National Front and the Northern League have so consistently defended such mechanisms of direct democracy as the regular use of referenda. The National Front has defended the establishment of a "Republic of referenda," and the Northern League launches regular referenda within its own group often in order to legitimize the direction announced by Bossi. The existence of a majority, instead of proportional, electoral system in both countries only enlarges the perception by these groups that their respective national governments operate through a *nominal* and not a *real* democracy. This element of demotic millennialism is a crucial component of the salvationist narrative that drives both movements. We will now look at the "sacred authority" of the messianic leader in guiding the embattled "chosen people" toward the millennium.

The Messianic Leader

My findings show that from the early beginnings of each movement there has been a process of mythologization of their respective leaders. I have referred to this process as an "industry" because it develops and maintains narratives that sustain the messianic status of the leader and invest him with a sacred authority. The work of collaborators, the discourse of the leader himself, and the personalization of the parties play a fundamental role in the construction of the image of the leader as a savior, a missionizing figure

---

1. This aspiration, however, entails the danger of totalitarianism. In *The Myth of the Nation and the Vision of Revolution*, Jacob L. Talmon wrote about the existence of an "unfathomable," "inescapable," and "ironic law" in history, "which causes revolutionary salvationist schemes to evolve into regimes of terror, and the promise of a perfect direct democracy to assume in practice the form of totalitarian dictatorship" (Talmon 1981, 535).

of historical proportions. I have detected six key images produced by these industries and I will discuss their implications.

The Leader as the Prophet. The faithful think that Le Pen and Bossi are men ahead of their times. They can read the "signs" of the present and reveal events lying in the future. These leaders, seeing what most cannot, shed light before the group. In the story told by these movements, different events are constantly interpreted as evidence of the leader's clairvoyance. In the party literature, influenced by and even drawing from the discourses of the leaders, one commonly finds such admiring expressions as "Le Pen was right," or "Bossi was right." Le Pen is heralded as someone who had the panoramic ability and the direct, penetrating insight to "see"—from the "evils" of communism to the emergence of a "dictatorial" European Union, and from the disruptive consequences of unhinged immigration to the Islamization of Europe—what no one else at the time saw or even could see. One finds the same legitimization of the leader's prophetic gift in the way his followers praise Bossi as someone who understood the path of history before others: the crisis of nation-states, the emergence of micro-nationalisms, the "chaotic" consequences of Third World immigration, the "evils" of globalization.

This prophetic dimension bestows upon both Le Pen and Bossi an aura of destiny while simultaneously transforming their visions into dogmas difficult for believers to question. The fact that the leader has "always" been right in the past legitimates his status as a sacred truth-teller in the present. Above all, the leader-as-prophet receives constant praise both for courage in stating the hard truths that ordinary mortals avoid and deny, and for tireless commitment, by the use of their courageous "word," to expose and shatter the lies of the dominant official paradigm. Writing about the prophets of the Hebrew Bible, Elie Wiesel notes that "the true power of the prophet derives from his moral conviction and from his courage and persistence in expressing it." He writes, "Anyone at any time may strike at him or humiliate him, and some have done just that. Nevertheless, nothing—neither seduction nor threat—can sway him. He never flatters, never aims to please; he is an enemy to all complacency: he is the bearer of truth and ethical concerns; and nothing and no one can make him say what he doesn't want to say, or silence him. Should he fall silent, his silence itself bears witness" (Wiesel 2003, 178).

Obviously the context of biblical prophets is different from today's context: The prophets of ancient Israel denounced corrupt monarchs who plundered the people and established idols in the land of the one God's chosen people; the prophets of contemporary European politics denounce purported democracies that allege to take care of their people while worshipping at the altar of utopian models for the continent.

This *ethical* aspect of prophecy, a claim that is central to the leader-follower dynamic sustaining these movements, can also be discerned in the way militants perceive the leader's resolution and steadfastness, amid inclement conditions, in the pursuit and exposition of the "truth." A driving force of this dynamic is the fact that the members of these groups perceive themselves as the powerless adherents to an ensemble of "speeches, gestures and practices" that constitute, in the definition of James C. Scott, a "hidden transcript"—regarding the complaints and "real" problems that affect both societies—that undermines the "official," *public* transcript promoted by the dominant elites and seemingly consented to or deferred by the subordinate groups (Scott 1990, 4). The attention paid by both the National Front and the Northern League to symbolism and ritual is a crucial aspect of this process of challenging hegemonic narratives and "stories." David Kertzer has stated that "[t]he struggle of groups seeking to delegitimize the new order involves a fierce struggle over symbolism" (1988, 178). In the same light, Scott writes that "whatever form it assumes—offstage parody, dreams of violent revenge, millennial visions of a world turned upside down" (1990, 9), this hidden transcript of subordinate groups is a constitutive part of power relations dynamics. Those who take up the role of "speaking truth to power" against official deception and lies, and who openly declare the "hidden transcript" (hence the repeated motto in these missionary movements of "saying out loud what people think in silence"), gain a charismatic dimension (and a powerful emotional attachment to them) in the eyes of those who recognize themselves in the leader's defiant words and actions (on this point see Scott 1990, 221–22). In the cases of Le Pen and Bossi, the leader's declaration of the hidden transcript was neither abrupt nor restricted to one single dramatic event, but was continuous and relentless, particularly because of being channeled through the alternative media created and organized by and within the parties. Thus the "prophetic" nature of the leaders—the mystique of possessing a "special relationship" with the truth so that *only they know* what the future holds—is enhanced by the manner in which, in the eyes of the militants, they shatter the false vision promulgated by the dominant groups and become the embodiment of those voices held "under domination."[2]

The Leader as the Moral Archetype. The respective narratives of these movements portray their leaders as exemplary figures. The power of the leader's example emanates both from his own personal qualities and from his life achievements. Le Pen is regularly portrayed as a man with a number of rare qualities worthy of admiration. He is a natural, driven leader and a gifted, magnetic orator whose perseverance in the pursuit of his ideals is worthy of admiration. He is above all the quintessential Frenchman and a true patriot. Further, his life achievements constitute the proof of his rare qualities. Though he founded the party with other people, he is heralded as the only true founder of the party and the man who, through his commitment, self-sacrifice, and unwavering loyalty to his ideals, was able to bring the National Front to a higher level of the political landscape. He belongs to the category of "Great Men" of history. In the narrative of the Northern League, Umberto Bossi is a leader of unique courage, intuition, and clairvoyance. He is also a powerful speaker with a spellbinding personality. His life achievements show that, though he had to confront powerful forces, he was able to create a revolutionary party.

Both leaders are the first militants of their respective parties. The story of how each created his party from scratch, and the activism that each has continually shown in the defense of his cause, make him the standard of militancy to which all other militants must conform. Le Pen's and Bossi's life stories, together with the personal qualities that they have manifested throughout, legitimate each as the role model and archetype for his entire community.[3] Eric Hoffer, in his study of mass movements of the twentieth

---

2. Obviously the hidden transcript is not necessarily moral or ethical. James Scott writes that it may not be a "pretty sight" and "might take the form of a previously muffled popular anti-Semitism, as appears to be the case in the post-*glasnost* Soviet Union" (1990, 223).

3. This image of the "exemplary leader" is not exclusive, of course, to contemporary populist movements. In his study on the charisma of George Washington, Seymour Martin Lipset, for instance, attaches a primordial importance to the "power of example," a model of

century, thought that the ability of the "exceptional leader" to personify "the certitude of the creed," and to evoke—by his own trajectory and actions—"the enthusiasm of communion" plays an important role in achieving a high mobilization and devotion among the "true believers" (Hoffer 1989, 114). In his study of Hitler, Ian Kershaw expresses a similar perspective on the leader's capacity to embody a "total commitment" and devotion to a goal as crucial aspects of his missionizing appeal. In Kershaw's words,

> Hitler repeatedly stated that he was uninterested in day-to-day issues. What he offered, over and over again, was the same vision of a long-term goal, to be striven after with missionary zeal and total commitment. Political struggle, eventual attainment of power, destruction of the enemy, and build-up of the nation's might were stepping-stones to the goal. But how it was to be then attained was left open. Hitler himself had no concrete notion. He just had the certainty of the fanatical "conviction politician" that it *would* be attained. (Kershaw 2001a, 290)

Both Le Pen and Bossi epitomize to their respective moral communities just such a total commitment and, as a consequence, serve as examples—in terms of their perseverance, iron will, and righteousness—for their respective publics to admire and emulate. Images and references to the leader's immaculate devotion to the mission abound in the internal literature of the parties.

The Leader as the Martyr. The scripts for these movements share a dominant theme of the leader's self-sacrifice for his beliefs and his cause. The respective biographies of Le Pen and Bossi constitute evidence of their self-sacrificing nature. Each gave up his own personal interests, well-being, and even health for the sake of the mission. In the case of Le Pen several biographical episodes are brought to the fore as evidence. The fact that Le Pen left the French parliament to go fight in Indochina showed how willing he

---

"public virtue" emanated by the first president of the United States. "Washington's greatest contribution was to keep [the army] viable, to command respect, and to maintain morale," wrote Lipset. "He showed no personal weakness and never gave his soldiers any reason to lose faith in him. He lived with his troops, drew no pay, and rejected opportunities to take even the briefest leave to visit Mount Vernon" (Lipset 1998, 29).

was to put his life in danger in defense of the nation. Both the 1976 bomb attack that destroyed Le Pen's Paris house and the fact that, according to the literature of the National Front, Le Pen lost an eye fighting political enemies demonstrate how easy and tempting, in the face of such risks, it would be for him to give up. Le Pen, however, persevered. He has many times mentioned the possibility of losing his life in the pursuit of his cause. Even more personal episodes such as Le Pen's losing his wife to another man are interpreted through the prism of sacrifice. A zealot for his cause, so committed to the party, he ended up neglecting his wife. Coupled with personal sacrifice is the theme of public sacrifice. The political parties, the mainstream media, the judiciary, and other forces of civil society, aware that Le Pen represents their only "true" opposition, ostracize and persecute his movement. Le Pen could have opted for compromise with the system and, therefore, been personally rewarded by the system. Although easier, he refused to be an "insider." In the narrative of the National Front this persecution constitutes a badge of honor and testifies to the self-sacrificing character of their leader.

One of the most prominent themes of the script of the Northern League is Bossi as the self-sacrificing son of Padania. Again we find a use of biography similar to that of the National Front to legitimate this image of sacrifice. Bossi is constantly portrayed as someone who gave up a comfortable life, possibly as a doctor, to fight for the communities of northern Italy. Bossi is described as someone who, from the very beginning, committed himself totally to his cause. Given particular emphasis are the early days of the League when Bossi, despite widespread challenges—financial, logistic, and from other political forces—managed to establish his own movement in the political landscape.

As in the case of Le Pen, Bossi is portrayed as someone who could have given in to the offers and temptations from the political establishment. However, he surrendered his selfish interests for the attainment of something higher: the creation of an independent Padania. Because of this "higher ideal" and his refusal to sell out his movement, Bossi is the "victim" of persecution—he has talked about the possibility of being jailed or even assassinated—by the judiciary, media, and political parties. This theme of unselfishness has remained unchanged even during the times when Bossi is a government official: Bossi entered the government not to fulfill personal interests but to fight for the cause of Padania. In the pursuit of his mission Bossi sacrificed his own health. In fact, his heart problems are usually described as the consequence of sleepless nights, tireless campaigning, and nonstop meetings, everywhere, with his militants. Bossi's suffering is viewed as the result of his missionary zeal. In both cases, images of personal affliction and martyrdom abound. Suffering increases the missionizing image of the leader as a heroic and stoic figure who endures great pain in order to fulfill his mission and who serves as an example of sacrifice for the followers.

The Leader as the People. The powerful dynamic of radical egalitarianism that crosses both movements is manifest in the way their narratives portray the leaders as personifications of common men with everyday qualities, attitudes, and lifestyles. They embody the radical anti-elitism of the movements they lead. They are hailed as the antithesis of the self-seeking and self-centered elites that the rank and file disdains and despises. Again, the use of biography serves to legitimize this demotic dimension of the leaders. Both had humble beginnings: Le Pen as the offspring of a family of fishermen and peasants; Bossi in the "simplicity and commonality" of the countryside. In the storyline of the movements both Le Pen and Bossi have an unassuming and unpretentious lifestyle. This simplicity of life is persistently stressed. Not only do they stay away from a luxurious lifestyle but also they regularly state that they do not need luxury, they do not need material possessions. Le Pen, for example, although he inhabits a mansion and has a considerable fortune, repeatedly stresses his ultimately frugal and austere nature. Intimately linked with the image of a common man is the image of the family man. Whether in party congresses, meetings with militants, or other public gatherings both leaders surround themselves with their families. Le Pen is seen many times with his wife and daughters, and Bossi with his wife and sons.

Their discourses emerge as the natural corollary of their dimension as simple people. Their language is direct and many times crude. In meetings with militants they adopt a conversational style, sometimes telling jokes, singing, and, particularly in the case of Bossi, swearing. It is worthwhile to note that even though their discourse is conversational in nature it has also a strong dimension of erudition, particularly in the rallies with militants, utilizing regular references to history and to cultural phenomena. This mix of informality and erudition provides the basis for a discourse of identity. At the same time their discourse is presented as an extension of common sense. The leaders, because they *are* from the people, have a direct link to what the people really think or really should think, no matter how much brainwashing and propaganda come from the "powerful." In this way it comes as no surprise that both parties are identified as the people's parties because they are the only ones who truly represent "the people." The demotic dimension of Le Pen and of Bossi is crucial for their strategy of self-legitimation as saviors of the community. It gives them the right qualities and credentials to "guide" the people.

The Leader as the Party. Both the National Front and the Northern League represent political parties geared toward preserving and maintaining the primacy of the leader and the personal attachment between the leader and the militants. Lately, political scientists have commented on the trend in European mainstream political parties toward a top-down model of party organization and increasingly leadership-driven parties. According to Peter Mair and colleagues, "The parties become their leaders. What this also implies, of course, is that the party appears more undifferentiated and standardized, speaking with just one voice and imparting just one message to the broader public" (Mair, Müller, and Plasser 2004, 265.) However, this trend by the mainstream parties is understood as a *response* to changing electoral markets, and therefore essentially as an electoral tool for the masses.

What distinguishes the personalization of the National Front and the Northern League is that it is part of the *nature* of these parties and has been a crucial component since their origins. The fact that each leader was present at the creation of the parties is crucial to understanding the highly personalized nature of each organization. Both parties are viewed as products of the leader's commitment and vision. This image of the leader as someone who almost single-handedly created and developed the party functions as a "myth of origins" for both parties, investing the leader with a natural sense of entitlement to decide about its structure and decision-making process.

From the very beginning both organizations were characterized by a hierarchical structure controlled by a leader with a discriminate power to appoint people to different offices. This power leads to a personalized structure that creates and encourages personal loyalty to the leader. The mandate of many in both parties, particularly for those in executive positions, depends on the goodwill of the leader. Both executive committees of the party testify to this personal hierarchy. Le Pen and Bossi appoint the members of their executive committees, and the criterion for appointment is loyalty to the leader, which encourages the development of a monolithic dynamic under a single guidance. Both leaders are triumphantly reelected in the party congresses by an acclamation that symbolizes the dynamics of the "true and direct democracy" pervading the ideology system of the collectivity. Strong because of overwhelming mandates from "the people," both leaders set the party agenda and decide in which direction they want to take the party, confident that the militants are in agreement.

This centralized structure of the party is deemed necessary because of the power and "mischievousness" of the group's supposed enemies. Fixated on destroying the group, these forces many times infiltrate it with agents to generate doubt and to weaken the group's solidarity; hence, doubt must be quelled. Every schism that happens is explained within this framework of the "enemy within." The possibility of internal betrayal is always present within the group and contributes to solidifying the primacy of the leader even more, with officials eager to demonstrate their agreement with and personal loyalty to the leader, and periodically jockeying for position around him. Angelo Panebianco describes a pure charismatic party as one being "formed by one leader who imposes himself as undisputed leader, conceiver and interpreter of a set of political symbols (the party's original ideological goals), which become inseparable from his person" (Panebianco 1988, 52). Both the National Front and the Northern League do seem to fit the category of "pure charismatic party." Even if an element of bureaucratization is present, the dynamics of "true democracy" within the party and the discriminatory power and legitimacy given to the leader keep the personal and charismatic allegiances flowing within those bureaucratic structures.

Because the personal charismatic leader is of such crucial importance, its disappearance raises valid questions regarding the survival of the social organization. In relation to the issue of routinization of charisma after the leader leaves the scene, it is inescapable to notice the setting off of dynamics of hereditary charisma in both movements. Le Pen has always given a special place in the party to members of his family and, in recent years, has unofficially appointed his youngest daughter as his "natural successor." Umberto Bossi, particularly after the deterioration of his health, has made clear that his family will continue to play a role in the movement, particularly through his sons. In these cases charisma is "transmitted" by heredity and it is perceived as a quality "that is participated in by the kinsmen of its bearer, particularly by his closest relatives" (Weber 1978, 248; see also Tucker 1970, 92; Schweitzer 1990, 40). As I have mentioned before, the issue of succession—and related emphasis on qualification by birth rather than by merit—is not settled for the two movements, but the leaders' insistence on the primacy of the family "after Le Pen" or "after Bossi" serves as a revealing indicator of the degree to which the charisma of the personal leader is enshrined, and therefore molds, the authority structure of each party.

The Leader as the Missionary. The central storyline produced by the Le Pen and Bossi industries is a sacralization of their respective leader as a prophetic figure driven by a sense of mission to save his community. This is the overriding theme in the scripts of the National Front and the Northern League. However, this missionizing dynamic is not merely connected with the proclamation of the leader's mission; it gains strength from the leader's capacity to embody the mission and to transmit the urgency of the times to his followers. It deals, at a deeper level, with the issue of authenticity. The biographical dimensions of the leader, and his early and consistent commitment and devotion to his cause, lend credibility to the leader's claims—reinforced by the inner core of militants—that he indeed *has* a mission. The leader of each movement is authentic, is worthy of being invested with the trust and belief of the faithful not only because he puts forward a storyline but also because he *embodies* this narrative. This is a crucial distinction as well as an important insight from studies that have focused on the process of leadership as a "narrative." Howard Gardner's conclusion that the most important weapon in the leader's arsenal is a set of stories of identity is confirmed by my case studies. Le Pen and Bossi, both by themselves and through their respective disciples, constantly generate "stories about themselves and their groups, about where they were coming from and where they were headed, about what to be feared, struggled against, and dreamed about" (Gardner 1995, 14).

But the extent to which each leader personifies the narrative is crucial; otherwise they risk being denigrated as hypocrites and manipulators, which, writes Gardner, "mutes the effectiveness of [their] stories" (1995, 10). From the outset of their careers both leaders have shown commitment and devotion to the cause, many times at the expense of their own self-interest and well-being, and have demonstrated that they possess the right and unique qualities to guide the group. They fulfill the role of the missionary, and they incarnate the spirit and substance of the mission. From this they derive the moral dimension of their leaderships. Their devotion, rectitude, and loyalty to their respective group set an ethical example of sacrifice and commitment to all followers and thus boosts their capital of trustworthiness within the community: Followers are more likely to accept shifts in strategy or policy because they *trust* that the leader, who *knows* what is best for the community, would *never* do anything to harm the community. Thus, for example, the core militancy of the Northern League followed the changes of policy direction by Umberto Bossi. The followers trust the leader's strategy because it is the *leader's* strategy. This dynamic is closely connected to the break with the rational order characteristic of the Weberian definition of charisma. It is important to remember the words of Weber: "Charismatic domination means a rejection of all ties to any external order in favor of the exclusive glorification of the genuine mentality of the prophet and hero. Hence, its attitude is revolutionary and transvalues everything; it makes a sovereign break with all traditional or rational forms: 'It is written, But I say unto you'"(Weber 1958, 250).

In the same vein, followers are also more likely to interpret electoral setbacks or internal crises as tests of their faith in the leader and of their devotion to the community. The follower's perception of Le Pen or of Bossi as a leader who is authentically and genuinely committed to the collective cause is fundamental to an understanding of the leader's missionary dimension and of the leadership capital that he gains from it. Such sacred authority calls not only for a strong belief but also a necessary leap of faith in the wisdom and rightness of the missionary leader.

THE SACRED COLLECTIVE

The actual construction and implementation of missionary politics is based on a paradigm of a redemptive outsiderhood. The group perceives and organizes itself as a separate and sacred entity existing on the periphery of the dominant profane rational-bureaucratic sphere that is ruled by "evil" forces and reliant for survival on the "passivity" and "ignorance" of the populace. This dynamic develops the group's self-perception as a transcendent, sacralized entity set apart from the ordinary world. Though these movements collaborate with the dominant, hegemonic paradigm (participating in elections or even joining governmental coalitions, as in the case of the Northern League), internally they always see themselves as constituting a people apart. This outsiderhood dynamic is never lost within these movements.

Narrative and Outsiderhood

The narratives employed by these movements stress the group's inherent uniqueness. As noted above, the members of the collective are hailed as the heirs to a specific historical tradition, a "chosen people" who, guided by their messianic leader, carry out the mission of saving their communities. This belief reinforces self-perceptions of exceptionality that set them apart from the mundane and ordinary world of politics. The narrative gives the group's members an alternative understanding of reality, providing them with a different belief system than the one promoted by the dominant paradigm. Therefore their values, principles, and beliefs acquire a deviant nature. They differ from the normative system and the accepted standards of society that are promoted by the "all powerful." The fact that they see the world through the lens of deviancy creates what Michael Barkun has named a "stigmatized knowledge." This type of knowledge runs counter to generally accepted beliefs. According to Barkun, "by *stigmatized knowledge* I mean claims to truth that the claimants regard as verified despite the marginalization of those claims by the institutions that conventionally distinguish between knowledge and error—universities, communities of scientific researchers and the like" (2003, 26). This stigmatized knowledge can have different varieties but as my findings on Le Pen and Bossi indicate, the overriding variety within both movements is clearly the one of *suppressed knowledge*. Here is how Barkun describes it:

> [Suppressed knowledge is] claims that are allegedly known to be valid by authoritative institutions but are suppressed because the institutions fear

the consequences of public knowledge or have some evil or selfish motive for hiding the truth . . . believers assume that when their own ideas about knowledge conflict with some orthodoxy, the forces of orthodoxy will necessarily try to perpetuate error out of self-interest or some other evil motive. The consequence is to attribute all forms of knowledge stigmatization to the machinations of a conspiracy. (Barkun 2003, 27)

In fact, in the discourse of the National Front and the Northern League there is a constant embracing of what are perceived as the taboos of the hegemonic paradigm promoted by the elites. From the time of their creation they have made their own themes that they have perceived to be excluded from use, approach, or mention by the authorities. As noted previously, the dominant paradigm in France stresses a specific historical tradition. The République Française is founded on the universalist ideals of the Enlightenment and on the concept of the nation as an open community where everyone is treated equally irrespective of race, color, and creed, under a unified republic. The National Front stresses a historical tradition primarily founded on a primordial ethnic vision of the nation, which is made up of members of the same ethnic group. Society is not an abstract group of citizens but a natural community of people who are bound by blood ties and a common culture. According to the National Front, the elites have ignored for decades the growth of culturally unassimilable immigrant communities, alien bodies that refuse to integrate with the wider French society and that have isolated themselves in a radical communalism. The National Front breaks the establishment's orthodoxy of assimilation of various cultures and ethnicities with a heterodox vision of monoculturalism, the safest way to keep the unity of the Republic. Further, in a break with the dogma of the laicization of the Republic, the National Front, even when it defends the need to keep the secularity of the state (in response to the growth of Islamic practices in the country), sets France's Christian heritage at the forefront of its political discourse. Concomitantly, the National Front embraces issues that it also perceives to be suppressed because they contradict the public scripts of the French Republic, such as, for instance, the heritage of the Vichy regime and colonialism.

The Northern League has always held close what it has perceived as the suppressed knowledge of the dominant Italian paradigm. To the faithful, this taboo originated in the nineteenth century with the historical unification of the Italian State known as *Risorgimento*. The centralized structure of Italy around its capital, Rome, and the related suppressing of local economies, cultures, and ethnicities became a dogma for the powerful elites. The continuing struggle of the Northern League has been against the powerful forces determined to preserve the orthodoxy. In this vein the Northern League has emphasized a heterodox vision of history that stresses the continuous tradition of freedom of the communities of northern Italy. The hegemonic paradigm operating in Italy is also guilty of imposing an artificial and disruptive model of multicultural society on the natural roots and traditions of the peoples. The Northern League breaks this taboo and offers its own model of a monocultural society.

The emphasis that both movements give to the creation of their own media and communications networks serves as good evidence of the crucial dynamics of suppressed knowledge that run through these movements. Academia and the mainstream media are invariably perceived as gatekeepers of the dominant paradigm and nothing more than tools of the orthodoxy.[4] That is the reason why these heterodox movements are ostracized, censored, ridiculed, and mischaracterized by major media outlets and universities, which, therefore, cannot be trusted. These movements felt compelled, from early times, to create their own media through which their suppressed knowledge may be channeled, free of distortion and censorship, to the members of the community. The National Front has created a publishing house that publishes party programs, photo books, and books by Le Pen and other major party figures. It has always promoted its own newspapers and magazines, and it was the first French political party to use the Internet as a tool of political propaganda. The Northern League has also created its own publishing

---

4. For these movements, knowledge produced by the academic world is viewed, in general, as *part* of elite rule, as tainted by nature, and thus is easily dismissed. Writing about the tendency of populist movements to resort to conspiracy theories, Taggart notes how "an academic investigation into whether a conspiracy exists is likely, for a conspiracy theorist, to be at best ineffective, and at worst in collusion with the conspiracy. This means that populists have yet another justification in dismissing overly theoretical and academic accounts of power" (Taggart 2000, 106).

house and has always given a crucial role to party newspapers in the combat for Padania. It has also acquired a radio and a television channel. The League has used the Internet from the beginnings. Both parties see the Internet as a powerful medium to circumvent what they perceive to be the bias of the media. Their websites are many times described as the last domains of freedom, against the censorship and mind control of public opinion promoted by the guardians of the dominant paradigm. I will now look at how the permanent use of rites serves to solidify and make transcendent the outsiderhood dimension of both movements.

Ritualism and Outsiderhood

From the very beginning, both the National Front and the Northern League, in order to cement their alternative world experientially, have engaged in ritualism. These repetitive and standardized actions and events have served both as demonstrations and inculcations of collective allegiance to the beliefs of the group and to the missionary leader, and have had the consequence of reinforcing its internal solidarity. Both movements have provided their militants with a comprehensive system of rites. As we have seen, they regularly organize parades and processions to historical places. The National Front, for example, holds an annual homage to its patron saint, Joan of Arc, which includes a procession to the streets of downtown Paris, Le Pen's laying a bouquet of flowers at a gilded statue of Joan of Arc riding a horse and waving the national flag, and a "solemn speech" of the leader to his militants in the Place de l'Opera. The party also holds an annual Festival of the Blue-White-Red where the militants of the party gather in celebration. Again, the crucial moment of the gathering is a speech by Le Pen.

The Northern League regularly organizes majestic parade-rallies to Pontida, the place where their ancestors had sworn to defend the freedom of the communities of the North. The central point of each rally in Pontida is Bossi's speech. The party also annually holds three days of rallies in the area surrounding the Po River, which delimitates the territory of Padania. These rallies end with a speech by Bossi in Venice.

These rites assume a form of pilgrimage, in which the militants go to a sacred place where they spend considerable periods of time together in anticipation of the words of the founder and leader of the group. The fact that the speeches of both Le Pen and Bossi are an integral part of the ritualistic procedures is an essential aspect. In his study of the "new political style" that emerged in the early nineteenth century from modern nationalism, Mosse explained the power of ritualistic speeches. By making the speech part of a ritual, in a sacred environment, the speech becomes a mere symbol among other symbols. In fact, both Le Pen and Bossi give their most militant, dramatic, and missionizing speeches in these rituals. Their words, as stated by Mosse, referring to ritualistic speeches of the past, "were thus actions, an integral part of the dramatization of the rite of national self-representation." In this manner "[the leader] was himself a living symbol who could commune with other symbols" (Mosse 1975, 201–2). The liturgy of both the National Front and the Northern League, made of processions, rallies in sacred places (truly sanctuaries), flags, posters, and slogans, help to invest the leader, as a symbol among other symbols in these "hours of worship," with an undisputable and sacred authority.

The Collective and Liminality

The sacralization of politics by both the National Front and the Northern League leads to a mythologization of the party narrative. As we have seen, the militants are seen as a chosen people, heirs to a sacred history, who are engaged in a salvationist mission and guided by a messianic leader. While the narrative becomes a myth in itself, the permanent use of rites, as we have seen, objectifies this mythic narrative and renders it a matter of personal and collective experience. In fact, through the use of myth, symbols, and rites, the community undergoes passage to what the anthropologist Victor Turner has called a "liminal situation." This process that Turner first applied to tribal societies but then expanded to postindustrial contexts (calling it specifically "liminoid") is characterized by a transcendent overcoming of the limits of everyday life and a suspension of the ordinary world. In these "threshold" moments, the ideal "world to come" is envisioned, which produces a sense of intense solidarity, which he characterized as *"communitas."* Therefore, liminality is "a time and place of withdrawal from normal modes of social action," (Turner 1977a, 167), and it is "any condition outside or on the peripheries of everyday life. It is often a sacred condition or can readily become one" (Turner 1979, 47). Turner defined the route from liminality to communitas in the following manner: "People who are similar in one important characteristic . . . withdraw symbolically, even actually, from the total system, from which they may in various degrees feel themselves 'alienated' to seek the glow of communitas among those with whom they share some cultural or biological feature they take to be their most signal mark of identity. Through the route of 'social category' they escape the alienating structure of a 'social system' into 'communitas' or social antistructure" (1977b, 47–48).

Liminality phases and communitas can develop on the fringes of the main structure, constitute the components of anti-structure or meta-structure, and are the "conditions for the production of [rival] root metaphors, conceptual archetypes, paradigms, models for, and the rest" (1979, 50). Turner's theory of collective rituals is too large and complex for a detailed exposition here. But the dynamic dialectic between structure, liminality, and communitas is useful for achieving a fuller understanding of the sacred dimension of the National Front and Northern League collectivities. Both communities, through a mythologized narrative and ritualism, undergo passage away from daily reality and into a liminal experience in which participants experience themselves immersed in a collective, unified body separated from the main hierarchical and divisive structure of society. As a consequence of this "threshold" situation, both the National Front and the Northern League constitute manifestations of communitas that are heightened during collective ritual performances.

We find here the same longing for wholeness that impels these movements, as we have noted before, to demotic millennialism and to forms of direct democracy in an attempt to make reality more fulfilling. The main structure referred to by Turner is a compartmentalized and rationalized society, where "the units are statuses and roles, not concrete human individuals. The individual is segmentalized into roles, which he plays" (1979, 237). These liminal movements break from this structure and form a different model of society, communitas, that in the words of Turner, "often appears culturally in the guise of an Edenic, paradisiacal, utopian or millennial state of affairs, to the attainment of which religious or political action, personal or collective, should be directed. Society is pictured as a communitas of free and equal comrades—of total persons" (Turner 1979, 237–38).

Communitas and Militancy

Against a segmented model of society, both the National Front and the Northern League offer to adherents a model of society that is an undifferentiated, homogenous whole where individuals are united by feelings of brotherhood, a shared belief system, and a common will. The internal dynamics of these missionary communities bespeak the centrality of kinship and affinity for its members. My findings, through analysis of party literature and interviews, attest to this aspect of the parties as a community of equals under the guidance of the missionary leader. The communities are insistently portrayed as communities of love in which affectivity between the members is a driving force. They constantly say that they are bound by love toward each other and toward the homeland that, in their view, has been betrayed and corrupted. They are moral communities that, in these times of tribulation, share a common idealism, faith, courage, sacrifice, and hope in the coming of their version of the millennium. The members share a feeling that they *belong together*, and have a sense of righteousness about themselves and about the absolute goodness of their mission. Those who defect are invariably characterized as moral failures and miscreants to the community.

Because of the fervor and solidarity generated by missionary politics, the commitment of the militants is total, which increases the effectiveness of their militancy. In the past few years several studies have shown that, in comparison to the heyday of mass parties, party membership in Europe, particularly in France and Italy, decreased substantially. One of the reasons, as stated by Peter Mair and Ingrid van Biezen, is that "as party identities have waned, and as partisan politics itself has become eroded, individuals citizens are themselves probably less likely to be willing to devote the time and energy that is often required by active party membership" (Mair and Biezen 2001, 14). To Mair, Müller, and Plasser, "today, however, the most pressing challenge to which the mainstream parties have to respond is that posed by popular disengagement and disaffection" (2004, 273). The activism of the militants of both the National Front and the Northern League runs against this trend in European politics in which political activism, at least through the traditional institutions, is not seen as rewarding anymore.

GROUP DYNAMICS, COMMITMENT, AND CONVERSION

The work of sociologists of religion Rodney Stark and Roger Finke regarding the formation and development of religious groups provides insights that may help in understanding the high level of commitment operating within the missionary community. These missionary communities are analogous to religious sects, groups whose members collectively exist in a high tension with their surroundings. They have norms and values different from those of the surrounding society and many times are met either by ridicule or by open hostility. As I have shown, militants of both the National Front and the Northern League set themselves apart from the rest of society, becoming subcultural deviants. Here is a fundamental reason to understand the high level of commitment of both groups. For Stark and Finke, "the higher its level of tension with its surroundings, the more extensive the commitment to a religious organization." As they explained, "The higher the tension of their religious group, the less distinction people draw between religious and secular matters: religious doctrines and practices impinge on everything else, defining with whom they associate, how they spend their leisure time, sometimes even how they dress and speak" (Stark and Finke 2000, 144).

At the same time, "the higher its level of tension with its surroundings, the more expensive it is to belong to a religious group," that is, the higher the material, social, and psychic costs of belonging to a religious group. Thus the group demands and requires more of its members. Finally, "the higher a group's level of tension with its surroundings, the higher its average level of member commitment" (Stark and Finke 2000, 145). For Stark and Finke there is a reciprocal relationship between expense and the value of the rewards of membership. In the case of the sects the greater value they offer in return for commitment is a close, personal, and responsive God.

In fact—from the standpoint of the militants of both movements—the sacred community offers indeed a greater value that justifies to the true believers all of the costs involved. It is an important insight to understand that the activism does not necessarily represent an irrational or demential attachment to the cause. The issue of "brainwashing" becomes a false issue. Most militants express the notion that, although the costs of belonging to these movements are extremely high in terms of emotional-physical commitment as well as of sacrifice, the reward of belonging to a "true community" that gives sense and a transcendental meaning to their lives alleviates all the trials they have to go through. The *fact* of belonging to a community of the righteous—the *knowledge* that the experience of membership invests the devotee with the power of a collective that is endowed with the vision of a charismatic leader and committed to a mission of salvation—justifies all costs (on this point see Stark and Finke 2000, 144–45). Although a cost-benefit analysis is manifestly insufficient to understand all the dynamics and shades of these missionary communities, it does not mean that such analysis should be altogether discarded if it takes into account benefits that are essentially spiritual and psychological in nature, even though these are hard to quantify. Nonetheless, the testaments and deeds of the participants demonstrate that these benefits can be intensely motivating.

A related issue has to do with the dynamics of growth and the possibility of these missionary communities' extending themselves from a core of supporters to the rest of society. This issue is related to the question of whether the charisma of the coterie can be expanded and transformed into mass charisma. The high levels of commitment of the members of these missionary communities lead them to proselytize and seek conversion of others. In reality, this need for conversion appears as a natural compensator for a movement that although it feels itself world-historical has the problem of validating its own marginality. The dynamics of close-knit group formation demonstrate that any new member will feel compelled to adapt their behavior and commitment to the average of the group. It is the power of example. As stated by Stark, "people take their cues from the example set for them by typical others. To the extent that most people around them display high levels of commitment and express their confidence that their religion is true and effective people will conform." At the same time because the religious group requires high costs of everyone it eliminates the problem of free-riders (Stark and Finke 2000, 147–48).

In his study of charismatic communities, Ron van Dooren acknowledges a similar dynamic in the newcomers of "spellbound communities." For him, the convergence of outsiders to the community—whom he calls *joiners*—stems from the enthusiasm of the core militants, whom he calls *seekers* (those charismatically committed), who set an "infectious spread of mood in a group motion." Their behavior "attracts the attention of others in the environment who may then either be carried away by the contagious display of enthusiasm or may interpret leader-adoration as the proper conduct in the given circumstances" (Dooren 1994, 253). In the final section I will discuss some of the contemporary trends that on the one hand can deepen the enthusiasm, commitment, and zeal within the missionary communities and, on the other, can facilitate the proselytizing of new converts by the militants outside of the missionary borders of their community. Whether such proselytizing will be contagious for the rest of society is outside of the scope of my book.

The essential point is that throughout their respective existences both the National Front and the Northern League have consolidated an outsiderhood dynamic—composed, as noted above, of various elements—that has developed each group's self-perception as an exceptional entity, set apart from the mundane and the ordinary. This liminal quality of these movements begets perceptions of a "true community" or communitas characterized by a different belief system, common values, and a different model of society than the dominant rationalized sociopolitical paradigm and bureaucratic structure. In the process the group acquired a transcendent dimension and the whole collectivity a sacred nature.

LEADERSHIP AND THE MISSIONARY MODEL

In sum, my data have shown that there is a sacralized framework—composed of a mythologized narrative and the creation and application of symbols and rites—in both the National Front and the Northern League that sustains the relationship between the charismatic leader, perceived as a "living symbol" of the movement, and his "chosen people." This structure supports and maintains the charismatic dynamics necessary for the cohesion of the missionary community. However, my focus on structure and on its function as a force of integration and group solidarity should not obscure the fact that agency has played and continues to play a fundamental role in creating and maintaining a missionary community. The importance of leadership in the construction of a missionary discourse anchored in ultimate concerns and in a quest for salvation has, in my view, been overshadowed in studies of contemporary political movements. This observation hinges on the question of whether the missionary leaders are essentially strategists who use sacral and symbolic resources in a rational manner for political gain and manipulation of followers or whether they are indeed genuine true believers.

Evidently, in the process of constructing a compelling view of reality, these leaders have at their disposal a full range of cultural resources that help to cement allegiances and mobilize people for collective action. For instance, Ann Ruth Willner has noticed how one of the driving forces of charismatic legitimacy is the capacity of the leader to "inadvertently or deliberately tap the reservoir of relevant myths in his culture," knowing how to "draw upon those myths that are linked to its sacred figures, to its historical and legendary heroes, and to its historical and legendary ordeals and triumphs" (Willner 1984, 62). The vast literature on social movements, drawing from the work of sociologist Erving Goffman,[5] has showed how these social movements have always been involved in the shaping, structuring, and construction of social life. By assigning meaning to events and conditions, these "framing processes" mobilize participants and "function to organize experience and guide action, whether individual or collective" (Snow and Benford 1986, 464). An important dimension of this framing of reality is, in the words of David A. Snow and Robert D. Benford, "narrative fidelity," or the way framing resonates with cultural narrations, that is, "with the stories, myths and folk tales that are part and parcel of one's cultural heritage and that thus function to inform events and experiences in the immediate present" (1988, 210).

As noted previously, the extent to which the National Front and the Northern League both portray themselves as the true defenders of the threatened cultural milieu of their nations and, therefore, have this dimension of cultural resonance with its symbols and myths, plays a crucial part in these movements' mobilizing potency. As seen in their writings and speeches, and

---

5. Goffman 1974. To Goffman, "When the individual in our Western Society recognizes a particular event, he tends, whatever else he does, to imply in this response (and in effect employ) one or more frameworks or schemata of interpretation of a kind that can be called primary" (1974, 21).

through the activities of their respective parties, both Le Pen and Bossi are aware that symbolism and culture constitute powerful vehicles for resource mobilization. Thus their efforts are in part calculated. At the same time they have seemed throughout their careers to display a spontaneous and genuine attachment both to their cause and to the missionary communities that they represent. Not only do they declare themselves to be true believers; they act as true believers and continue to commit themselves to their movements in a total manner, as "true" militants should. Herein lies, as noted, a major reason that these leaders continue to appeal to their followers. Both leaders frame reality and mobilize resources to maximize this appeal. But what ultimately matters most toward a missionary politics is the way that *leaders are perceived as genuine true believers by the other members of the community*. And from this perception, the relationship "leader-followers" gains its inner strength and durability, as well as reinforces charismatic dimensions within the group. I share Roy Wallis's view regarding the need to focus on the social construction of charisma, and particularly agree with his contention that "[b]ecoming charismatic is not a once and for always thing." Charisma "must be constantly reinforced and reaffirmed or it no longer exists. The charismatic leader, and those around him, must find means constantly to secure the reaffirmation required" (Wallis 1982, 35). The leader's proven devotion to the cause is part of this charismatic construction. My focus on the implementation and actual operation of missionary politics in my case studies has demonstrated how crucial a role agency plays in the process of the construction of a reality, an organic whole, which integrates individuals and their leaders. But although missionary politics is a construction, an element of authenticity lies at the very heart of the attachment to the community. Followers should not be seen as trapped or manipulated by the missionary community. They are willing members of the community, in the sense that they are willing to be carried away by the emotional benefits offered by the community. It is not the missionary structure that imposes on the individual his or her allegiance to the group. This structure facilitates and sustains the allegiance. But it is the member's ideology, the power of belief, the emotional reality of experience, and the deeply felt perception of the moral value of the mission that lie at the very root of and underpin the allegiance to the community.

5
The Future of Missionary Politics

In this book I have showed the inner dynamics of political movements in contemporary Europe that cast themselves as the sacred defenders of their communities, driven toward a holy mission and composed of a devoted followership around a charismatic leader. In a time when European politics is regularly portrayed, particularly in the media, as the dominion of "grey bureaucrats" and "dull politicians," and in which pragmatic and legalistic discussions prevail, I have opened the view to the other side of the politics of the old continent where militancy, fervor, and attachment to politico-religious movements are very much alive.

Will missionary politics continue to have a hold on considerable numbers of people in Western Europe? If my case studies of the National Front and the Northern League serve as an indication, the future promises more, not less, missionary politics and charismatic leadership. In this chapter I bring to attention current trends that, because of my research into both the National Front and the Northern League, I believe are potential incubators of general public anxieties and, therefore, would increase the number of those seeking refuge from a rapidly changing reality in political movements that offer a telos of salvation from a threatening and increasingly global environment. The path of the movements I have categorized as "missionary" is, obviously, not preordained, and global trends are not immutable per se—social reality always contains the possibility of changes that would curtail the enchanting power of these movements. Yet these are the trends (at least the major ones) that will guide, shape, and ultimately determine the future of missionary politics in Europe.

GLOBALIZATION

Anti-globalization rhetoric has become a prime mover in the development of missionary politics. In the paradigm that I have outlined, globalization is perceived to be an inexorably malign project promoted by powerful elites recklessly determined to achieve world domination. In this vision, globalization is a utopian project, rooted in an inhuman economic vision of the world and with the final goal of a uniformity of peoples, cultures, and practices, all united in worship of the market. Policies of depopulation and open borders are an essential part of this calculated project to disintegrate ethnicities and uproot cultures, which are pictured as the last bastions of authentic human experience.

This apocalyptic portrait of globalization—linked with the pervasive conspiratorial theme of a "New World Order"—offers a grand narrative to missionary movements, which portray themselves as locked in a meta-historical struggle against the forces of evil. This narrative also increases millenarian expectations. In this manner the mission, from a local or national setting, evolves into a global struggle, with both movements claiming to play a global role.[1]

America's pitch for total power and domination over a global market that meets its burgeoning needs for products and services is perceived to be the driving force behind this wicked and vicious globalization. In order to achieve and consolidate its preeminence over the rest of the world, America—through the government, global corporations, or shadowy groups—exerts its influence over domestic policies of other countries, destroying any vestiges (such as indigenous attachment to local and national identities) that might interfere with the final goal of "making the world safe for the market."

Globalization is ultimately and forcefully rejected by these movements because it is thought to lead to the devaluation of man, who is exploited and reduced to an undifferentiated commodity at the mercy of global capitalist needs. This critique invests their anti-globalization narratives with a crucial

---

1. Writing on the international opposition to globalization, Ronald Niezen has pointed out that "it has become nearly impossible to effectively assert community values without recourse to ideas with global reach, directed toward an international audience (2004, 58).

ethical dimension, and contains the reason why the denunciation by these movements of globalization is indistinguishable from their excoriation of the materialism and vacuity of modern society. Thus, calls for a purification and renewal of the now exceedingly materialistic West abound. This rhetoric of cleansing implies a holistic, and not a pragmatic, vision of politics. Missionary politics has therefore found in its combat against globalization a fertile ground, appealing to a larger population afraid of losing its identity in the anonymous, global marketplace.

ISLAMIZATION

The National Front and the Northern League share a deep foreboding about the increasing number of Muslim immigrants to Europe, whose influx each party views as a grave threat to Europe's traditional Christian culture. The fear of an "Islamization" of the continent has gained ground in the narratives of each party, and has fueled apocalyptic dynamics that present the end of European culture as a real possibility. Over the last few years, the Northern League has been particularly vehement in its defense of the Christian roots of Europe (it felt the need to readjust its discourse in a more Christian-oriented direction), while the National Front has increasingly framed the issue less in terms of religion (though references to Christianity remain salient) and more in terms of the inevitable disruption caused by uncontrolled immigration (a trajectory in tune with the strategy of Le Pen's likely successor—his daughter—to present a less traditionalist and more modern party). But in the long term, this theme of the rise and fall of a Christian Europe that will be replaced by a Muslim Europe has the potential to outlast any short-term strategies and to have primacy over other themes in the narrative of missionary movements.

Both the National Front and the Northern League have taken the lead in fighting against the construction of mosques and Muslim schools in their countries. A running theme of these parties—particularly visible, for instance, in the European elections of 2004—is resistance to the entry of Turkey into the European Union, which both interpret as a potential cataclysm for the Christian-rooted culture of Europe. An electoral poster of the National Front revealed the growing importance of this theme. "Did you like immigration?"

it states, and then promises, "Well, you're going to love Islamization!"² The demographic decline of Europe and the filling of this demographic void with Muslim immigrants have increased the drama and the sense of urgency that each movement records in its propaganda. From the perspective shared by the National Front and the Northern League, the coupling of these two factors in the not so distant future will spell doomsday for Europe.

In recent years the French and the Italian governments have undertaken efforts to facilitate the integration of Muslim communities within the broader society. With the largest Muslim population in Western Europe—an estimated five million,³ or 7 to 8 percent of the total population—France created in 2002/2003 a Conseil Français du Culte Musulman (French Council for the Muslim Religion), made up of experts and representatives of mosques and Muslim federations, and dedicated to representing concerns related to the Muslim religion within the French State (for example, the allocation of prayer spaces). A similar path was followed in 2005 by Italy—whose own Muslim population, between 1 and 2 percent of the total population, is slim compared to that of France—which created a government-appointed body, the Consulta per l'Islam italiano (Consultative Council for Islam), under the direct authority of the Ministry of the Interior. This body goes beyond mere religious issues (as in the French case) by having as founding goals the "facilitation of [an] institutional dialogue with the Italian Muslim community" toward its "harmonious" insertion into the national community.⁴ In both cases the aim has been to encourage the development of a homegrown,

---

2. "Le 13 Juin dites non à la Turquie dans l'Europe," May–June 2004. This poster was available at the National Front's website.

3. There are no definite numbers on the Muslim population in France because France does not keep official statistics on people by religious affiliation. On this issue see Jonathan Laurence and Justin Vaisse (2006, chap. 1). The December 2006 European Monitoring Center on Racism and Xenophobia (EUMC) report, *Muslims in the European Union: Discrimination and Islamophobia*, estimated the Muslim population in France as (unofficially) 3,516,824; in Italy, also unofficially, as 723,188. The report, however, states that this represents the "best available information" (EUMC 2006). Dispute over the real number of Muslims in both countries (especially in France) remains.

4. See *Ministero dell'Interno—Decreto 10 Settembre 2005*, <http://www.interno.it/legislazione/pages/articolo.php?idarticolo=691>.

mainstream, and official Islam in order to prevent further Muslim alienation and to undercut the appeal of a more radical and extremist Islam.

The reader should not be surprised that both missionary movements have derided these integration attempts as further "proof" that the "Islamic march" in Europe is being aided and abetted by the ruling elites. The National Front announced that these efforts marked the end of the separation between church and state, and the start of the official financing of Islam in France under the pressure of its burgeoning "migrant and demographic force" (Le Pen 2006a; see also M. Le Pen 2006, 317–19). The Northern League, on the other hand, criticized the creation of the new body as one more example of the political establishment's dangerous "delusion" about and "blindness" toward the "domineering" and "conquering" nature of Islam. The right approach, instead, would be to reinforce (in the Constitution) the Christian identity of the country against the risk of an Islamic takeover (*La Repubblica*, September 10, 2005; *Lega Nord* 2006b).

This denunciation of Islamic practices on European soil is often tied with dire predictions—both in European nationalist movements and in other conservative intellectual circles (regularly echoed in the blogosphere)—of Europe's potential transformation into a new geopolitical entity called "Eurabia."[5] Regardless of how many studies or statistics are published to dispel such fears, the specter of a Muslim Europe hangs over the missionary

---

5. Middle Eastern and Islamic scholar Bernard Lewis, for example, asserted that Muslims "seem to be about to take over Europe." "Will it be an Islamized Europe or Europeanized Islam?" is the only relevant question, he declared in an interview (*Jerusalem Post,* January 29, 2007). British author Bat Ye'or's book *Eurabia: The Euro-Arab Axis* (2005) has become a reference in the "Islamization of Europe" perspective. Bat Ye'or describes the emergence—with the collaboration of the elites—of a new European civilization of *dhimmitude,* of subordination and subjugation to the new Muslim "masters" of Europe. In *While Europe Slept: How Radical Islam Is Destroying the West from Within,* Bruce Bawer warns against what he sees as the ongoing "colonization" of Europe by Islamism, and its consequences for the Western world (2006, 231). For a similar, somber view of the future of Europe, see Claire Berlinski's *Menace in Europe: Why the Continent's Crisis Is America's Too* (2006). Berlinski writes, "As someone who *has* spent time thinking about Europe and its history, I do not prophesy the imminent demise of European democratic institutions, nor do I predict imminent catastrophe on European soil. But I don't rule out these possibilities either. Europe's entitlement economy

movements that I have focused on in this book. According to the tenet of *suppressed knowledge* of both the Northern League and the National Front, studies that come from governmental agencies, academia, or the media are dismissed as and proclaimed to be invalid, because their aim is to manipulate public opinion, distort reality, and consolidate the dominant paradigm. Thus Umberto Bossi announced on the eve of the 2006 general elections that, with a victory by the center-left, Italy would become an "Islamic-Communist Republic" (*La Padania*, April 7, 2006). Further, Le Pen has pointed out that "there are more veiled Muslim woman in France than in Tehran," and accused the political establishment of being beholden to religious minorities (and the Muslim minority in particular). "Soon," he added, "their numbers [will] increase even more," as will their political leverage and power at the expense of that currently enjoyed by the indigenous French population (*Les Français d'Abord!,* July 5, 2006).

Therefore, recognition by the state (in both countries) of the need for a more proactive approach in order to integrate Muslim communities and avoid further estrangement is seen as part of the problem and not of the

---

will collapse. Its demography *will* change. The European Union may unravel. Islamic terrorists may succeed in taking out a European city. We have no idea what these events would herald, but it is possible and reasonable to imagine a very ugly outcome" (Berlinski 2006, 246). Among those who connect the unfolding of Eurabia with a popular reaction that might bring back fascism to Europe is Canadian columnist Mark Steyn. In *America Alone: The End of the World as We Know It,* he writes, "How bad is it going to get in Europe? As bad as it can get—as in societal collapse, fascist revivalism, and then the long Eurabian night, not over the entire Continent but over significant parts of it. And those countries that manage to escape the darkness will do so only after violent convulsions of their own" (Steyn 2006, 105). Though rejecting the predictions of an Islamic Europe by the end of the twenty-first century, historian Walter Laqueur asserts that a declining Europe will need to reach a policy of "appeasement" with its Muslim population. "But as nations have failed to take a strong stand that might have prevented the current crisis when it was still possible," he writes, "what are the alternatives now, as immigrants of Muslim background become the majority in certain cities, regions, and subsequently perhaps even entire countries?" (2007, 217). The issue of the rise of a Muslim Europe is covered regularly in weblogs (mostly on the right). An influential voice is Norwegian blogger Fjordman, who wrote a four-part series titled "The Eurabia Code," where he documents the creation of Eurabia as "one of the greatest betrayals in the history of Western civilization." This essay can be read online at <http://gatesofvienna.blogspot.com/2006/10/eurabia-code_19.htm>.

solution.⁶ In this manner, within both the Northern League and the National Front—and other political parties across Europe⁷—the sense of impending doom regarding the long-term consequences of Muslim settlement and visions of a slow Muslim takeover of the institutions and values of European countries are likely to deepen, and will increase the popular appeal of missionizing calls for political salvation from a future of intimidation, subjugation, and cultural loss.

DEMOGRAPHIC DECLINE

A powerful underlying force pervading the discourse of these missionary movements is a sense of deep urgency to combat the ongoing decline of Europe's population. Both parties' programs vow to face what is characterized as a "true demographic time bomb" with pro-traditional family policies, and both accuse the political establishment of contributing decisively (and wittingly) to the current demographic crisis. Fertility levels in European nations have since the 1970s declined to below-replacement level. Coupled with a steady increase in the elderly population, this trend will make it impossible for societies to replenish themselves and will lead to a shrinking European population in the future. While Italy has one of the lowest fertility rates in Western Europe, France has one of the highest, though this is still at subreplacement level.⁸ In more recent times, both the French and to a lesser extent

---

6. There has been growing research on the issue of Muslim integration in Europe. See, for example, Toensing 2005; Laurence and Vaisse 2006; Giry 2006; and Pfaff and Gill 2006. On Islam and Muslims in Europe, see also the Web site Euro-Islam <http://www.euro-islam.info>.

7. For instance, Filip Dewinter, one of the prominent leaders of the Flemish party Vlaams Belang, when asked in an interview in *Jewish Week* about his party's xenophobia, replied, "Xenophobia is not the word I would use. If it absolutely must be a phobia, let it be a islamphobia. Yes, we are afraid of Islam. The Islamization of Europe is a frightening thing. Even distinguished Jewish scholars as Bat Ye'or and Bernard Lewis warned about this. If this historical process continues, the Jews will be the first victims" (October 28, 2005). For these comments he was prosecuted by the Belgian authorities for "inciting hatred" (*EJP* 2005).

8. The European Union average fertility rate was 1.52 children per woman in 2005. The average birth rate in France was 2.00 children per woman in 2006, the highest in thirty years (Insee 2007), while in Italy it was 1.30 children per woman in 2005 (Istat 2006). The

the Italian governments have embarked on policies to buck this trend—for example, cash and fiscal incentives to couples with more than one child (see *Il Corriere della Sera*, July 17, 2003; CNN, October 25, 2005). Another solution to offsetting the economic and social consequences of falling birthrates (and maintaining both a competitive economy and a sustainable welfare state) would be to loosen even further restrictions on immigration.

The continuation of these demographic trends accentuates the fear within the missionary communities that the native population will be soon replaced, slowly but steadily, by foreigner groups; they are alarmed moreover by the fact that immigrant communities have higher birthrates than native-born women.[9] According to this rationale, even if European countries further tighten restrictions on immigration, the source of replacement is *already* present within each society. This factor triggers a deep-seated sense of cultural despair in which combat against these demographic trends is felt as and understood to be a struggle for survival of the "original" ethnic nations.

Within the inner world of the missionary communities, the decades-long radical anti-family policies and their related anti-life, pro-contraceptive, pro-homosexual offshoots are just a symptom of an underlying disease. These developments are associated with globalization and its onslaught on such "natural" attachments of mankind as that to one's community, nation, or family, in order to create a uniform and easily transferable population at the mercy of the needs and directives of the global market. The bearers of intellectual and institutional authority are dismissed as willing participants

---

level of fertility at which a population replaces itself (replacement level) is 2.1 children per woman. See *2004 Revision of World Population Prospects,* Population Division of the Department of Economic and Social Affairs of the United Nations Secretariat, <http://www.un.org/esa/population/publications/WPP2004/WPP2004_Volume3.htm>. At the same time mass immigration across borders will dramatically increase. Recent figures from the United Nation's Population Division predict that for the period 2007–2050 "the population of the more developed regions is expected to remain largely unchanged at 1.2 billion and would have declined were it not for the projected net migration from developing to developed countries, which is expected to average 2.3 million persons annually." Most of these immigrants will come from Asia and Africa (see United Nations 2007).

9. There is evidence though of decreasing fertility rates among Muslim women, at least in France. On this point, see Laurence and Vaisse 2006, chap. 1.

in this global project and therefore lack the genuine will or legitimacy to put in place pro-family policies, regardless of how well they mask their true intentions. Many times the economic implications of the current demographic trends take a secondary role in these movements' discourses, which focus instead on their cultural and ethnic dimensions, which foreshadow a catastrophe for the communities and, more broadly, the passing of European civilization.

EUROPEANIZATION

Like globalization and Islam, the emergence and widening of a European Union policy is seen as a direct threat to the diversity of continental cultures. The push by the "elites" to build a postmodern bureaucratic paradise is portrayed in the missionary rhetoric as an attack against the people. Both the National Front and the Northern League have positioned themselves against the "Brussels Eurocrats" whom they see as fanatically determined to regulate and bring under control every aspect of the lives of European Union citizens. Both parties attack what they perceive to be a dangerous and artificial process of "social engineering" that is hell-bent on destroying the natural roots and allegiances of traditional European societies. Thus they reject the proposal to criminalize across EU countries behavior deemed racist or xenophobic and the creation of a European arrest warrant, on the basis that the true intention is to create an intrusive, oppressive judicial system that silences any voices that go against the dominant orthodoxy, to stifle dissent, and to impose a European-wide de facto censorship. Therefore, the European Union is increasingly derided as a "superstate" that is by nature tyrannical, totalitarian, and ruled by a class of bureaucrats.

In order to boost the legitimacy of the European project, the European Union has made a continued effort to foster not just a *civic* (in terms of popular attachment to EU institutions and laws) but also, increasingly, a *cultural* European identity with a shared cultural and historical legacy (Bruter 2005). The dissemination of pan-European symbols (flag, anthem, passport, "Europe Day," for example) and championing of the EU cosmopolitan, peaceful, and tolerant founding values (that leave to the past the era of aggressive and selfish nationalisms) are seen by some scholars as catalysts for the emergence—and continuing growth—of a "mass European identity," or "the evolution of Europeanness as a mass phenomenon" (Bruter 2005, 166–78). The strengthening of a pan-Europe is interwoven with the notion of a new, unified continent, as, in the words of an early supporter of the project, an "exemplar of a new stage in political civilization" (Duchêne 1973, 19),[10] a true civilian power (as opposed to military) in the stage of global governance.[11] Thus there is an ongoing clash of cultural views about Europe, in the sense that contemporary missionary movements also hold the defense of (the decidedly Christian and ethnically more homogenous than that promoted through the EU ethos) European civilization and legacy as one of their founding goals.

In this light, European Union–wide policies are envisioned as nothing more than a top-down and illegitimate attempt to coerce the citizens, legally and morally, to accept a deracinated version of society. This perception of a Europe-wide rule of bureaucrats—dismissed many times as vassals of antinational global designs—has the potential to increase the already widening distance between the citizens and the institutions of power, and to strengthen the internal dynamics of marginalization and localism within the respective European nations.

---

10. It should be stressed that before the official creation of the European Union, a significant number of modern authors and statesmen, both from within and outside of Europe, stressed the revolutionary potential of a unified Europe. In 1929, American journalist (and future editor-in-chief of the Protestant periodical *Christian Century*) Paul Hutchinson described to an American audience the efforts being made—by such people as Count Richard N. Coudenhove-Kalergi, hailed as "the Prophet of Pan-Europe," and Aristide Briand, "probably the most powerful single figure in the political life of the continent"—to give birth to the U.S.E, the United States Of Europe. Hutchinson noted, however, that a crucial condition for the success of the project as the unshakable basis of peace for future European generations was a necessary "meeting of Europe's masses." Such "must be a genuine meeting—not for a day or a month, but a continuous meeting, in which men look at each other as fellow-workers towards one goal" (Hutchinson 1929, 223).

11. On an ambitious conception of Europe as a "civilian power," see Telo 2006.

6
Conclusion

As I stated in the introduction, my method of investigating and explaining the phenomenon of contemporary sacralized politics has been based on the construction of a heuristic device, an ideal type of politics that I claim to be "missionary." Starting with the empirical reality of the movements, my method has taken the acts and rhetoric of both leadership and rank and file seriously, and then has put forward a model of characteristic patterns and structures within each group.

I propose that this missionary form of politics be understood as a cluster concept; defined as a political religion; and characterized by a dynamic interaction between charismatic leadership, a soteriological narrative of outsiderhood and ritualization, and the creation of a moral community invested with a collective mission of combating conspiratorial enemies and redeeming the nation from its putative crisis.

The National Front and the Northern League, though close to ideal typical cases of missionary leadership, do not replicate the pure type of missionary politics that, as an ideal type, will always remain a constructed utopia. Nonetheless, an ideal type analysis allows some of the most difficult-to-understand aspects of these extraordinary social movements to be elucidated and systematized. The question then arises of whether other political leaders and movements, either right or left, can be considered cases of contemporary missionary politics. There are obviously other European political movements in Europe—such as the independentist Flemish party Vlaams Belang (Flemish Interest) or Austria's Freedom Party—that merit scrutiny through the prism of missionary politics. The same can be said about movements on the left, particularly those with an anti-globalization outlook. Another fertile ground for these movements can eventually be found in Eastern Europe. Vladimir Tismaneanu has written about the development of "fantasies of salvation" and the mythologization of politics in post-communist countries; studies by other social scientists have already demonstrated the resurgence of charismatic leaderships in that region (Tismaneanu 1998; Eatwell 2002). Only further study of such movements across both political boundaries and academic disciplines will determine whether or not such fit the ideal type as well as do the National Front and the Northern League, and which specific factors are responsible for the various trajectories. Another avenue of research would be to address the issue of whether the missionary model of analysis may be extended to cases beyond populist movements. Though a deeper investigation, if not a settlement, of these issues is beyond the scope of my study, they undoubtedly merit being brought to attention.

In any case, in the interest of comparative research, the ideal type of missionary politics should be utilized not only as a yardstick against which reality can be compared and measured, but also as a theoretical framework against which specific case studies may be tested, conceptually framed, and evaluated as either warranting or not warranting the "missionary" label. This theoretical model of missionary politics may thus be extended to other cases and contribute to the field of comparative politics.

The examples of the National Front and the Northern League offer proof that faith-based secular movements remain strong and may become even stronger in reaction to felt threats to localized identity. Within these movements, the sacralization of both the group and its collective mission is achieved in such a comprehensive manner that it gives members a way of re-enchanting the world with myth, ritual, and a redemptive vision. In this manner politics, no longer a managerial or expedient activity, transforms itself into a sacred worldview that injects both a sense of meaning and a revitalized identity into all touched by the sacred mission. In conclusion, it seems that a sacralized form of politics, far from absent in the modern or postmodern era, is destined to remain salient, and perhaps even to increase in importance. The primacy given by missionary leaders and groups to the aforementioned global and societal trends and to a secular-nationalist form of religious experience bespeaks the potential appeal of missionary politics or "politics not as usual," at least in contemporary Western Europe. Missionizing politics is here to stay for the foreseeable future.

REFERENCES

INDEX

References

BROADCAST MEDIA

AFP. 2003. "Le Pen se voit comme 'un médecin en période d'épidémie.'" Nov. 10.
AGI—Agenzia Giornalistica Italia. 2006. Oct. 2.
BBC News. 2005. Jan. 13, <http://news.bbc.co.uk/2/hi/europe/4170761.stm>.
———. 2006. Feb. 18, <http://news.bbc.co.uk/2/hi/europe/4727606.stm>.
CNN. 2005. "French Incentives to Produce Larger Families." Oct. 25, <http://transcripts.cnn.com/TRANSCRIPTS/0510/25/i_ins.01.html>.
EJP—European Jewish Press. 2005. "Complaint Against Extreme-right Leader for 'Islamophobia,'" Nov. 24, <http://www.ejpress.org/article/4336>.
———. 2007. "Extreme-right Politician Sentenced for Gas Chamber Comments." Jan. 18, <http://www.ejpress.org/article/13061>.
France 2. 2004. "Question Ouverte—Invité Jean-Marie Le Pen." Jan. 29.
France 3. 2006. "Journal: Région Centre." Oct. 29.
France 5. 2006. "Ripostes sur France 5." Nov. 26, <http://www.france5.fr/ripostes/#>.
JTA—Jewish Telegraphic Agency. 2004. "French Politico Faces Firing for Calling Existence of Gas Chambers Debatable." Oct. 15, <http://www.jta.org/cgi-bin/iowa/news/article/20041015Frenchpoliticoface.html>.
Reuters. 2006. "French Leader Denounces Islam." Apr. 24.

NEWSPAPERS AND MAGAZINES

Corriere della Sera, Il
Daily Telegraph
Famiglia Cristiana
FDA: Le magazine de Jean-Marie Le Pen
Federalismo, Il
Figaro, Le

Figaro-Magazine, Le
Français d'Abord!, Les
Gente
Giornale, Il
The Guardian
Identité: Revue d'Études Nationales
International Herald Tribune
Jerusalem Post
Jewish Week
Jewish World Review
Lega Nord–Padania Indipendente
Libération
Lombardia Autonomista
Monde, Le
National-Hebdo
New York Times
New Yorker
Padania, La
Panorama
Parisien, Le
Paris Match
Point, Le
Présent
Quaderni Padani
Repubblica, La
Scotsman, The
Stampa, La
Wall Street Journal

BOOKS, ARTICLES, AND SPEECHES

Alexander, Jeffrey C., Bernhard Giesen, and Jason L. Mast. 2006. *Social Performance: Symbolic Action, Cultural Pragmatics and Ritual.* Cambridge, UK: Cambridge Univ. Press.

Aminzade, Ron, and Doug McAdam. 2001. "Emotions and Contentious Politics." In *Silence and Voice in the Study of Contentious Politics,* edited by Ron Aminzade et al., 14–50. New York: Cambridge Univ. Press.

Antony, Bernard, and Yves Daoudal. 2005. *L'islam sans complaisance: Mythes et réalités*. Paris: Éditions Godefroy de Bouillon.

Apter, David E., 1963. "Political Religions in the New Nations." In *Old Societies and New States*. edited by Clifford Geertz. New York: Free Press of Glencoe.

Aron, Raymond. 1945. *L'Age des Empires et L'Avenir de la France*. Paris: Éditions Defense de la France.

Baiocchi, Giuseppe. 1999. Preface to *La Lega: 1979:1989*, by Umberto Bossi. Milan: Editoriale Nord.

Ballaman, Edouard. 2005. *La Piccola Guida alla Cultura Islamica*. Lega Nord Federazione Padana, <http://www.padaniaoffice.org/pdf/scuola_politica_federale/bellaria_sestri/Libro_Ballaman.pdf>.

Bariller, Damien, and Franck Timmermans. 1994. *20 ans au Front. L'histoire vraie du Front National*. Paris: Éditions Nationales.

Bariller, Franck, D. Lefort, and F. Marest. 1995. "Français Passionnément: La Vie de Jean-Marie Le Pen en Bande-Dessinée." Paris: Éditions Nationales.

Barkun, Michael. 2000. "Politics and Apocalypticism." In *The Encyclopedia of Apocalypticism*. Vol. 3: *Apocalypticism in the Modern Period and the Contemporary Age*, edited by Stephen J. Stein, 442–60. New York: Continuum.

———. 2003. *A Culture of Conspiracy: Apocalyptic Visions in Contemporary America*. Berkeley: Univ. of California Press.

Bat Ye'or. 2005. *Eurabia: The Euro-Arab Axis*. Madison, N.J.: Farleigh Dickinson Univ. Press.

Bawer, Bruce. 2006. *While Europe Slept: How Radical Islam Is Destroying the West from Within*. New York: Doubleday.

Bell, Daniel. 1977. "The Return of the Sacred? The Argument on the Future of Religion." *British Journal of Sociology* 28, no. 4 (Dec.).

Bellah, Robert. 1967. "Civil Religion in America." *Daedalus, Journal of the American Academy of Arts and Sciences* 96, no. 1 (Winter).

Bensman, Joseph, and Michael Givant. 1975. "Charisma and Modernity: The Use and Abuse of a Concept." *Social Research* 42, no. 4.

Berger, Peter L., ed. 1999. *The Desecularization of the World: Resurgent Religion and World Politics*. Grand Rapids, Mich.: William B. Eerdmans Publishing Company.

Berlinski, Claire. 2006. *Menace in Europe: Why the Continent's Crisis Is America's Too*. New York: Crown Forum.

Berzano, Luigi. 1994. *Religiosità del nuovo areopago: credenze e forme religiose nell' forma postsecolare*. Milan: FrancoAngeli.

Betz, Hans-Georg, and Stefan Immerfall. 1998. *The New Politics of the Right: Neo-Populist Parties and Movements in Established Democracies.* New York: St. Martin's Press.

Biorcio, Roberto. 1997. *La Padania Promessa: La storia, le idée la logica d'azione della Lega Nord.* Milan: Il Saggiatore.

Blot, Yvan. 1992. *Baroque et Politique.* Paris: Éditions Nationales.

Bobbio, Norberto. 1987. *The Future of Democracy: A Defense of the Rules of the Game.* Translated by Roger Griffin. Minneapolis: Univ. of Minnesota Press.

———. 1998. "Attenti al carisma, la violenza viene dal 'capo.'" *Reset,* no. 48, May.

Bossi, Umberto. 1990. "Discorso di Pontida." Pontida, May 20.

———. 1991a. "1 Congresso Lega Nord." Pieve Emanuele, Milan, Feb. 8-9-10.

———. 1991b. "Discorso di Pontida." Pontida, June 16.

———. 1993. "Second Congress of Lega Nord, Intervento di chiusura del Segretario Federale." Dec. 11, 12.

———. 1994. "Discorso del Segretario Federale on. Bossi, al II Congresso Federale della Lega Nord." Feb. 4.

———. 1995. *Tutta la verità.* Milan: Mondadori.

———. 1996. *Il mio progetto. Discorsi su federalismo e Padania.* Milan: Sperling and Kupfer.

———. 1997. "Intervento del Segretario Federale." 3 Congresso Federale, Milan, Feb. 15, <http://www.leganord.org/segretariofederale/discorsi_assemblee/1997_15febbraio.pdf>.

———. 1998a. "Intervento del Segretario Federale." Milan, Congresso Federale, Mar. 28, <http://www.leganord.org/segretariofederale/discorsi_assemblee/1998_28marzomilano.pdf>.

———. 1998b. "Lettera di Bossi ai militanti: si ritorna all'attacco!!!" Aug., <http://www.prov-varese.leganord.org/articoli.asp?ID=332>.

———. 1998c. "Intervento del Segretario Federale." Ponte di Legno, Sept. 7.

———. 1998d. "Intervento del Segretario Federale." Brescia, Congresso Federale, Oct. 25, <http://www.leganord.org/segretariofederale/discorsi_assemblee/1998_25ottobre_congresso.pdf>.

———. 1999. *La Lega, 1979-1989.* Milan: Editoriale Nord.

———. 2000a. "Intervento del Segretario Federale." Pontida, June 4, <http://www.leganord.org/segretariofederale/discorsi_pontida/2000_4giugno.pdf>.

———. 2000b. "Intervento del Segretario Federale." Venice, Sept. 17.

———. 2002. "Intervento del Segretario Federale." Venice, Sept. 15, <http://www.leganord.org/segretariofederale/discorsi_venezia/2002_15settembre.pdf>.

———. 2003a. "Intervento del Segretario Federale." Pontida, May 4, <http://www.leganord.org/segretariofederale/discorsi_pontida/2003_4%20maggio.pdf>.
———. 2003b. "Intervento del Segretario Federale." Venice, Sept. 21, <http://www.leganord.org/segretariofederale/discorsi_venezia/2003_21settembre.pdf>.
Bossi, Umberto, and Daniele Vimercati. 1992. *Vento del Nord*. Milan: Sperling and Kupfer.
———. 1993. *La rivoluzione. La Lega: storia e idée*. Milan: Sperling and Kupfer.
———. 1998. *Processo alla Lega*. Milan: Sperling and Kupfer.
Bossi-Fini. 2002. "Modifica alla normativa in materia di immigrazione e di asilo." July 30, <http://www.parlamento.it/leggi/021891.htm>.
Bourdieu, Pierre. 1987. "Legitimation and Structured Interests in Weber's Sociology of Religion." In *Max Weber: Rationality and Modernity*, edited by Sam Whimster and Scott Lash. London: Allen and Unwin.
Bracher, Karl Dietrich. 1984. *The Age of Ideologies: A History of Political Thought in the Twentieth Century*. New York: St. Martin's Press.
Bruce, Steve. 2002. *God Is Dead: Secularization in the West*. Oxford, UK: Blackwell Publishing.
———. 2003. *Politics and Religion*. Cambridge, UK: Polity Press.
Bresson, Gilles, and Christian Lionet. 1994. *Le Pen: Biographie*. Paris: Éditions du Seuil.
Brigneau, François. 1984. "Le Passeur d'eau." In *L'Album Le Pen: Images d'un Français*, edited by Patrick Buisson and Alain Renault. Ecully, France: Intervalles.
———. 1992. *La Haine Anti–Le Pen*. Paris: Publications FB.
Bruter, Michael. 2005. *Citizens of Europe? The Emergence of a Mass European Identity*. New York: Palgrave Macmillan.
Buisson, Patrick, and Alain Renault. 1984. *L'Album Le Pen: Images d'un français*. Ecully, France: Intervalles.
Burleigh, Michael. 2000. *The Third Reich: A New History*. New York: Hill and Wang.
Burns, James MacGregor. 2003. *Transforming Leadership: A New Pursuit of Happiness*. New York: Atlantic Monthly Press.
Burrin, Philippe. 1997. "Political Religion: The Relevance of a Concept." *History and Memory* 9, nos. 1–2:321–49.
Camus, Jean-Yves. 1997. *Le Front National: Histoire et Analyses*. Paris: Éditions Laurens.
Canovan, Margaret. 1999. "Trust the People! Populism and the Two Faces of Democracy." *Political Studies* 47, no. 1 (Mar.): 2–16.

———. 2002. "Taking Politics to the People: Populism as the Ideology of Democracy." In *Democracies and the Populist Challenge*, edited by Yves Mény and Yves Surel, 25–44. New York: Palgrave.

Caravita, Federico. 1993. *Lega Nord: Storia Fotografica*. Legnano, Italy: EdiCart.

Carlyle, Thomas. 1962. *On Heroes and Hero Worship*. 1841. Reprint. New York: E. P. Dutton and Co.

Carter, Elisabeth. 2005. *The Extreme Right in Western Europe, Success or Failure*. Manchester, UK: Manchester Univ. Press.

Cassirer, Ernst. 1961. *The Myth of the State*. 1946. Reprint. New Haven, Conn.: Yale Univ. Press.

Cavalli, Luciano. 1987. "Charisma and Twentieth-Century Politics." In *Max Weber, Rationality and Modernity*, edited by Sam Whimster and Scott Lash, 317–33. London: Allen and Unwin.

———. 1996. *Carisma*. Rome: Istituto della Enciclopedia Italiana, Enciclopedia delle scienze sociali.

Cohn, Norman. 1970. *The Pursuit of the Millennium: Revolutionary Millenarians and Mystical Anarchists of the Middle Ages*. 1957. Reprint. New York: Oxford Univ. Press.

Daoudal, Yves. 2002a. *La Face Cachée de Le Pen*. Paris: Éditions Godefroy de Bouillon.

———. 2002b. *Le Tour Infernal: 21 Avril–5 Mai 2002, Analyse d'une fantasmagorie électorale*. Paris: Éditions Godefroy de Bouillon.

Datops. 2004. "Le Front National dans les Newsgroups." <www.datops.com>.

Diamanti, Ilvo. 1996. *Il Male del Nord, Lega, Localismo, Secessione*. Rome: Donzelli.

Donegà, Claudio. 1994. "Strategie del Presente. I volti della Lega." In *Figli di un benessere minore: La Lega 1979–1993*, edited by Giovanni de Luna, 81–135. Florence: La Nuova Italia.

Dooren, Ron van. 1994. *Messengers from the Promised Land: An Interactive Theory of Political Charisma*. Leiden, Netherlands: DSWO Press, Leiden Univ.

Douglas, Mary. 2002. *Purity and Danger: An Analysis of Concept of Pollution and Taboo*. 1966. Reprint. London: Routledge Classics.

Duchêne, François. 1973. "The European Community and the Uncertainties of Interdependence." In *A Nation Writ Large? Foreign Policy Problems Before the European Communities*, edited by Max Kohnstamm and Wolfgang Hager, 1–21. London: Macmillan.

Durkheim, Émile. 2001. *The Elementary Forms of Religious Life*. Translated by Carol Cosman. 1912. Reprint. New York: Oxford Univ. Press.

Eatwell, Roger. 2002. "The Rebirth of Right-Wing Charisma? The Cases of Jean-Marie Le Pen and Vladimir Zhirinovsky." *Totalitarian Movements and Political Religions* 3, no. 3 (Winter): 1–23.

———. 2004. "Introduction: The New Extreme Right Challenge." In *Western Democracies and the New Extreme Right Challenge*, edited by Roger Eatwell and Cas Mudde, 1–17. London: Routledge.

Emrich, C. G., H. H. Brower, J. M. Feldman, and H. Garland. 2001. "Images in Words: Presidential Rhetoric, Charisma and Greatness." *Administrative Science Quarterly* 46, no. 3 (Sept.): 527–57.

EUMC—European Monitoring Center on Racism and Xenophobia. 2006. "Muslims in the European Union: Discrimination and Islamophobia." Dec., <http://www.eumc.eu.int>.

Evans, Richard J. 2006. *The Third Reich in Power*. New York: Penguin Books.

Famiglia Cristiana. 1997. No. 24, June 11, <http://www.sanpaolo.org/fc97/2497fc/2497fc24.htm>.

Fassini, Morena. 1998. *La Vera Storia della Lega Nord: "Federalismo E Liberta" Dalle Origini Ad Oggi*. Milan: Ufficio Elettorale Federale, Lega Nord.

Fjordman. 2006. "The Eurabia Code," <http://gatesofvienna.blogspot.com/2006/10/eurabia-code_19.htm>.

Flanagan, Thomas. 2000. "Modernity and the Millennium: From Robespierre to Radical Feminism." In *Essays on Twentieth-Century Millenarianism*, edited by Martha F. Lee. Westport, Conn: Praeger.

Gabler, Neal. 1998. *Life: The Movie, How Entertainment Conquered Reality*. New York: Vintage Books.

Gardner, Howard. 1995. *Leading Minds: An Anatomy of Leadership*. New York: Basic Books.

Geertz, Clifford. 1973. *The Interpretation of Cultures: Selected Essays*. New York: Basic Books.

Gentile, Emilio. 2006. *Politics as Religion*. Translated by George Staunton. 2001. Reprint. Princeton, N.J.: Princeton Univ. Press.

Giner, Salvador. 2003. *Carisma y Razón*. Madrid: Alianza Editorial.

Girardet, Raoul. 1986. *Mythes et Mythologies Politiques*. Paris: Éditions du Seuil.

Giry, Stephanie. 2006. "France and Its Muslims." *Foreign Affairs*, Sept.–Oct.

Glassman, Ronald M. 1986 "Manufactured Charisma and Legitimacy." In *Charisma, History and Social Structure*, edited by Ronald M. Glassman and William H. Swatos, Jr., 115–29. New York: Greenwood Press.

Goffman, Erving. 1974. *Frame Analysis: An Essay on the Organization of Experience*. New York: Harper Colophon Books.
Gollnisch, Bruno. 2003. *La Réaction c'est La Vie!* Paris: Éditions Godefroy de Bouillon.
Graumann, Carl F. 1987. "Conspiracy: History and Social Psychology—A Synopsis." In *Changing Conceptions of Conspiracy*, edited by Carl F. Graumann and Serge Moscovici, 245–51. New York: Springer-Verlag.
Gregor, James A. 2006. "Roger Griffin, Social Science, Fascism, and the Extreme Right." In *Fascism Past and Present, West and East: An International Debate on Concepts and Cases in the Comparative Study of the Extreme Right*, edited by Roger Griffin, Werner Loh, and Andreas Umland, 115–22. Stuttgart, Germany: ibidem-Verlag.
Griffin, Roger. 1991. *The Nature of Fascism*. New York: St. Martin's Press.
———. 2005. "Cloister or Cluster? The Implications of Emilio Gentile's Ecumenical Theory of Political Religion for the Study of Extremism." *Totalitarian Movements and Political Religions* 6, no. 1 (June): 33–52.
Gurian, Waldemar. 1952. "Totalitarian Religions." *Review of Politics* 14, no. 1 (Jan.): 3–14.
Habbad, Said. 1998. "Le Pen, sujet et object de discours." Ph.D. diss., Université Lumière Lyon II.
Halman, Loek. 1999–2000. *The European Values Study: A Third Wave*. Tilburg, Netherlands: Tilburg University. <http://spitswww.uvt.nl/web/fsw/evs/documents/Publications/Sourcebook/EVS_SourceBook.pdf>.
Hayes, Carlton J. H. 1926. *Essays on Nationalism*. New York: Macmillan.
———. 1960. *Nationalism: A Religion*. New York: Macmillan.
Herf, Jeffrey. 1986. *Reactionary Modernism: Technology, Culture, and Politics in Weimar and the Third Reich*. 1984. Reprint. Cambridge, UK: Cambridge Univ. Press.
Holeindre, Roger. 2001. Preface to *Le Pen*. Edited by Yann Maréchal and Nicolas Gauthier. Paris: Objectif France SARL.
———. 2003. *SOS Hystérie II*. Paris: Godefroy de Bouillon.
Hoffer, Eric. 1989. *The True Believer: Thoughts on the Nature of Mass Movements*. 1951. Reprint. New York: Harper Perennial.
Hofstadter, Richard. 1967. *The Paranoid Style in American Politics and Other Essays*. New York: Vintage Books.
Hogg, Michael A., and Barbara A. Mullin. 1999. "Joining Groups to Reduce Uncertainty: Subjective Uncertainty Reduction and Group Identification." In *Social*

Identity and Social Cognition, edited by Michael A. Hogg and Dominic Abrams, 249–79. Malden, Mass.: Blackwell.

Hutchinson, Paul. 1929. *The United States of Europe.* Chicago: Willett, Clark and Colby.

Iacopini, Roberto, and Stefania Bianchi. 1994. *La Lega ce l'ha crudo! Il linguaggio del Carroccio nei suoi slogan, comizi e manifesti.* Milan: Mursia.

Ignazi, Piero. 2003. *Extreme Right Parties in Western Europe.* Oxford, UK: Oxford Univ. Press.

Igounet, Valerie. 2000. *Histoire du négationnisme en France.* Paris: Éditions de Seuil.

Inglehart, Ronald, and Pippa Norris. 2004. *Sacred and Secular: Religion and Politics Worldwide.* Cambridge, UK: Cambridge Univ. Press.

INSEE. 2007. "Bilan démographique 2006: Un excédent naturel record." <http://www.insee.fr/fr/ffc/ipweb/ip1118/1p1118.html>.

ISTAT. 2006. "Population Projection." Mar. 22, 2006, <http://demo.istat.it/altridati/previsioni_naz/idex_e.html>.

Jenkins, Philip. 2002a. "Christianity's New Center." *Atlantic Monthly,* Sept.

———. 2002b. "The Next Christianity." *Atlantic Monthly,* Oct.

———. 2003. *The Next Christendom: The Coming of Global Christianity.* Oxford, UK: Oxford Univ. Press.

Jouve, Pierre, and Ali Magoudi. 1988. *Les dits et les non-dits de Jean-Marie Le Pen: Enquêtes et Psychanalyse.* Paris: Éditions La Découverte.

Kalberg, Stephen. 1994. *Max Weber's Comparative-Historical Sociology.* Chicago: Univ. of Chicago Press.

Katz, Richard, and Peter Mair. 1995. "Changing Models of Party Organization and Party Democracy: The Emergence of the Cartel Party." *Party Politics* 1 (Jan.): 5–28.

Kershaw, Ian. 2001a. *Hitler: 1889–1936, Hubris.* London: Penguin Books.

———. 2001b. *Hitler.* Harlow, UK: Pearson Education Limited.

———. 2004. "Hitler and the Uniqueness of Nazism." *Journal of Contemporary History* 39, no. 2: 239–54.

Kertzer, David. 1988. *Ritual, Politics, and Power.* 1988. Reprint. New Haven, Conn.: Yale Univ. Press.

Kitschelt, Herbert. 1995. *The Radical Right in Western Europe: A Comparative Analysis.* Ann Arbor: Univ. of Michigan Press.

Koenker, Ernest B. 1965. *Secular Salvations: The Rites and Symbols of Political Religions.* Philadelphia: Fortress Press.

Lacouture, Jean. 1970. *The Demigods: Charismatic Leadership in the Third World.* New York: Alfred A. Knopf.

Lafont, Valérie. 2001. "Les Jeunes Militants du Front National: Trois Modèles d'Engagement et de Cheminement." *Revue Française de Science Politique* 51, nos. 1–2 (Feb.–Apr.): 175–98.

Landes, Richard. 2004. "Millennialism." In *The Oxford Handbook of New Religious Movements,* edited by James R. Lewis, 333–59. New York: Oxford Univ. Press.

La Padania. "La Storia di Marco D'Aviano," <http://old.lapadania.com/news/RUBRICHE/la_storia_di_marco_d.htm#4>.

Laquer, Walter. 2007. *The Last Days of Europe: Epitaph for an Old Continent.* New York: Thomas Dunne Books.

Laurence, Jonathan, and Justin Vaisse. 2006. *Integrating Islam: Political and Religious Challenges in Contemporary France.* Washington, D.C.: Brookings Institution Press.

Lecoeur, Erwan. 2003. *Un néo-populisme à la française.* Paris: Éditions La Découverte.

Lega Nord. 1988–95. "Cronistoria della Lega Nord dalle origini ad oggi. Seconda Parte," <http://www.leganord.org/ilmovimento/storia/02_lega_nord_storia88_95.pdf>.

Lega Nord. 1996–98. "Cronistoria della Lega Nord dalle origini ad oggi. Terza Parte," <http://www.leganord.org/ilmovimento/storia/03_lega_nord_storia96_98.pdf>.

Lega Nord. 2006a. "Articolo." Sept. 21, <http://www.leganord.org/dblog/articolo.asp?articolo=132>.

Lega Nord. 2006b. "Le Radici Cristiane," <http://www.leganord.org/specialeelezioni/politiche/schede_tematiche/scheda_radici_cristiane.pdf>.

Lega Nord Flash. 2004. "Un referendum per dire: I Turchi no!" No. 52, Dec., <http://www.leganord.org/Lega%20Nord%20Flash%20nuovo%20logo/Fl-52%20Turchi%20no%20-%20nuovo%20logo.pdf>.

Lega Nord Flash. 2006. "Cittadinanza per avere il loro voto." No. 58, Sept., <http://www.leganord.org/leganordflash/Fl-58%20cittadinanza.pdf>.

Lega Nord Piemonte. 2006. "Circoncisione. Rossi: 'Presto l'Asl pagherà anche l'infibulazione?'" Mar. 21, <http://www.gruppoleganord.piemonte.it/comstampa/2006-21-03c.html>.

Le Pen, Jean-Marie. 1979. "Le Front National." In *La Droite Aujourd'hui,* edited by Jean-Pierre Apparu. Paris: Éditions Albin Michel.

———. 1984. *Les Français d'abord.* Paris: Éditions Carrere-Michel Lafon.

———. 1985. *La France est de retour.* Paris: Éditions Carrere-Michel Lafon.
———. 1989a. *L'Espoir.* Paris: Éditions Albatros.
———. 1989b. "La Politique: Une vision au service du people." *Identité: Revue d'Études Nationales,* Sept.–Oct.
———. 1990. "Le cri du muezzin." *Identité: Revue d'Études Nationales,* Mar.-Apr.
———. 1991. *Le Pen 90: Analyses et propositions.* Maule, France: Éditions de Présent.
———. 1992a. *Le Pen 91: Analyses et propositions.* Maule, France: Éditions de Présent.
———. 1992b. "Le Discours de Jean-Marie Le Pen à La Trinité." *Présent,* Sept. 2–3.
———. 1992c. "Le Discours du Serment de Reims." *Présent,* Sept. 14–15.
———. 1993. "La mort en face: Un livre pour tous les Français qui ont donné leur vie pour la France." In *La Mort en Face,* by Marcel Hasquenoph et al. Paris: Publications François Brigneau.
———. 1995. "Le Discours de Jean-Marie Le Pen aux BBR." *Présent,* Oct. 4–5.
———. 1996a. Préface to *In Clovis Roy des Francs—célébration nationale du 1500 anniversaire,* by Jean-Marc Brissaud. Paris: Éditions Nationales.
———. 1996b. "Le Pen: Defendre en toute occasion l'interet des Francais." *National-Hebdo,* Mar. 21–27.
———. 1996c. "Entendez le Chant du Peuple Français." *Présent,* Sept. 5–6.
———. 1997. "17ème Fête des Bleu-Blanc-Rouge." Sept. 26, <http://www.frontnational.com/doc_interventions_detail.php?id_inter=2>.
———. 1998. "Fête de Jeanne d'Arc." May 1, <http://www.frontnational.com/doc_interventions_detail.php?id_inter=7>.
———. 1999a. "Manifestation contre le traité d'Amsterdam à Versailles." Jan. 17, <http://www.frontnational.com/doc_interventions_detail.php?id_inter=10>.
———. 1999b. "Ralliez-vous à mom panache tricolore." *National-Hebdo,* Jan. 14–20.
———. 1999c. "Fête de Jeanne d'Arc." May 1, <http://www.frontnational.com/doc_interventions_detail.php?id_inter=9>.
———. 1999d. Université d'été 1999 du Front National à Orange." Sept. 3.
———. 2000. "Fête de Jeanne d'Arc." May 1, <http://www.frontnational.com/doc_interventions_detail.php?id_inter=12>.
———. 2001a. "Le Pen à la Trinité: Une grande journée entre symboles et espoirs." *National-Hebdo,* Aug. 23–29.
———. 2001b. "21ème Fête des Bleau-Blanc-Rouge." Sept. 23, <http://www.frontnational.com/doc_interventions_detail.php?id_inter=15>.
———. 2002a. "immigration et souveraineté." Jan. 27, <http://www.frontnational.com/doc_interventions_detail.php?id_inter=19>.
———. 2002b. "Fête de Jeanne d'Arc." May 1.

———. 2002c. "Meeting de Marseille." May 2, <http://www.frontnational.com/doc_interventions_detail.php?id_inter=17>.

———. 2002d. "Université d'été du Front National à Annecy." Aug. 30, <http://www.frontnational.com/doc_interventions_detail.php?id_inter=20>.

———. 2003a. "Discours de clôture du Congrès du FN à Nice." Apr. 21, <http://www.frontnational.com/doc_interventions_detail.php?id_inter=5>.

———. 2003b. "Fête de Jeanne d'Arc." May 1, Paris.

———. 2003c. "Discours de lancement de la campagne Le Pen PACA 2004." Sept. 18, Nice.

———. 2003d. "Conseil National du Front National." Sept. 20, <http://www.frontnational.com/doc_interventions_detail.php?id_inter=25>.

———. 2004a. "Fête de Jeanne d'Arc." May 1, <http://www.frontnational.com/doc_interventions_detail.php?id_inter=31>.

———. 2004b."Université d'été du Front National à Enghein." Aug. 28, <http://www.frontnational.com/doc_interventions_detail.php?id_inter=32>.

———. 2005. "22ème Fête des Bleu-Blanc-Rouge au Bourget." Oct. 9, <http://www.frontnational.com/doc_interventions_detail.php?id_inter=3>.

———. 2006a. "Discours de Jean-Marie Le Pen à Valmy." Sept. 20, <http://www.frontnational.com/doc_interventions_detail.php?id_inter=43>.

———. 2006b. "Guerre et Paix—discours du candidat Jean-Marie Le Pen aux Herbiers (Vendée)." Oct. 22, <http://www.frontnational.com/doc_interventions_detail.php?id_inter=47>.

———. 2006c. "Aujourd'hui il faut d'abord éviter le pire." *National-Hebdo*, Nov. 2–8.

———. 2006d. "Le Pen s'y croit déjà; Présidentielle." *Le Point*, Nov. 2.

———. 2006e. "Le Bourget—Projet Presidential." Nov. 12, <http://www.frontnational.com/doc_interventions_detail.php?id_inter=51>.

———. 2007. "Déclaration de Jean-Marie Le Pen après le second tour des élections Législatives," Apr. 22, <http://www.frontnational.com_interventions_detail.php?id_inter=84>.

Le Pen, Marine. 2006. *Á Contre Flots*. Paris: Éditions Grancher.

Lindholm, Charles. 1990. *Charisma*. Cambridge, Mass.: Basil Blackwell.

Linz, Juan. 2004. "The Religious Use of Politics and/or the Political Use of Religion: Ersatz Ideology versus Ersatz Religion." In *Totalitarianism and Political Religions: Concepts for the Comparison of Dictatorships*, edited by Hans Maier and Jodi Bruhn. London: Routledge.

Lipset, Seymour Martin. 1998. "George Washington and the Founding of Democracy." *Journal of Democracy* 9, no. 4 (Oct.): 24–38.

Loewenstein, Karl. 1966. *Max Weber's Political Ideas in the Perspective of Our Time*. Translated by Richard and Clara Winston. Amherst: Univ. of Massachusetts Press.

McCarthy, Patrick. 1997. "Italy: A New Language for a New Politics." *Journal of Modern Italian Studies* 2, no. 3 (Fall): 337–57.

Maier, Hans, and Jodi Bruhn, eds. 2004. *Totalitarianism and Political Religions: Concepts for the Comparison of Dictatorships*. London: Routledge.

Mair, Peter, and Ingrid van Biezen. 2001. "Party Membership in Twenty European Democracies, 1980–2000." *Party Politics* 7, no. 1:5–21.

Mair, Peter, W. Müller, and F. Plasser, eds. 2004. *Political Parties and Electoral Change: Party Responses to Electoral Markets*. London: Sage.

Marcilly, Jean. 1984. *Le Pen Sans Bandeau*. Paris: Jacques Grancher.

Maréchal, Yann, and Nicolas Gauthier, eds. 2001. *Le Pen*. Paris: Objectif France SARL.

Maroni, Roberto. 1994. "Come la vedo io, di Roberto Maroni." In *Il grande camaleonte. Episodi, passioni, avventure del leghismo*, by Giovanna Pajetta. Milan: Feltrinelli.

Marshall, P. David. 1997. *Celebrity and Power: Fame in Contemporary Culture*. Minneapolis: Univ. of Minnesota Press.

———, ed. 2004. "Fame." *M/C: A Journal of Media and Culture* 7, no. 5 (November).

Martinez, Jean-Claude. 2006. *Á tous les Français qui ont déjà voté déjà une fois Le Pen*. Paris: Lettres du Monde.

Masson, Louis. 2003. *Les 15 Jours de Jean-Marie Le Pen*. Paris: Éditions de l'Æncre.

Mauge, Roger. 1988. *La Vérité sur Jean-Marie Le Pen*. Paris: Éditions France-Empire.

Mayer, Nonna. 2002. *Ces Français Qui Votent Le Pen*. Paris: Flammarion.

Mazzoleni, Gianpietro, J. Stewart, and B. Horsfield, eds. 2003. *The Media and Neo-Populism: A Contemporary Comparative Analysis*. Westport, Conn.: Praeger Publishers.

Mégret, Bruno. 1990. *La Flamme: Les voies de la renaissance*. Paris: Éditions Robert Lafont.

———. 2002. "Les dangers de l'islamization—Intervention au colloque 'Les femmes et l'islam.'" Feb. 7, <http://www.m-n-r.net/discours93.htm>.

———. 2007. "VŒux de Bruno Mégret pour l'année 2007." Jan. 10, <http://www.m-n-r.net/discours168.htm>.

Mény, Yves, and Yves Surel, eds. 2002. *Democracies and the Populist Challenge*. London: Palgrave.

Monnerot, Jules. 1976. *The Sociology of Communism*. Translated by Jane Degras and Richard Rees. 1949. Reprint. Westport, Conn.: Greenwood Press.

Monnier, Pierre. 1994. *Le Pen, Le Peuple et la Petite Fille Espérance*. Paris: Éditions Nationales.

Morgan, Philip J. 2006. "Recognizing the Enemy." In *Fascism Past and Present, West and East: An International Debate on Concepts and Cases in the Comparative Study of the Extreme Right*, edited by Roger Griffin, Werner Loh, and Andreas Umland, 156–60. Stuttgart, Germany: ibidem-Verlag.

Mosse, George L. 1975. *The Nationalization of the Masses: Political Symbolism and Mass Movements in Germany from the Napoleonic Wars Through the Third Reich*. New York: Howard Fertig.

———. 2000. *Confronting History: A Memoir*. Madison: Univ. of Wisconsin Press.

Mouffe, Chantal. 2005. "The 'End of Politics' and the Challenge of Right-wing Populism." In *Populism and the Mirror of Democracy*, edited by Francisco Panizza, 50–71. London: Verso.

National Front. 1991. *Militer au Front*. Institut de Formation Nationale. Paris: Éditions Nationales.

———. "Identité: la France." In *300 Mesures pour la Renaissance de la France*, <http://www.frontnational.com/doc_id_france.php>.

———. 2007a. "François Bayrou et l'identité nationale—Communiqué de presse de Jean-Marie Le Pen." March 9.

———. 2007b. "Le vrai symbole d'Epinal—Communiqué de presse de Jean-Marie Le Pen." July 13.

Neumann, Franz. 1957. *The Democratic and the Authoritarian State: Essays in Political and Legal Theory*. Glencoe, Ill.: Free Press.

Niezen, Ronald. 2004. *A World Beyond Difference: Cultural Identity in the Age of Globalization*. Malden, Mass.: Blackwell.

Northern League. 2002a. "Federalismo e Devoluzione." *Segreteria politca federale*. Sept., <http://www.prov-brescia.leganord.org/documenti/Federalismoedevoluzione.pdf>.

———. 2002b. "La Battaglia della Lega Nord contro la prostituzione di strada, la pedofilia e la pornografia." *Segreteria Politica Federale*, Sept., <http://www.padaniaoffice.org/pdf/documentazione/battaglia_LN.pdf>.

———. 2002c. "Ragionare sull' Immigrazione: La Nuova Legge Bossi." <http://www.padaniaoffice.org/pdf/approfondimenti/Ragionaresull_immigrazione.pdf>.

———. 2004. "Programma per le elezione Europee 2004." *Segreteria Politica Federale*. May, <http://www.padaniaoffice.org/pdf/Programma_Europee_2004.pdf>

Oakeshott, Michael. 1996. *The Politics of Faith and the Politics of Scepticism.* New Haven, Conn.: Yale Univ. Press.

O'Leary, Stephen D. 1994. *Arguing the Apocalypse: A Theory of Millenial Rhetoric.* New York: Oxford Univ. Press.

Ottaviani, Achille, and Rafaello Canteri. 1992. *I cento giorni della Lega.* Verona: Euronobel.

Panebianco, Angelo. 1988. *Political Parties: Organization and Power.* Cambridge, UK: Cambridge Univ. Press.

Panizza, Francisco. 2005. "Introduction: Populism and the Mirror of Democracy." In *Populism and the Mirror of Democracy,* edited by Francisco Panizza, 1–31. London: Verso.

Paxton, Robert. 2004. *The Anatomy of Fascism.* New York: Alfred A. Knopf.

Payne, Stanley G., 2002. "Emilio Gentile's Historical Analysis and Taxonomy of Political Religions." *Totalitarian Movements and Political Religions* 3, no. 1 (Summer): 122–30.

Pedahzur, Ami, and Avraham Brichta. 2002. "The Institutionalization of Extreme Right-Wing Charismatic Parties: A Paradox?" *Party Politics* 8, no. 1:31–49.

Pfaff, Steven, and Anthony J. Gill. 2006. "Will a Million Muslims March? Muslim Interest Organizations and Political Integration in Europe." *Comparative Political Studies* 39, no. 7 (Sept.): 803–28.

Piat, Yann. 1991. *Seule, Tout en Haut à Droite.* Paris: Éditions Fixot.

Pinto, Antonio Costa, Stein Ugelvik Larsen, and Roger Eatwell, eds. 2006. *Charisma and Fascism.* London: Routledge.

Plekhanov, Georgi V. 2003. *The Role of the Individual in History.* 1898. Reprint. Honolulu: University Press of the Pacific.

Plenel, Edwy, and Alain Rollat. 1984. *L'Effet Le Pen.* Paris: Éditions La Découverte.

Poliakov, Léon. 1980. *La Causalité Diabolique: Essai sur l'Origine des Persécutions.* Paris: Calmann-Lévy.

———. 1992. "Causalité, Demonologie et Racisme: Retour à Lévy-Bruhl?" In *Les Protocoles des Sages de Sion: Faux et Usages d'un Faux II,* edited by Pierre-André Taguieff, 417–56. Paris: Berg International Éditeurs.

Quaderni Padani. 1998. Vol. 4, n. 17, May–June, <http://www.laliberacompagnia.org/pubblicazioni/qp_pdf/qp_17.pdf>.

Riggio, Ronald E. 2004. "Charisma." In *Encyclopedia of Leadership.* Vol. 1, edited by George R. Goethals, G. J. Sorenson, and James MacGregor Burns. Thousand Oaks, Calif.: Sage Publications.

Rosanvallon, Pierre. 2006. *Democracy Past and Future.* Edited by Samuel Moyn. New York: Columbia University Press.

Ross, Marc Howard. 1997. "Culture and Identity in Comparative Political Analysis." In *Comparative Politics: Rationality, Culture and Structure,* edited by Mark Irving Lichbach and A. S. Zuckerman. Cambridge, UK: Cambridge Univ. Press.

Rousseau, Jean-Jacques. 1987. *On the Social Contract.* Translated by Donald A. Cress. 1762. Indianapolis: Hackett Publishing Company.

Rustow, Dankwart A. 1970. "The Study of Leadership." In *Philosophers and Kings: Studies in Leadership,* edited by Dankwart A. Rustow, 1–32. New York: George Braziller.

Ruzza, Carlo. 2005. "The Northern League: Winning Arguments, Losing Influence." In *Movements of Exclusion: Radical Right-Wing Populism in the Western World,* edited by Jens Rydgren, 65–85. New York: Nova Science Publishers.

Rydgren, Jens, ed. 2005. *Movements of Exclusion: Radical Right-Wing Populism in the Western World.* New York: Nova Science Publishers.

Sartori, Giovanni. 1987. *The Theory of Democracy Revisited.* Chatham, N.J.: Chatham House Publishers.

Scaliati, Giuseppe. 2006. *Dove va la Lega Nord: Radici ed Evoluzione Politica di un Movimento Populista.* Milan: Zero in Condotta.

Schain, Martin, Aristide Zolberg, and Patrick Hossay, eds. 2002. *Shadows Over Europe: The Development and Impact of the Extreme Right in Western Europe.* New York: Palgrave Macmillan.

Schlesinger, Arthur, Jr. 1960. "On Heroic Leadership and the Dilemma of Strong Men and Weak Peoples." In *Encounter* 15, no. 6 (Dec.): 3–11.

Schonhuber, Franz. 1998. *Le Pen, L'indomptable.* Ploufragan: Éditions Les Presses Bretonnes.

Schweitzer, Arthur. 1990. "Democracy and Charisma." *Sociologia Internationalis* 28, no. 1:27–41.

Scotsman, The. 2006. May 12, <http://thescotsman.scotsman.com/international.cfm?id=708932006>.

Scott, James C. 1990. *Domination and the Arts of Resistance: Hidden Transcripts.* New Haven, Conn.: Yale Univ. Press.

Shannon, Jasper B. 1949. "The Study of Political Leadership." In *The Study of Comparative Government: An Appraisal of Contemporary Trends,* edited by Jasper B. Shannon. New York: Appleton-Century-Crofts.

Shils, Edward. 1975. *Center and Periphery: Essays in Macrosociology.* Chicago: Univ. of Chicago Press.

Sironneau, Jean-Pierre. 1982. *Sécularisation et religions politiques*. Paris: Mouton Éditeur.

Smith, Anthony D. 1979. *Nationalism in the Twentieth Century*. New York: New York Univ. Press.

———. 2003. *Chosen Peoples*. New York: Oxford Univ. Press.

Smith, Philip. 2000. "Culture and Charisma: Outline of a Theory." *Acta Sociologica* 43, no. 2:101–11.

Snow, David A., and Robert D. Benford. 1986. "Frame Alignment Processes, Micromobilization, and Movement Participation." *American Sociological Review* 51, no. 4:464–81.

Snow, David, and Robert D. Benford. 1988. "Ideology, Frame Resonance, and Participant Mobilization." In *From Structure to Action: Comparing Social Movement Research Across Cultures*. Vol. 1, edited by B. Klandermans, H. Kriesi, and S. Tarrow, 197–217. Greenwich, Conn.: JAI Press.

Souchard, Maryse, S. Wahnich, I. Cuminal, and V. Wathier. 1998. *Le Pen Les mots: Analyse d'un discours d'extrême droite*. Paris: Éditions Le Monde, 1998.

Stark, Rodney, and Roger Finke. 2000. *Acts of Faith: Explaining the Human Side of Religion*. Berkeley: Univ. of California Press.

Stella, Gian Antonio. 1996. *Dio Po: Gli uomini che fecero la Padania*. Milan: Baldini and Castoldi.

Steyn, Mark. 2006. *America Alone: The End of the World as We Know It*. Washington, D.C.: Regnery Publishing.

Tabladini, Francesco. 2003. *Bossi la grande illusione*. Rome: Editori Riuniti.

Taggart, Paul. 2000. *Populism*. Buckingham, UK: Open Univ. Press.

Tal, Uriel. 2004. *Religion, Politics and Ideology in the Third Reich. Selected Essays*. London: Routledge.

Talmon, Jacob L. 1981. *The Myth of the Nation and the Vision of the Revolution*. Berkeley: Univ. of California Press.

Telo, Mario. 2005. *Europe: A Civilian Power? European Union, Global Governance, World Order*. New York: Palgrave Macmillan.

Thiriart, Jean. 1964. *Europe, an Empire of 400 Million People: A Nation Built from a Historic Party*. Brussels: Imprimerie Sineco.

Tismaneanu, Vladimir. 1998. *Fantasies of Salvation: Democracy, Nationalism, and Myth in Post-communist Europe*. Princeton, N.J.: Princeton Univ. Press.

Tocqueville, Alexis de. 1955. *The Old Regime and the French Revolution*. 1856. New York: Doubleday Anchor Books.

Toensing, Chris, ed. 2005. "Europe and Islam: The Challenge of Inclusion." *Middle East Report,* no. 235 (Summer).

Tucker, Robert C. 1970. "The Theory of Charismatic Leadership." In *Philosophers and Kings: Studies in Leadership,* edited by D. Rustow, 69–94. New York: George Braziller.

Turner, Victor. 1977a. *The Ritual Process: Structure and Anti-Structure.* 1969. Reprint. Ithaca, N.Y.: Cornell Univ. Press.

——. 1977b. "Variations on a Theme of Liminality." In *Secular Ritual,* edited by Sally F. Moore and Barbara G. Myerhoff, 36–52. Amsterdam: Van Gorcum.

——. 1979. *Dramas, Fields and Metaphors: Symbolic Action in Human Society.* Ithaca, N.Y.: Cornell Univ. Press.

United Nations. 2007. "World Population Division Prospects: The 2006 Division." <http://www.un.org/esa/population/publications/wpp2006/2pp2006_highlights.pdf>.

Valle, Alexandre del. 1997. *Islamisme et Etats-Unis, une alliance contre l'Europe.* Lausanne, Switzerland: L'Age d'Homme.

Vimercati, Daniele. 1990. *I Lombardi alla nuova crociata.* Milan: Mursia.

Voegelin, Eric. 1986. *Political Religions.* Translated by T. J. DiNapoli and E. S. Easterly III. 1938. Reprint. New York: Edwin Mellen Press.

Wallis, Roy. 1982. "The Social Construction of Charisma." *Social Compass* 29, no. 1.

Wall Street Journal. 2005. November 19, <http://www.opinionjournal.com/editorial/feature.html?id=110007576>.

Weber, Max. 1958. *From Max Weber: Essays in Sociology.* Edited by Hans Gerth and C. W. Mills. New York: Oxford Univ. Press.

——. 1978. *Economy and Society: An Outline of Interpretative Sociology.* 2 Vols. Edited by Guenther Roth and Claus Wittich. 1922. Reprint. Berkeley: Univ. of California Press.

——. 2002. *The Protestant Ethic and the Spirit of Capitalism.* Translated by Stephen Kalberg. 1904–5. Reprint. Los Angeles: Roxbury Publishing Company.

Whimster, Sam, and Scott Lash. 1987. *Max Weber, Rationality, and Modernity.* London: Allen and Unwin.

Wiesel, Elie. 2003. *Wise Men and Their Tales: Portraits of Biblical, Talmudic, and Hasidic Masters.* New York: Schocken Books.

Willner, Ann Ruth. 1984. *The Spellbinders, Charismatic Political Leadership.* New Haven, Conn.: Yale Univ. Press.

Zanzi, Carlo. 1994. *Maroni L'Arciere.* Varese, Italy: Lativa.

Index

Italic page number denotes illustration.

Agnelli, Giovanni, 130
Aliot, Louis, 72, 84
America Alone: The End of the World as We Know It (Steyn), 238n. 5
Antaeus, 157
Antony, Bernard, 49n. 5, 109
Apocalyptic scenarios: cataclysmic/transformational, 202; discourse and, 90–91; dynamics of salvation and, 199–210
Apter, David E., 15
Aron, Raymond, 12

Babbini, Giuseppe, 151
Bainville, Jacques, 41
Ballaman, Edouard, 127n. 1
Barbarossa, Federico (emperor), 1, 117, 165
Barkun, Michael, 203, 221
Barrès, Maurice, 41
Bawer, Bruce, 237n. 5
Belang, Vlaams, 239n. 7, 243
Bell, Daniel, 17, 17n. 9
Bellah, Robert, 14n. 7
Benedict XVI (pope), 134
Benford, Robert D., 231
Bensman, Joseph, 21
Berger, Peter L., 3
Berlinski, Claire, 237n. 5

Berlusconi, Silvio, 128, 136, 163
Bertotti, Elisabetta, 148
Betz, Hans-Georg, 22
Bildelberg Group, 50
Binder, Patrick, 73, 106
Biological imagery, 203
Birthrates, declining, 54–55
Blot, Yvan, 64, 68, 69, 73
B'nai B'rith, 52, 53
Bobbio, Norberto, 23, 208
Bompard, Jacques, 109
Bonaparte, Napoléon, 75, 95, 131
Bossi, Renzo (son), 185n. 8
Bossi, Ricardo (son), 185n. 8
Bossi, Umberto, 1, 30, 30n. 17, 33, 34, *152, 167, 185,* 190; biological imagery and, 203; charisma and, 181–82; clairvoyance and, 149–50; Federal Council and, 161–62; industry of, 146–54; inner circle of, 147–63; leader's discourse and, 154–60; messianic leader and, 210–20; moral community and, 173–81; mythologizing, 146–63; Northern League and, 115–89; personalized party and, 160–63; political-religious symbolism, 164–82; rhetoric and, 164; rituals and, 164–73; as savior, 146–87; self-sacrifice and, 215–16; succession of charismatic leader and, 182–87

Boumedienne, Houari, 55
Bourdieu, Pierre, 23
Bracher, Karl Dietrich, 13, 13n. 5
Brasillach, Robert, 80
Brenno, 174n. 7
Briand, Aristide, 242n. 10
Brigneau, François, 63, 67, 70, 73, 101
Bruce, Steve, 3, 19
Brutus, 74
Bruyas, Jacques, 57
Burleigh, Michael, 14, 14n. 6
Burns, James MacGregor, 21
Burrin, Philippe, 17, 17n. 10
Bush, George W., 135

Cadoudal, George (general), 95
Caesar, 74
Calderoli, Roberto, 128, 128n. 3, 184
Calling. *See* Vocation
Cambronne, Pierre (general), 75
Canovan, Margaret, 26, 27, 209
Carlyle, Thomas, 6
Carroccio. *See* Northern League
Carter, Elisabeth, 23
Cassandra, 99
Cassirer, Ernst, 1
Castellazzi, Franco, 163
Castelli, Roberto, 183
Catholics, 5
Cattaneo, Carlo, 119
Cavalli, Luciano, 17
Cavour, Camillo Benso di, 153
Charisma, 70–71, 213n. 3; missionary forms of, 25; political-religious symbolism and, 108, 181–82; popular/superficial forms of, 10, 18, 20, 21, 22, 24, 25
Charismatic leadership, 6, 18, 20–21; calling, 8; despair/hope and enthusiasm's relation to, 8–9, 23; mission concept

and, 7; new, 22; political, 10, 11–12; postcolonial states' demigods and, 15; resembling biblical prophets, 7; resurgent literature on, 23; succession of, 108–10, 182–86; weakening of, 19
Chirac, Jacques, 53, 57, 61
Chosen people, 197–99
Chrétienté Solidarité, 109
Christianity, 4, 5
Church attendance, 5
Churchill, Winston, 42, 153
Civic religion, 11, 14, 15
Clairvoyance, 70–71, 149–50
Clemenceau, George, 84
Clinton, Bill, 139
Clovis I (king), 1, 36, 41, 73, 194
Cluster concept, 27–28
Cohn, Norman, 204, 205, 206
Communion, 13, 19
Communism, 12, 13, 46, 53–55
Conspiracy, 199–204, 223n. 4; and Bossi, 135–37, 140–41, 146; and Le Pen, 50, 51, 53, 58, 100
Cota, Roberto, 149
Coudenhove-Kalergi, Richard N. (count), 242n. 10
Council on Foreign Relations, 50
Cultural analysis, 28–30

Da Giussano, Alberto, 117, 167, 194
D'Amato, Federico Umberto, 137
Daoudal, Yves, 49n. 5, 69, 71, 100
D'Aviano, Marco, 127n. 1
De Béjarry, Louis-Armand, 104, 106, 107
De Brem, Jean, 41, 41n. 2
De Gaulle, Charles (general), 38, 75, 153
Del Valle, Alexandre, 139, 139n. 5
Descartes, René, 69

Despair, 8–9, 23
D'Estaing, Giscard, 39, 40
De Villiers, Philippe, 49n. 5, 99n. 14
Dewinter, Flip, 239n. 7
Diên-Biên-Phû, 37, 38
Disenchanted world, 2, 3; reenchanting of, 6–21
Djebbour, Ahmed, 69
Dogmas, 12
Domard, Eric, 68, 105
Douglas, Mary, 207
Dufraisse, André, 107n. 17
Dupâquier, Jacques, 57
Duprat, François, 52n. 6, 107n. 17
Duran, Pierre, 71
Durkheim, Émile, 11–12, 14n. 7

Eatwell, Roger, 22, 23, 32
Ecclesia, 8
Economy and Society (Weber), 7
Eisner, Kurt, 9n. 3
Emrich, C. G., 32
Énarques, 68, 69
Encyclopedia of Leadership, 19
Eurabia: The Euro-Arab Axis (Ye'or), 237n. 5
Europeanization: missionary politics and, 241–42
European Union, 5, 46, 47, 58, 89, 132, 141–42, 239–40n. 7, 242n. 10
Evangelicalism, 3
Evans, Richard J., 16
Evil, 201–2, 206, 207

Faith, 12, 13, 19, 26, 103, 175, 176
Fallaci, Oriana, 129, 129n. 4
Fascism, 12, 13n. 5, 14, 24
Faverio Simonetta, 153, 178

Federal Council, 161–62
Fertility rates, declining, 240n. 9
Fête des Bleu-Blan-Rouge, 91
Finke, Roger, 228
Fjordman, 238
Flanagan, Thomas, 205, 206
Followers, 7, 10, 23
Français d'Abord, Les (J. Le Pen), 87
Français d'Abord! Les (newspaper), 68, 86
Freemasons, 51, 53, 136, 137
French National Front: holy rituals and, 1

Gardner, Howard, 219, 220
Garibaldi, Giuseppi, 154
Geertz, Clifford, 28
Gentile, Emilio, 14, 18, 27, 29
Giner, Salvador, 15, 18
Giorgetti, Giancarlo, 150, 151, 161, 185
Girardet, Raoul, 200
Givant, Michael, 21
Gladstone, William, 9n. 3
Glassman, Ronald M., 21
Globalization: missionary politics and, 234–35; National Front and, 55; Northern League and, 138, 142
Gobbo, Giampaolo, 182
God, exclusion of, 6
Goffman, Erving, 231
Gollnisch, Bruno, 52n. 6
Graumann, Carl F., 199, 200
Griffin, Roger, 14, 24, 27
Grimoldi, Paolo, 153
Groups: Bildeberg, 50; definition of, 41–43; missionary models, commitment, conversion and dynamics of, 228–30; National Front and, 36–62, 105; Northern League and, 116–46; opposition, 105; under siege, 44–58
Gurian, Waldemar, 13n. 4

Harlan, Veit, 130n. 4
Hayes, Carlton J. H., 190
Hegel, Georg Wilhelm Friedrich, 118
Herf, Jeffrey, 206
History: creation of alternate, 38–41, 96; sacred, 194–97; Weber on disenchanted world and philosophy of, 2–3
Hitler, Adolf, 32, 100, 214
Hoffer, Eric, 213
Hofstadter, Richard, 204
Holeindre, Roger, 65, 70, 73, 100n. 15
Holocaust denials, 52n. 6
Homer, 68
Hope, 8–9, 23, 102
Human rights, 51
Hutchinson, Paul, 242n. 10

Ignazi, Piero, 22
Iliad (Homer), 68
Il Mercante di Pietre, 130n. 4
Immigration, 48, 53–55, 57, 126, 135, 136, 141
Inglehart, Ronald, 4
International Monetary Fund, 46
Islam, 3
Islamization: missionary politics and, 235–39

Jenkins, Philip, 4, 5
Jewish Week, 239n. 7
Joan of Arc, 37, 41, 73, 75, *76*, 88, 89, 91, 102, 193, 194, 224
John Paul II (pope), 90, 134
Jud Süss (film), 130n. 4

Kalberg, Stephen, 25
Kershaw, Ian, 16, 32, 214

Kertzer, David, 212
Kitschelt, Herbert, 22
Knowledge: power of collective and, 229; stigmatized, 221; suppressed, 221–22
Kosovo, 135, 139

Lacouture, Jean, 15
Lafont, Valérie, 108
Landes, Richard, 202
Lang, Carl, 72, 84
La Rochejaquelein (general), 75
Leaders: charismatic, 6–9, 10, 11–12, 15, 18, 19, 20–23; democratic, 20; discourse of, 74–82, 154–60; martyr as, 214–16; messianic, 210–20; missionary, 219–20; missionary models and, 230–32; moral archetype, 213–14; party, 217–19; people, 216–17; prophet, 211–13; quasireligious relationship between followers and, 7, 10, 23; succession of charismatic, 108–10, 182–86
Leadership. *See* Leaders
Lega Lombarda, 117, 146, 148
Lega Nord, 30, 115
Leninism, 13n. 5
Lenin, Vladimir, 75
Leoni, Giuseppe, 148, 150
Le Pen, Jean-Marie, 1, 23, 30, 30n. 17, 33, 66, *76, 92,* 190; apocalyptic scenarios and, 90–91; biological imagery and, 203; charisma and, 108; clairvoyance and, 70–71; on Communism, immigration, declining birthrate, and globalization, 53–56; family life of, 70, 79; industry of, 62–86; inner circle of, 62–73; leader's discourse and, 74–82; messianic leader and, 210–20; moral community and, 102–8; mythologizing, 62–74; National Front

and, 34–114; personalized party and, 82–86; political-religious symbolism and, 86–108; racial hatred against Muslims and, 80n. 11; rhetoric and, 86–91; rituals and, 91–102; as savior, 62–110; self-sacrifice and, 214–15; succession to charismatic leader and, 108–10; word choice of, 80
Le Pen, Marie-Caroline (daughter), 109
Le Pen, Marine (daughter), 50, 52n. 6, 59n. 7, 70, 71, 83, 108–10
Le Pen, Yann (daughter), 70
Lettre de Jean-Marie Le Pen, La, 86
Lewis, Bernard, 237n. 5, 239n. 7
Ligue des Droits de l'Homme, 51
Ligue Internationale contre le Racisme et l'Antisémitisme, 51
Lincoln, Abraham, 75
Lindholm, Charles, 23, 32
Linz, Juan, 16, 17
Lipset, Seymour Martin, 213n. 3
Loewenstein, Karl, 20
Lombardia Autonomista, 115, 118, 165
Louis XVI (king), 94
Lustiger, Jean-Marie (cardinal), 90

Magic: missionary politics and, 1
Mair, Peter, 217, 227
Malaguti, Christina, 147
Mandela, Nelson, 188
Maoism, 13n. 5, 18
Marcilly, Jean, 63, 68
Maréchal, Samuel, 109
Marin, Jean-Claude, 60n. 7
Maroni, Roberto, 129–30n. 4, 147
Martin, Dominique, 70, 106
Martinelli, Renzo, 129, 130n. 4
Martinez, Jean-Claude, 109, 110n. 18
Mauge, Roger, 64

Maurras, Charles, 41
Mayer, Nonna, 108
Mazzoleni, Gianpietro, 22
Mégret, Bruno, 49n. 5, 63, 67, 73, 74, 85, 85n. 12, 90, 91
Menace in Europe: Why the Continent's Crisis Is America's Too (Berlinski), 237n. 5
Mény, Yves, 22
Methodology: of missionary politics, 22–33
Methuselah, 84
Metternich, Klemens von, 153
Michael (archangel), 88
Millennialism: collective/terrestrial/imminent/total/miraculous, 205; political, 205; restorative/progressive, 206; sacredness and, 204–10
Mission, 7, 9, 10
Missionary models: elements of sacredness in, 190–220; framework of analysis with, 190; group dynamics, commitment, conversion, and, 228–30; leadership and, 230–32; National Front and, 110–14, 190–232; Northern League and, 186–89, 190–232; politics as salvation and, 110–14, 186–89; sacred collective and, 220–28
Missionary politics: anomalies to dominant rationalist paradigm and, 22–24; approach/methodology to, 22–33; book's plan and, 33; case studies, 30–33; cluster concept and, 27–28; cultural analysis and, 28–30; demographic decline and, 239–41; de-sacralization of politics and, 16–21; disenchantment of world and, 2–6; Europeanization and, 241–42; future of, 233–42; globalization and, 234–35; ideal type of approach/methodology and, 25–27; introduction,

Missionary politics (*cont.*)
1–33; Islamization and, 235–39; magic and, 1; mission in secular religions and, 9–16; as political religion, 27; reenchanting of world and, 6–21; secularization theory and, 2–6; Weber, charismatic leadership and, 6–9

Moncalvo, Gigi, 151, 166, 182

Monnerot, Jules, 12

Monnet, Jean, 50, 137

Monnier, Pierre, 64, 65, 67, 68, 70, 71, 101

Montand, Yves, 80

Moral community, 102–8, 173–81

Mosse, George L., 191, 192, 199, 225

Mouffe, Chantal, 29

Mouvement National Républicain, 49n. 5

Mouvement pour la France, 49n. 5

Müller, W., 227

Muslims: decreasing fertility rates and, 240n. 9; Northern League's stance against, 129; racial hatred against, 80n. 11

Myth of the Nation and the Vision of Revolution, The (Talmon), 210n. 1

Myth of the State, The (Cassirer), 1

Myths, 12, 19, 190, 191; ethnic election and, 192; Jean-Marie Le Pen and, 62–74; ritual, communion, faith, secular religions and core of, 13; Umberto Bossi and, 146–63

Nabucco, 96, 173

Nation, the, 34–35, 56, 190–94

National Front, 22n. 12, 30, 31; alternate histories created by, 38–41, 96; apocalypticism, dynamics of salvation and, 199–210; apocalyptic scenarios and, 90–91; biological imagery and, 203; B'nai B'rith and, 52, 53; *bureau politique/exécutif* of, 82; celebrated historical figures and, 36–37; chosen peoples and, 197–99; clairvoyance and, 70–71; Communism and, 46, 53–54; crisis: rejection of present time and, 34–36; declining birthrate and, 54–55; definition of group and, 41–43; as elect group, 36–62; evil/purification/renewal and, 201–2, 206, 207; exceptionality of, 58–62; Fête des Bleu-Blan-Rouge and, 91; Freemasonry/Grand Orient and, 51, 53; globalization and, 55; *grand discours* and, 91; group dynamics, commitment, conversion and, 228–30; as group under siege, 44–58; historical continuity and, 36–41; Holocaust denials and, 52n. 6; human rights stance of, 51; immigration and, 48, 54, 57; industry of, 62–86; inner circle, 62–73; internal/external enemies of, 45–46; Islamic culture opposed by, 48, 49n. 5; leadership and, 230–32; Le Pen and, 34–114; Le Pen as savior and, 62–111; messianic leader and, 210–20; missionary model and, 110–14, 190–232; moral community, 102–8; myth of ethnic election and, 192; "nation" concept and, 34–35, 56; opposition groups, 105; politics as salvation and, 110–14; *rentrée politique* and, 91; rhetoric, 86–91; rituals, 91–102; sacred collective and, 220–28; sacred geography and, 193, 196; shock rhetoric and, 53–55; succession of charismatic leader and, 108–11; threats to France according to, 53–55; tribute to Joan of Arc and, 91; *Université d'été* and, 91

National-Hebdo, 69, 73, 101

Nationalization of the Masses, The (Mosse), 191
Nazism, 12, 13, 14, 16, 18, 32, 38, 59
Neumann, Franz, 199
New Radical Right, 22
Next Christendom, The (Jenkins), 4
Niezen, Ronald, 234
Norris, Pippa, 4, 5
Northern League, 22n. 12, 30, 31; anti-Muslim stance and, 129; apocalypse, dynamics of salvation and, 199–210; biological imagery and, 203; Bossi and, 115–89; Bossi as savior and, 146–86; centralist state and, 140–41; charisma and, 181–82; chosen peoples and, 197–99; clairvoyance and, 149–50; crisis: renunciation of present and, 115–16; definition of group and, 120–23; enemies of, 125–32; European Union and, 132, 141–42; evil/purification/renewal and, 201–2, 206, 207; exceptionality of, 144–46; Federal Council and, 161–62; Freemasons and, 136, 137; globalization and, 138, 142; group as vanguard, 116–46; group dynamics, commitment, conversion and, 228–30; group under siege and, 123–44; historical continuity of, 116–20; holy rituals and, 1; immigration and, 126, 135, 136, 141; industry of, 146–54; inner circle of, 147–63; leadership and, 230–32; Lega Lombarda and, 117, 146, 148; *Lombardia Autonomista* and, 115, 118, 165; messianic leader and, 210–20; missionary model and, 186–89, 190–232; moral community and, 173–81; myth of ethnic election and, 192; Padania and, 116–17, 121–23, 134, 136, 138, 142, 143, 156, 166, 171; *La Padania* and, 127n. 1, 130n. 4, 147, 149, 150, 151, 166, 168, 172, 181, 183, 188; Padania Youth and, 154, 173, 177, 180; *Partitocrazia* and, 125; personalized party and, 160–63; political-religious symbolism and, 164–82; politics as salvation and, 186–89; rhetoric and, 164; *Risorgimento* and, 118–19, 188, 223; rituals and, 164–73; sacred collective and, 220–28; sacred geography and, 193, 196; *Sole delle Alpi* and, 172; succession of charismatic leader and, 182–86; Turco-Napolitano and, 127. *See also* Lega Nord

Oakeshott, Michael, 26, 27
Old Regime and the French Revolution, The (Tocqueville), 11
O'Leary, Stephen D., 202, 204
Oneto, Gilberto, 179
On the Social Contract (Rousseau), 10

Padania, 116–17, 121–23, 134, 136, 138, 142, 143, 156, 166, 171
Padania, La, 127n. 1, 129–30n. 4, 147, 149, 150, 151, 166, 168, 172, 181, 183, 188
Padania Youth, 154, 173, 177, 180
Pagliarini, Giancarlo (senator), 148
Panebianco, Angelo, 218
Partitocrazia (partitocracy), 125
Pascal, Blaise, 69
Passionately French: The Life of Jean-Marie Le Pen in Cartoon Strips (National Front), 72
Paul (apostle), 7, 154
Paxton, Robert, 14n. 6
Payne, Stanley G., 18
Péguy, Charles, 80, 102, 113
Peltier, Martin, 64

Pétain, Marshal, 38
Piaf, Edith, 80
Piat, Yann, 83
Piazzo, Stefania, 147
Piccola Guida all Cultura Islamica, La (Short Guide to Islamic Culture, A), 127n. 1
Pisati, Carlo, 149
Plasser, F., 227
Plekhanov, Georgi, 6
Poliakov, Léon, 201
Political religions, 13–19, 27
Political-religious symbolism: charisma and, 108, 181–82; moral community and, 102–8, 173–81; rhetoric and, 86–91, 164; rituals and, 91–102, 164–73
Political sphere, 13
Politics: missionary, 1–33, 190–242; missionary politics and de-sacralization? of, 16–21; missionary politics and sacralization of, 190–232; salvation, missionary models and, 110–14, 186–89; skepticism and, 26
"Politics as a Vocation" (Weber), 8
Pozzi, Filippo, 150, 180
Protestant Ethic and the Spirit of Capitalism, The (Weber), 2
Protestants, 5
Protocols of the Elders of Zion, 140
Pursuit of the Millennium, The (Cohn), 204

Ras Le Front, 105
Reagan, Ronald, 46n. 3
Realissimum, 13n. 4
Reenchanting of world: de-sacralization of politics and, 16–21; missionary politics and, 6–21; mission in secular religions and, 9–16; Weber, charismatic leadership and, 6–9, 10

Religions: civic, 11, 14, 15; Durkheim on, 11–12; follower/leader relationships linked to, 7, 10, 23; link between modernization and decline in, 5; as marketplace product, 4; mission in secular, 9–16; political, 13–19, 27; secular, 9–16; secularization theory and, 2–3; sphere of, 13
Religious sphere, 13
Renan, Ernest, 35
Rhetoric, 53–55, 86–91, 164
Riggio, Ronald E., 19
Risorgimento, 118–19, 188, 223
Rites, 190, 191
Rituals, 19, 190; French National Front and holy, 1; National Front, 91–102; Northern League, 164–73; sacred collective, outsiderhood and, 224–25; secular religions, mythical core, communion, faith and, 13
Rivoluzione, La (U. Bossi), 187
Robespierre, Maximilien, 39
Rocchetta, Franco, 149
Rockefeller, David, 51, 53
Rosanvallon, Pierre, 208
Ross, Marc Howard, 28
Rousseau, Jean-Jacques, 10, 39

Sacred collective, 220; collective/liminality and, 225–27; communitas/militancy and, 227–28; narrative/outsiderhood and, 221–24; ritualism/outsiderhood and, 224–25
Sacredness: apocalypticism, dynamics of salvation and, 199–210; belief in regenerative power of sacrifice and, 192; chosen peoples and, 197–99; collective, 220–28; importance of celebrating community/heroes and,

192; messianic leader and, 210–20; millennialism and, 204–10; missionary model and elements of, 190–220; myth of ethnic election and, 192; sacred history and, 194–97; sacred nation and, 190–94; terrains of, 192; yearning to recover spirit of golden age and, 192
Saint-Just, Louis de, 39
Salvadori, Bruno, 154
Salvation, 110–14, 186–89, 190, 199–210
Salvini, Matteo, 177, 180
Sarkozy, Nicolas, 78, 99, 99n. 14
Sartori, Giovanni, 208
Schlesinger, Arthur, Jr., 20
Scott, James C., 212, 213n. 2
Secularization theory: individualism and, 2; missionary politics and, 2–6; outer/inner world asceticism and, 2; postindustrial societies and, 5n. 1; rational-choice theory and, 4; Reformation, Enlightenment and, 2; religion and, 2–3
Secular religions: dimensions of religious phenomena in, 13; global interpretation of events and, 12; mission in, 9–16; mythical core, ritual, communion, faith in, 13; party's fraternal community and, 12
Self-sacrifice, 214–16
Shannon, Jasper B., 20
Shils, Edward, 15
Sironneau, Jean-Pierre, 13, 18
Skepticism, politics of, 26
Smith, Anthony D., 192, 195
Smith, Philip, 29
Snow, David A., 231
Sociology of Communism, The (Monnerot), 12
Sohm, Rudolph, 7

Sole delle Alpi, 172
SOS Racisme, 51, 59n. 7
Spengler, Oswald, 57
Staglieno, Marcello (senator), 150
Stalinism, 13n. 5, 18
Stark, Rodney, 4, 228, 229
Stefani, Stefano, 152, 168, 182–83
Steyn, Mark, 238n. 5
Stirbois, Jean-Pierre, 83, 85, 85n. 12
Submission (film), 127
Surel, Yves, 22
Sylla, Fodé, 59n. 7
Symbolism, political-religious, 86–108, 164–82

Tabladini, Francesco, 161, 174
Taggart, Paul, 30n. 17, 223
Taine, Hippolyte, 35
Tal, Uriel, 16n. 8
Talmon, Joseph L., 210n. 1
Terroni (pejorative term for Southerners), 126
Terrorists, 47, 135
Thiriart, Jean, 48n. 4
Tismaneanu, Vladimir, 243
Tocqueville, Alexis de, 11
Toynbee, Arnold, 57
Trilateral Commission, 50, 53
Tucker, Robert C., 23
Turco-Napolitano, 127
Turner, Victor, 226

Van Biezen, Ingrid, 227
Van Dooren, Ron, 229
Van Gogh, Theo, 127n. 1
Vatican, the, 123, 133, 201
Vercingétorix, 36, 194
Verde, Camisa, 150

Verdi, Giuseppe, 96, 173
Verhaeren, Émile, 73, 80
Vérité sur Jean-Marie Le Pen, La (Mauge), 66
Victoria (queen of England), 9n. 3
Vimercati, Daniele, 119
Vocation, 8
Voegelin, Eric, 13n. 4

Wallis, Roy, 232
Washington, George, 213n. 3
Weber, Max, 11, 17, 20, 23, 25, 26, 28, 112, 220; philosophy of history, "disenchanted world" and, 2–3; "reenchanting of world," charismatic leadership and, 6–9, 10; on succession, 182; "value-free sociological analysis" and, 9n. 3
While Europe Slept: How Radical Islam Is Destroying the West from Within (Bawer), 237n. 5
Wiesel, Elie, 211
Willner, Ann Ruth, 24, 231
World: disenchanted, 2, 3; reenchanting of, 6–21
World Bank, 46

Ye'or, Bat, 237n. 5, 239n. 7

Zilio, Giovanni Meo, 149, 153, 154